# Aesthetic Collectives

This book focuses attention on groups of performing people that are unique aesthetic objects, the focus of an artist's vision, but at the same time a collective being; a singular, whole mass that exists and behaves like an individual entity.

This text explores this unique experience, which is far from rare or special. Indeed, it is pervasive, ubiquitous and has, since the dawn of performance, been with us. Surveying installation art from Vanessa Beecroft & Kanye West, Greek tragedy, back-up dancing groups and even the mass dance of clubbing crowds, this text examines and names this phenomenon: *Aesthetic Collectives*. Drawing on a range of methods of investigation spanning performance studies, acting theory, studies of atmosphere and affect and sociology it presents an intervention in the literature for something that has long deserved its own attention.

This book will be of great interest to scholars, students and practitioners in performance studies, theatre, live art, sociology (particularly of groups and subcultures), cultural studies and cultural geography.

**Dr. Andrew Wiskowski** is a lecturer and artist in performance, having recently been in the faculty of Creative and Digital Industries at Lambeth College, London Southbank University.

# Routledge Advances in Theatre & Performance Studies

This series is our home for cutting-edge, upper-level scholarly studies and edited collections. Considering theatre and performance alongside topics such as religion, politics, gender, race, ecology, and the avant-garde, titles are characterized by dynamic interventions into established subjects and innovative studies on emerging topics.

**Shakespeare's Contested Nations**
Race, Gender, and Multicultural Britain in Performances of the History Plays
*L. Monique Pittman*

**Performing the Wound**
Practicing a Feminist Theatre of Becoming
*Niki Tulk*

**Butoh America**
Butoh Dance in the United States and Mexico from 1970 to the early 2000's
*Tanya Calamoneri*

**Deburau**
Pierrot, Mime, and Culture
*Edward Nye*

**Performance at the Urban Periphery**
Insights from South India
*Cathy Turner, Sharada Srinivasan, Jerri Daboo and Anindya Sinha*

**Australian Metatheatre on Page and Stage**
An Exploration of Metatheatrical Techniques
*Rebecca Clode*

For more information about this series, please visit: https://www.routledge.com/Routledge-Advances-in-Theatre-Performance-Studies/book-series/RATPS

# Aesthetic Collectives
On the Nature of Collectivity
in Cultural Performance

**Andrew Wiskowski**

LONDON AND NEW YORK

First published 2022
by Routledge
4 Park Square, Milton Park, Abingdon, Oxon OX14 4RN

and by Routledge
605 Third Avenue, New York, NY 10158

*Routledge is an imprint of the Taylor & Francis Group, an informa business*

© 2022 Andrew Wiskowski

The right of Andrew Wiskowski to be identified as author of this work has been asserted in accordance with sections 77 and 78 of the Copyright, Designs and Patents Act 1988.

All rights reserved. No part of this book may be reprinted or reproduced or utilised in any form or by any electronic, mechanical, or other means, now known or hereafter invented, including photocopying and recording, or in any information storage or retrieval system, without permission in writing from the publishers.

*Trademark notice*: Product or corporate names may be trademarks or registered trademarks, and are used only for identification and explanation without intent to infringe.

*British Library Cataloguing-in-Publication Data*
A catalogue record for this book is available from the British Library

*Library of Congress Cataloguing-in-Publication Data*
A catalog record has been requested for this book

ISBN: 978-1-032-07135-0 (hbk)
ISBN: 978-1-032-07155-8 (pbk)
ISBN: 978-1-003-20566-1 (ebk)

DOI: 10.4324/9781003205661

Typeset in Bembo
by MPS Limited, Dehradun

To my father, Michael Wiskowski.

Before his death I wrote this and hope it was known:

*Might you never forget or be unaware of how important and superlative you are. If I ever give you cause to forget or be unaware, I ask you to forgive me. I love you.*

Having lost him I now think of how different life is being-not-with and how much I took for granted the being-with.

Thank you.

# Contents

| | |
|---|---|
| *Acknowledgements* | ix |
| **Introduction—The Aesthetic Collective** | 1 |

**PART I**
**Precis**     21

**1   Proximity and Prägnanz—Space, Order, Touch**     25

*Insides/Outsides, Proxemics and Containment 28*
*Aesthetic Fields, Collective Domains 33*
*Proximity and Prägnanz 36*
*The Discharge 43*
*Touch—Known, Unknown; Security, Threat 50*
*Communitas and Affect Transmission 56*

**2   Similarity—Authority and Agency**     62

*VB16, VB35, VB45, VB46, VB48 66*
*Manipulating Agency and Authority 72*
*Directions/Instructions—Explicit and Implied 79*

**3   Common Fate—Objective, Agency and Essence**     92

*Choreography and Rhythm 97*
*Dialogue 101*
*Rôle/Character 105*
*Agentic States 109*

viii    *Contents*

**PART II**
# Precis                                                                    119

## 4    Character and Contagion                                             127

*Character as Roles and Dramatis Personae 128*
*Essence and Essentialisation 134*
*Characterisation, Characterising, Mood 141*
*Contagion 147*

## 5    Mood, Affect, Feeling, Emotion                                      154

*Mood-Making 155*
*Affective Dimensions 160*
*Mood Setting/Contagion 165*

## 6    Encountering Atmospheres                                            175

*The Encounter 176*
*Immersion 184*
*Foam Structures—Atmospheres 192*
*Conditioning 195*
*Climate and Human Weather 199*

## Conclusion                                                              210

*Bibliography*                                                             218
*Appendix A*                                                              226
*Appendix B*                                                              228
*Appendix C*                                                              229
*Index*                                                                   232

# Acknowledgements

I would like to thank my PhD advisor Martin Welton for his outstanding guidance through this research. His advice, our conversations and his empathic academic understanding was essential in ensuring that the research grew but also that I felt supported and safe. I would also like to thank Josephine Machon and Cormac Power for their advice and suggestions in preparing the text for submission. The experience of having them as examiners was both enjoyable and productive! Thank you all.

# Introduction—The *Aesthetic Collective*

*I sit at the Tower of London on 21 July 2018 watching* Storming the Wall, *a site-installed performance of dance directed and choreographed by Hofesh Schechter. I sit in the raised viewing area of the Tower on its west wall watching the stage, below in the moat, before which there is a built seating area. There are 202 young dancers and musicians performing in the production. The dance is composed in a way that alternates between scenes of intense group-centred activity and focus and scenes of isolation or individuated dance and narration. There is no true narrative to the work, although all the dance is composed of scenes playing with elements of narrative drawn from stories linked in part to the tower or the imperial histories loosely associated with it: military enlistment and sacrifice, mass migration and the slavery diaspora, British (English) power as displayed through military prowess, the tower's long history with execution and its spectacle.*

*The dance is remarkable in and of itself—performed by under-25s drawn from the residences of east London. There is a strong presence of Schechter's choreographic style running through all the sections (each, save one, actually choreographed by others under his direction). It is impressive that 202 dancers have adopted and routinised this style of dance and that all have been able to realise in performance one common vision of performance. Through every section there is a display of collective dance. All the dancers are harmonised and homogenised. They move in the same ways, at the same times, with the same directives, goals, intentions and appear to be having highly similar, if not the same, emotional experiences in their dance. They move in this way as groups, traversing the stage as a unit or at times occupying the entirety of the stage by spreading out. Their presence here eclipsed only by the expanse of the greyish, stone Tower itself and the threatening stormy sky backdropping them.*

*This mass appears like a singular entity. This collective movement and presence bring to mind experiences of watching murmurations of starlings I had seen years prior in Wiltshire, or National Geographic videos of schools and shoaling fish. Their co-ordination and fluidity of action seem to be driven by some superseding authority, some agency that is controlling them. I even consider the beat of the music as the beat of this authority/agency's very heart. This notion dominates my thinking. I cannot stop a preoccupation with how they are operating in this way, and what it means. This body of performers is made further collective in its appearance by the in and out appearance of solo dancers, themselves dancing alternately 'with' the collective body and in contrast to it.*

DOI: 10.4324/9781003205661-1

## 2    Introduction—The Aesthetic Collective

*Their juxtaposition in either case only highlighting in my mind the socialised nature of the performers who dance as one body and the individual dancers' demonstrations of individuality and personal narrative. The choreography embodies before us, the audience, a thoroughly collective endeavour.*

*I hesitate to label this dancing collective body an aesthetic object, for it is no object. I can point to the individual bodies of the performers and illustrate the pattern and organisation of their actions. Nonetheless, this collective body exists in some sort of psycho-perceptual form, something non-materialist. It is something I 'see' happening before me, but it is only 'seen' within my own conceptualising mind. If anything, the dancing body creates in the space of this performance something, some effect I perceive and experience. I would even say that at times I feel transfixed by it, caught within the scope of its effect. For this performance, it operates as its true aesthetic object. The individual dancers, who in other contexts might be the focus or 'stars' of the performance, are here merely incidental characters against whom this larger and more powerful collective character expresses itself, dominating the stage and our attention.*

*Even as I consider that I ask myself if 'character' is the right term here. Can this conceptualised body be a character? Or am I resorting to the term 'character' in its broader form—the character/isation that they are giving to the experience? I feel that both are true. I am reading them as a character (role) within the partial narratives unfolding—they do things, they participate in the advancement of the story, they are affected by and affect the other groups and individual performers—but they are also like a cloud energy, working with the scene, the sky, the weather to produce a tone to the performance and my experience of it; they are creating an atmosphere. That tone I can only summarise in affective terms, something of feeling and emotion. In this space of time, I have come to be affected by this dancing body, and that sensation of being-affected-by is by far made strongest by this collective body in its various permutations than with any of the singular or individual dancers. As the narrative constructs, deconstructs and reconstructs itself in my mind I am washed over with feelings and an emotive experience precipitated by this dancing body. From my removed position in the audience, I begin to feel their experience both subjectively as my own experience and objectively as an experience I can process and think about.*

Like other natural phenomena, this collective body of dancers moves about the stage with a type of mystique and fascination that grasps attention. Like a murmuration of birds, a school of fish or a swarm of insects, there is something primal about it. That they seem simultaneously non-human and all too human. They do not work or appear as individual performers, but rather as coordinated, homogenised and even conformed agents or elements of a larger structure. Like a swath of silken fabric moving about in a breeze, the group is more fluidic or aeriform. It has a beauty and a calmness, but like a swarm it also induces discomfort and even a type of terror—all these things being together, so controlled but working with no seen control.

I have witnessed this kind of performance feature often in all different artistic disciplines. It takes many shapes and forms: for instance, staged crowds or assemblages, static installed groups, khoroi and choruses,[1] dancing ensembles, back-up dancing groups, flashmobs, immersive performance/audience masses

Introduction—The Aesthetic Collective 3

and so on. They pop up and occur all over, equally in contained, formalised performances as in non-formalised public spaces. They command images of power in protest demonstrations, military parades or political campaign events. They are playful, entertaining and filled with hope in Olympic ceremonies or sports half-time shows. Their distinctive collectivising effect deindividuates the individual participants, we do not comprehend the individuals as discrete actors, but as constituent members of a greater whole—they are a mass and that mass is contained within the mass body. The gestalt of the group foregrounds and the individual and their individuality is subsumed, maybe even lost, within that gestalt.

Encountering such groups or being a part of them creates unique reactions and experiences. Such subsuming of individuals within larger conforming bodies carries with it a range of feelings and thoughts: they can be hypnotic and mesmerising; freeing, liberating and embracing; unsettling, scary or terrifying; they can create polarised thoughts of the utopian collective, dystopian social prisons, communal bliss, fascistic enslavement. Different from other collective bodies, like the aforementioned protests, military parades or political campaign bodies, I am narrowing in on those determined or produced in and for aesthetic, performance contexts. This is to say a human, cultural practice, something that we create for deliberative, considered experiencing and/or spectating. They are one step out of natural behaviour of human beings into constructed behaviour. They are re/presentational. They reflect attributes of the human experience as social entities.

A name is needed for these kinds of groups. I invent the term *aesthetic collective* to denote them and this text serves to explore what defines them, how they are used and what they can tell us about human nature and specifically the instinct of masses to watch masses. We generally perceive collectives as a singular body, as a gestalt or whole. There are an enormous number of collectives in the geography of human experience. We generally gather and group in collectives. There are more sociological phenomena such as mobs, crowds or organisational bodies like armies, business boards or even athletics teams. However, I draw a definitive and delimiting circle around a type of collective—those produced and created in or for artistic, designed and performance experiences. Such performance collectives purposefully re-present human collectivity and sociality; performance, and art writ large, seeks to reflect back to us, an audience, that which exists in the world, but in heightened and aesthetically transformed ways. In this text, I will further narrow to the disciplines of theatre, dance, installation art or entertainment media and experiences. Certainly, much of what I will discuss is already directly applicable to non-artistic collectives as well—and such correlations and conclusions are put forward. Nonetheless, the scope of consideration is fixed to, in as broad a category I can use, performance. Crucially, this includes audiences/spectatorship. These collectives constitute or become an 'object' of artistic spectatorship. While almost all elements of life are aestheticised in some way and all collectives likewise have aestheticised dimensions, attention here is

4    *Introduction—The* Aesthetic Collective

on these events' aesthetic and objectified ends, intentions. Hence, my use of the qualifying term *aesthetic*, to delineate that these phenomena are concerned with intentional, designed and performed contexts. They are phenomena of artistry. They are collectives, but they are a subset of collectives with aestheticised experiences as their motivation and output.

In writing this text, using the term 'object', as above, problematised me. Such an ontological term posed philosophical problems for me considering human beings in such a way. In performance or live arts, questions arise as to how we can consider a group of performers/participants who constitute such aesthetic collectives objects. While I can *objectify* people, I cannot really reduce them, the individuals, to the status of an object, nor can I ascribe the totality subject status. This is a pervading problem and one that I will come to address: the ontological status of an aesthetic object composed of live people that is plural, not singular, yet experienced as a singular gestalt. Subjectivity is present in at least the individuals who form collectives, but a group is not a subject in the way that a person is. Groups have no single intelligence, central nervous system or centralised phenomenological being. Consequently, discussion of subjecthood and objecthood is vari-focal and unset. Addressing a collective as an object in this way in part strips the members' subjectivity away. Neither *subject* nor *object* is a proper term for an aesthetic collective. Usually when something does not easily sit within either of those two categories we call them 'things'. Instead of pursuing encampment in such expansive categories, I embrace and foreground their in-betweenness, between objects and subjects. Following Bill Brown's 'Thing Theory',[2] I resolve that aesthetic collectives, broadly speaking, are complex types of *things*. More specifically, I view them as *quasi-things*, a term taken from Tino Griffero.[3] As will be seen, aesthetic collectives operate with a principle feature of being betwixt and between categories. While this can be initially frustrating it does better define them and affords a greater purchase on what we are encountering, what the intersubjective experience of aesthetic collectives is or can be.

Intersubjectivity also occurs here in multiple, different experiential perspectives. Aesthetic collectives offer experience from three main potential perspectives: (1) from inside the collective as a participant; (2) from outside as an audience; or (3) some mixed perspective vacillating between those two. This extends and holds true whether in live or recorded formats as well; in both, there are still participants and audiences—or the audience perspective is present and assumed. Recorded media is a particularly rich place in which to find aesthetic collectives. Indeed, there are dozens of examples in popular culture, particularly in comic books, television and film and they are a favourite trope of science/speculative-fiction and horror. A passing glance at popular culture finds aesthetic collectives as zombie hordes, clones, cybernetic hive-mind aliens or fleets of human-androids presented, respectively, in TV shows such as *The Walking Dead, Orphan Black, Star Trek*'s the Borg and *Westworld* or *Battlestar Galactica*; in literature, one can look to the scary children of *The Midwich Cuckoos* or the psychic mutant Stepford Cuckoos of *X-men*. By way of passing mention,

Introduction—*The* Aesthetic Collective     5

these are all excellent examples. While *aesthetic collective* expands to include further virtual or transmodal collectives where technological mediation is necessary for engagement I am going to exclude them here. They stand well within my concern in explicating the idea, but the technological mediation involved is a lateral concern to the present task. For the present work, I will look across disciplines in the performing arts and determine the specific dimensions of aesthetic collectives through a series of experienced instances (i.e. cases). I have highlighted dancing crowds in club culture, installed live art ensembles specifically looking at the work of Vanessa Beecroft and Kanye West, Greek khoros in theatre performance and back-up dancing groups in music videos (specifically from videos by Janet Jackson, Sia and Lady Gaga).

In many ways, they are all like versions of khoros—perhaps humanity's first formalised artistic collective. From its inception in 6th century B.C.E., Greece khoros was simultaneously a political, religious and sociological tool used to concretise polis structure. It was/is the democratic body on display. In each Greek tragedy, a khoros is present that represents a mass, and often marginal, demographic (soldiers, the aged men, women, slaves, religious celebrants and so on). They watch the action of the scenes and acting between the drama of the scenes and the audience perspective, they comment, dance and sing about the action and its meanings. Crucially, khoros comes from sacred practices.[4] Apprehended from religion and transplanted into the pseudo-religious artistic setting of the theatre (remaining today as Greek tragedy, comedy and satyr play) khoros became a bedrock aspect of society. The institution of the khoregia would become a defining attribute of Greek culture and most notably Athenian society. At a surface level, all my instances of aesthetic collectives have obvious similarity; at a depth, however, there are even more evocative connections. Dancing crowds in clubs pursue the ecstasy of communal dance; Beecroft's installations present form and rigid rules of communal identity-making; back-up dancing groups literally present backgrounds of emotive dance in and between the lyrical episodes of song.

I am not saying these are all khoroi. Rather, these are versions of a similar trope of performance that cuts both ways through the heightened aesthetics of the world of performance and the performative worlds of social, cultural acts and events. Clubbing crowds, for instance, link in this continuum of aesthetic experiences with Greek khoroi and back-up dancers, as phenomena with roots and underpinnings in dancing for ecstatic release. Clubbing crowds are potentially problematic in comparison with the other instances, and are a unique inclusion here. Do we even consider that performance? As social dance, how do they fit with what is otherwise obvious, more formalised performance? Is there an audience? Well, yes they are performance, yes they fit in and yes there is an audience of sorts. What might seem problematic in them is actually an opportunity for better analysis. They are designed cultural experiences and their resulting crowds are objects caught in and perpetuated through artistry. The dance, neither scripted nor agreed in any explicit way, is evocative dance, communally done and under the artistic influence of at least one key

6   *Introduction—The* Aesthetic Collective

artist—the DJ. Their context as social gathering venues/experiences indeed differs from standard presentational contexts for performance work: galleries, theatres, digital platforms. While not explicitly performance events in the same way as my other instances, they are heavily performative events. As to audience, no, they do not define or position an audience as such, but one auto-emerges as a mixed participant/audience body. Dancers dance both for themselves *and* with/for others. There is definite watching happening. These features underpin and are addressed in discussion in chapter 1 and serve to illustrate how pervasive aesthetic collectives are in various corners of life, while also clarifying, and even testing, definitional parameters. In a sense, they stand as a limit case, at the very edges of what is considered planned, constructed or designed and audience-based in the same way as theatrical or artistic performances.

Observationally, aesthetic collectives have unifiers. All have an audience experiencing subjects in contexts in which the *entitativity* of a collective body is created (*entitativity* will be explained shortly); design is used to condition and construct all the experiences had; they all play with the relationship between and interface of audience and aesthetic collective-as-art-object; they all involve space and spacing as a key element of construction. Looking just at the collectives there are a few further common, key attributes—uniformity, conformity, and similarisation. These are some of the first things noticed when seeing an aesthetic collective. Individual identity and presence are adumbrated by or even lost in the identity and presence of the collective totality. A group mentality appears to be dominant and pervading. Behaviour, speech, action, affect and attitude all harmonise in various ways to that of the collective. As individuality dissipates the plural totality foregrounds. These attributes are central to understanding not just what an aesthetic collective is, but how they work. To grasp these inner workings, it is necessary to take the experience as an audience to these encounters and to become a participant (that is, where possible have the experience of existing and being within them). It is also necessary to consider the spaces in which these encounters happen. Reduction to the purely human element mistakenly neglects the essential non-human, post-human or new-materialist elements that collaborate in these phenomena. From internal and external perspectives this book observes, reports and queries the ways in which audience, participant and space/ matter collaboratively construct these entitative collective personae and their entailed experiences.

My interest here emerged from a realisation that performance studies does not really address this. While not directly addressing aesthetic collectives, the fields of sociology, psychology, phenomenology, and studies of atmosphere are more helpful and in-tune with their ideas and explore concomitant concepts like groups, crowds, hive-mind behaviour, perceived entitativity and atmosphere. Sociology in particular brought my attention to *entitativity* and *atmospheric* effect—we perceive them like entities and they behave like/create atmosphere in their artistic situations. However, there is again a lacking degree

*Introduction—The* Aesthetic Collective    7

of scholarship on performance bodies. Khoros is certainly historically analysed, but such scholarship limits itself to performance methods, a history of khoros, politics and social relevance. Disappointingly, there is little to help advance consideration of their entity-like presentation and effect. Significantly, this constellating of ideas frames them within an aesthetics of atmosphere. Moving analysis through these two fields and lenses, entitativity and atmosphere, is something not yet noted in the literature nor fully explored in performance studies. While atmosphere studies is rapidly growing at the moment (we now speak of 'the turn to atmosphere'), again no one seems to be considering atmosphere and entitativity as linked concepts with regard to social bodies in performance. Such thinking has an enormous benefit to performance studies, situating aesthetic collectives within a continuum of active and emergent research and discourse in audience theory, affect theory, the transmission and effect of affect in groups and the relationship between those groups and artistic environments.

Collectives are composed like and have properties of atmosphere: they have field properties. Encountering them is like immersion in an energy field or cloud. Immersion occurs both physically (with respect to the material bodies) and psychologically or intersubjectively, we *feel* inside them. This assertion draws heavily on the aesthetics of atmosphere posited by Gernot Böhme and Peter Sloterdijk. Both discuss atmosphere not as a thing, but as a happening; atmospheres are the already and always present contour and texture of experience on the affective level. They also highlight how atmosphere is at least bimodal that we bring them with us AND that we enter them as pre-existing conditions—we affect the atmosphere, and we are affected by it. Sloterdijk goes further than bimodality, and I follow him in this, considering the atmospheric engine to be polyvalent and occurring in an infinity of affect/be affected trajectories. How we share and transmit affect in this way is a science all its own, and affect theory labours at this. I apply affect theory to unpack such thinking, modelling my own notions particularly after work by Ben Anderson and Theresa Brennan, looking at biophysical possibilities, but more so psycho-emotional ones. It would be a disservice not to include bio-physical grounds, but while such information is alluring, drawing on science and quantifiable, tested data, I tend to move away from it. This is because the encounter of performance is first and foremost a qualitative experience and must be assessed on those terms. Also, such science is vastly difficult to implement as experimental apparatus. Such is the complexity of affect theory and studies of atmosphere; but also a strength—they force us to consider our own experience as valid, informative and to be held on equal footing with concrete scientific data. A significant next move here is how encounters with these aesthetic collectives allow us (as participants, audiences or both) to experience, explore and contemplate notions of plurality in being and subjectivity. Ultimately, this leads to an understanding of the human project in creating and encountering aesthetic collective happenings to experience and re-experience

8    *Introduction—The* Aesthetic Collective

ideas and sensations of 'being-with' and of how that state is reflective of on-going existence outside the performance realm.

The text is in two large parts. The first part explores live performances of aesthetic collectives and presents observations of how they can be conceptualised as entities: as objects, oriented, contained, cohesive, similarised and finally as commonly motivated. Each chapter explores how *entitativity* is achieved or happens in collectives. Together, the first three chapters describe and contribute to a clear and defining image of aesthetic collectives. Throughout, this concept of *entitativity,* posited by Donald T. Campbell in 1958, denotes the perception of entitative states and how this happens.[5] It defines the quality of being, or being like, an entity; something that exists and has definite reality and substance, independent from other things and self-contained. Campbell coined and developed the term to discuss and analyse groups, such as communities, mobs, masses of creatures and protest groups, that we experience and treat like singular beings. In general, gatherings and ensembles of disparate pieces that make up a greater whole. Entitativity and the granting of entitative status involves four procedural analytic tasks that Campbell appropriated from gestalt psychology and implanted in the term's rubric of analysis. He outlines that we grant entitativity on a scale or spectrum based on *proximity, prägnanz,*[6] and *common fate.* Each of the initial three chapters analyses these elements in sequence. *Proximity* and *prägnanz* dominate discussion of clubbing crowds in chapter 1; *similarity* I examine in chapter 2 through Beecroft and West's installations; *common fate* I examine in chapter 3 in relation to Greek khoros. While related terms of Campbell's *entitativity* borrow heavily from Gestalt Theory, I specifically follow his conception, arguments and the use of the terms as well as related and consequent literature.

Although I elaborate and expand these terms in their chapters, a clarification of them is also useful at the outset as I use them throughout and the notion of entitativity drives much of the discourse in this text. First, Campbell states that parts of a whole can be associated and considered part of a totality (a gestalt) by virtue of their *proximity*, nearer together parts being more connected than distanced ones. Second, he outlines how containment and organisation of parts creates a sense of outline, border or edge and more connection to those contained parts. Order or pattern in positioning and relationships also implies coherence and relation. Since no clearer term covers all these aspects, the gestalt term *prägnanz* is used. Campbell anglicised the term to *pregnance* but since this word is not recognised by most scholars or dictionaries I will use the original *prägnanz* throughout this text (as many social scientists in this tradition do). Third, Campbell explains how parts that bear resemblance to each other in appearance and mode of being (that is potential action and qualities of execution) we perceive as similar and thus more together than things that appear different; this he terms *similarity.* Lastly, he outlines how parts that move in the same direction and towards the same purpose or objective we perceive as connected and unified. 'Movement' here does not simply mean physical mobilisation but it can also relate to speech, intentions, goals or

Introduction—*The* Aesthetic Collective    9

elements of identity in and through time. This he terms *common fate* or *joint destiny*. One of the key features of this term is that it is very much a temporal measure. It gives a sense of connected past and future to the presently perceived whole.

These chapters elaborate audiences and spectator perspectives as well. Discussion of aesthetic collectives progresses from contexts in which the audience/art divide is non-existent or exists at the choice of the participant (chapter 1) to one in which the divide and distinction is defined (chapter 2) and then finally aesthetically formalised (chapter 3). In chapter 1, club-crowd audiences have objectifying power and experiential agency over their experiences by controlling their role and performance in the work (free movement in space, ability to communicate, choice of how long to experience, etc.). In chapter 2, we move to the gallery setting and the divide is concrete; audiences are spatially and experientially clearly determined and distinct from the artworks. In chapter 3, we move to theatre audiences, placed in more receptive, silent and mostly immobile roles watching the 'art-object'. Beginning with clubbing crowds as limit studies, where the defining attributes of aesthetic collectives are most indistinct, I centripetally progress into the analysis of cases that are more obvious and definite.

Chapter 1 analyses club-based, rave and DJ experiences. Aesthetic collectives emerge in immersive, entertainment-focused and aesthetically directed spaces in the form of an organically emerging dancing crowd. We first need to understand aesthetic collectives as spatially conceptualised entities. To do so, I construct a theory of space, spatialisation and territorialisation drawn, in the main, from Edward T. Hall.[7] Participants attend these events, are physically contained in a designed space and through mingling, interacting and dancing with/for each other become part of a large dancing crowd. There is no 'art-object' as such. However, all the components of the experience are themselves designed and artistic: the space, the lighting, the music, the air, dress code and so on. In some (but not all) respects, this is not dissimilar to an immersive theatre event in which the artistic vision of the company and director entirely surrounds and involves an audience. In fact Punchdrunk, for instance, routinely ends their immersive performances with a club-dance party; the club-dance feel synthesising the immersive experiences in a social dance format. Issues of immersivity pervades the first part of the text. However, despite my comparison to immersive theatre, my use of the term *immersivity* is primarily descriptive in nature and denotes discussion of feelings of being within/without. It is not an explicit correlation to immersive theatre/performance as a production style which, as David Shearing defines it, is 'concerned with experiential, embodied approaches to performance reception; such practices include promenade, site-specific, one-on-one, audio walks and installation. Immersive theatre privileges the promise of intimacy over distant spectatorship'.[8] While these club-based crowds do indeed involve attributes of these practices—notably feelings of embodied experience and participation—my concern and use of *immersive* is more about being situated within/without and

## 10 Introduction—The Aesthetic Collective

feelings of containment. It includes both physical and psychological entrance to, and audience interaction with, the aesthetic collectives. In some dancing crowds, audience members can interact with the aesthetic collective; in some they do not; in some they can physically enter the aesthetic collective; in some they do not.

The use and application of *immersivity* in Part 1 is more earnestly returned to and directly analysed in chapter 6, where I address larger issues of the encounter, intersubjective experiences and ontological status of aesthetic collectives—whether as a concept they are a subject, object, thing or something else. As I already mentioned, none of these terms quite works, but what does work is considering them as atmospheric entities, something that exists betwixt and between these notions. What is the *art-object* or *aesthetic object* here? In chapter 1, it is the attending audience itself as they dance and perform with and for each other. Everything is designed to facilitate immersion in the event aesthetics and to induce activity with the dancing crowd. The boundary between performer and audience blurs and is effaced to create a common ground of experience. The participant is a self-directing entity who may choose to participate or to watch overtly and/or covertly.

Chapter 2 moves into the live art installation/performance world and explores the work of one particular artist, Vanessa Beecroft, as well as some of her contemporary collaborative work with Kanye West. Attention moves to the individual participants and their similarisation. Looking at Beecroft's practice from the early 1990s and early 2000s, she developed and mounted live art installations of groups of people arranged in spatial patterns, doing no action, usually lasting approximately three hours. From around 2003 on an evolution occurs in her approaches; her aesthetic collectives have progressively more stringent instructions about their appearance, action, affect and general type of embodiment. Spatially, they are not to move from their places while an audience navigates about and watches as they manage and endure the strain of, what will be shown to be, a fairly demanding performance. Considering her work exposes means and methods of transforming a plurality of smaller singularities (people) into larger compound entities (aesthetic collectives).

Beecroft's installations typify the aesthetic collective at an extreme as she works on the allowed activity of the participants, their physical appearance and, crucially, manipulates/controls their agency. In transforming them, often severely, she creates deindividuated clones: removing individuality from the participants to strengthen the collective identity. From 2008 to the present, Beecroft has been working under/with Kanye West, directing and designing his fashion shows, album 'listening parties', some of his music videos and assisting in his creative process in more general ways. I will touch on this and give some attention to West's work, his collectivising techniques and the outcomes of some of his collaboration with Beecroft, but not delve too deep (that is by far an entirely other piece of work). The chapter raises issues in similarising members, how physical and agentic transformations are done and the entailments of what such transformation might mean. Moreover, the

*Introduction—The* Aesthetic Collective 11

elaboration of spectatorial perspectives as defined audience-to-art-object contexts, as opposed to the fully fluid clubbing experience contexts, shows the participants and audience are here clearly cleaved into two different bodies.

The realm of theatre performances and Greek khoros forms the majority of discussion in chapter 3 Theatre and khoros, as mentioned, is a striking example of aesthetic collectives. Surveying four specific performances in London, UK in 2015–2016, the chapter explores khoroi in *Medea* and a *Bakkhai* at the Almeida Theatre, *Oresteia* at Shakespeare's Globe, and *Chorus* from the *Iphigenia Quartet* at the Gate Theatre.[9] Ancient Greek khoros is the aesthetic collective of theatre par excellence, exemplifying its most codified and historically long-lasting artistic practice. In khoroi, we come to see synchronicity, uniformity, conformity and anonymity at their extremes: the embodiment of a collective over the individual. Speech, action, appearance, identity and temporal existence are all similarised to create a group who are equal and the same. While a fascinating area of study all its own, this text only explores these elements as a means to construct a background for khoros. Through examples of khoros we can more intently focus on issues of functionality with aesthetic collectives, how they demonstrate common objective, goal or purpose and how these lend them a temporal existence. Here too I will look into practices (for performers) that are germane to the execution of Greek khoros and the means of producing such objectives in contemporary Greek khoros.

Arising from this discussion of common fate is another feature, of *essence* (and *essentialisation*), to aesthetic collectives. This notion is advanced and broadened in chapter 4, but here stands as a critical outcome of collectives as entitative bodies. The broader literature on essence is overwhelmingly voluminous, expansive and reaches across many disciplines. The term and my restricted discussion/use of *essence,* is defined mainly through the literature on entitativity—which itself is pulling on theory from psychology and phenomenology. For my purposes, *essence* is a present sense or experience of the ontological notion of *being* in an entity.[10] *Being*, notions of which are themselves wide and varied, is the metaphysical centre of an entity comprised of the distinguishing features that define it as an autonomous entity. In an aesthetic collective, an actual being is ambiguously absent, never actualisable in tangible form, only as *perceived* or *sensed* in/through manifestations. As a feature of internalised, immutable reality of self, essence is ascribed to such entities that can only be sensed, perceived or otherwise acknowledged through its *recognition in* more concrete expressions and experiences. These include aspects of identity, appearance, action, vocalisation of thought, intersubjective engagement, physicality and so on. Essence, then, is a present yet always absent attribute of subject entities. In my concluding thoughts, I will draw on Jean-Luc Nancy's interpretation of *being* as *being-with* to detail how aesthetic collectives and their ontological status, and hence their essence, leads to them being a material illustration of *being* as first and foremost *being-with*, and that essence is entitative presence of being with and in the world.[11]

12  *Introduction—The* Aesthetic Collective

Having established their entitativity and achieved presence like an individual actor or agent, the second part of the text moves to more involved discussions of a variety of ontological issues associated with aesthetic collectives. Throughout Part 2, I cast attention on the use and function of aesthetic collectives: what they do or contribute. This part also broadens and details the conceptualisation of aesthetic collectives. I observe how our conceptualising process personifies them as things and, specifically, substances. Returning to immersivity, I note how being *like* substances (mostly liquids and gases) we feel immersed in them. This leads to my ultimate consideration of their atmospheric properties.

Chapter 4 reviews the first part, detailing uses/functions/purposes of aesthetic collectives. Centrally, as characters, as essentialised things, and as characterising, mood-makers. First, they can function as characters within performances. I use the term *character* in the specific meaning of role. This is easy enough to conceive of in the theatre examples where characters are components of the plays. Outside of such scripted or narrative contexts, this was equally the case, though. Beecroft installations clearly construct a character/character type for the models and the clubbing crowds allow situations for fluid and open performative enactment of character types. Second, character role implies an intersubjective experience—that audience and participant are engaging with some subjectivity or the assumption of it. I frame this in terms of a notion of essence and essentialisation drawn, in the main, from research authored and co-authored by social scientist Yoshihisa Kashima—itself an outgrowth of Campbell's concept of entitativity.[12] Within that framework, the idea of essence emerges in higher levels of entitativity as the thing that we ascribe to inhabited, subject-like entities. It is something we can grant or project onto non-subject, non-human things to engage with them like we engage with human subjects. Third, I laterally expand the notion of character from a noun, character-as-role, to a verb, character-as-acting-quality, and examine how aesthetic collectives create a character/istic to their encounter. Lastly, this character/istic element exposes aesthetic collectives as mood-makers.

Chapter 5 addresses recorded media cases drawn from music videos of Janet Jackson (*Rhythm Nation*), Sia (*The Greatest*) and Lady Gaga (*Bad Romance* and *Alejandro*).[13] I expand observation to include recorded media, music videos, as a place where aesthetic collectives also appear (sometimes as unobserved dominant elements). In shifting to recorded media issues of liveness and ways of viewing are diversified. Here we (the viewer/s) have complete control over the video playback and timecode. Turning to Philip Auslander,[14] I consider the impact this has, which is otherwise not the case in live performance contexts. Each of these videos is a cornerstone piece of art in music video culture and has made a significant impact on the industry and popular culture writ large. The function, use and purpose of aesthetic collectives create or supply *mood* for their aesthetic events—mood is something powerful, pervasive and essential in performance. As I turn to what constitutes mood, I begin to

*Introduction—The* Aesthetic Collective   13

examine affect, feeling, emotion and atmosphere. A central feature of the chapter is in formalising concepts of atmosphere and affect, affective reality and affect exchange/transmission.

I focus discussion through contemporary angles in affect theory centring on ideas of affective experiences, transmission and convergence. This is concentrated mostly on work by Sigal Barsade (on her own and with others),[15] Theresa Brennan[16] and Ben Anderson.[17] This in turn accesses and uses two dominant threads in affect theory, one from Silvan Tomkins and the other from Gilles Deleuze.[18] As Gregory Seigworth and Melissa Gregg note, '[w]ith Tomkins, affect follows a quasi-Darwinian "innate-ist" bent toward matters of evolutionary hardwiring [...] traduc[ing ...] influences borne along by the ambient irradiation of social relations'.[19] I agree with such biophysiological dimensions to social relations; clearly, we as organisms use biology to perceive and affect our environments. I also, and more substantively, consider a Deleuzian perspective that 'locates affect in the midst of things and relations (in immanence) and, then, in the complex assemblages that come to compose bodies and worlds simultaneously'.[20] As I progress and move into chapter 6, both affective vectors are used to give a 'certain inside-out/outside-in difference in directionality: affect as the prime "interest" motivator that comes to put the drive in bodily drives (Tomkins); affect as an entire, vital, and modulating field of myriad becomings across human and nonhuman (Deleuze)'.[21] chapter 7 mainly observes how aesthetic collectives, as artistic things, are affectively unique in their intentional affect exchange and transmission and, as such, are special cases of directed atmospheric phenomena.

In chapter 8, I examine the encounter itself. I return to the issue of the audience and how in spectating aesthetic collectives we have the unique situation of masses viewing masses, one mass body watching/performing for/ with another mass body. Starting with an overview of encounter types between audience and participant bodies, with each other and themselves, I then pursue the intersubjectivity that aesthetic collectives provide/can provide. A notable deviation from most study of intersubjectivity, is that they create multiple intersubjective experiences that happen simultaneously—I refer to this as *plural intersubjectivity*. This is another notion that, outside of philosophy, is not unpacked in performance studies: the concept of intersubjectivity occurring in multiple directions in pluralised states of being. Intersubjectivity here occurs with a plural-yet-singular body, both in the form of the audience body and the collective 'subject'. Again, not really a subject, but exuding features of subjectivity, the collective body demonstrates a field property of subjective presence—the thing in which and with an intersubjective occurrence takes place. Here, I turn to Peter Sloterdijk to expand this kind of intersubjectivity, heavily adopting his philosophical reimagining of human interaction and metaphysics in spherology.[22] The whole of *Spherology* is massive. Spanning three volumes and approximately 3000 pages of text, Sloterdijk's perspective could not possibly be used in totality. I selectively use a few central notions, mainly drawn from his third volume, *Foam*.

14  *Introduction—The* Aesthetic Collective

Key tenets of Sloterdijk's philosophical framework underpin a macro-level conceptual architecture for aesthetic collectives and intersubjective experiences of them. He conceives of intersubjective experiences in novel ways. First, he posits that subjecthood begins and is modelled after a plural existence in the first instance; that from conception the individual is not alone and subjectivity is not solipsistic, rather the individual is *with-* (a mother, a placenta, a twin, etc.) and that after birth a spacing and differentiating of the self from others creates individuality. Thus, we might link our fascination and disquiet with collectives in performance in terms with this inceptive notion of *being* as actually *being-with*. Second, Sloterdijk puts forth a notion of reality as being like foam in structure and intersubjective geometry. From this perspective, individuals are like bubbles, self-contained spheres inclusive of our physical, inhabited territory and filled with our presence. Our bubbles, though, press up against other bubbles. We press up against the inhabited spheres of other people, but this expands beyond into new-materialist, posthuman horizons. We are also caught against, within and around spheres of influence and force. The nature of these spheres might be material (living spaces, cubicles, transportation structures), social (groupings by sociological category [race, gender, sexuality, etc.] or membership in groups), conceptual (status/economics/law/politics), virtual (media, communications, digital existences, avatar realities) or even entirely imagined (psychology, mental health). In a globalised and technologically mediated world, we no longer exist in *a* sphere (and perhaps we never did), but in a multiplicity of spheres all touching, connecting and interacting: in foam structures. Foam is the larger picture of how these spheres interact, affect and are affected by each other, like a confluence of bubbles. This differs from networks and network theory in that there are no nodes here, no centres and no axial movements. Instead, everything occurs in fields of presence and influence and multiply, imbricated or simultaneous ways. This theory exquisitely defines and explains the geometry of plural intersubjectivity at work in aesthetic collectives. They are foam structures with foam properties. As such, the notion of immersion returns again on several overlapping levels and depths.

To establish exactly what I mean, or can be meant, by *immersive* in aesthetic collectives I look to Gareth White[23] and Catherine Bouko.[24] Pulling from two of their key texts, I mean *immersive* as something different than simply physically moving amongst or interacting with the performed work. This is a general tendency of assumption with audiences. Again, this is not a commentary on immersive theatre as a style of performance reception (indeed, most of these works would not be classed as immersive theatre); this is a descriptive term addressing feelings of being engulfed, contained or subsumed within or the opposite (being outside).[25] Aesthetic collectives are immersive events that may work on their audiences in this physical way, but also, and more importantly, in terms of the reach of their field of presence—their affective dimension. Such immersion I distil down to three general types of encounter: *being immersed* or *participating* in an aesthetic collective; *witnessing*

*Introduction—The* Aesthetic Collective    15

immersion of participants within an aesthetic collective; *feeling immersed* or part of the aesthetic collective *as a result of acts of witnessing.*

All three are determined by the context and interactive format of the performance. In contexts where you are a member or participant in an aesthetic collective, like clubbing crowds, you are immersed by being a part of them, through physical subsumption, by participating. It is possible as well to shift roles here, being an audience or participant. This allows both interacting/participating and witnessing. Where aesthetic collectives are physically distinct from the audience (theatre, galleries, video), you, as audience, may witness the immersion and experience of the participants within the collective. As a result of this, you might also have an experience of immersion by absorption—feeling brought into it. That is, being immersed in the aesthetic collective by psychological projection into it. These types of immersion are not simply how we interact with this performance phenomenon, but they also condition the intersubjective experience and ontological grasping that occurs.

Conditioning I further elaborate in the latter part of chapter 6, where aesthetic collectives as atmospheric phenomena as an idea is fully unpacked. Returning to Sloterdijk, *being-with* occurs in *conditioned* spaces, which he first refers to as climates and then as atmospheres. I elaborate the idea of conditioning and how space (and the material of space, air) is conditioned and that it conditions our sensations and experiences. In a reciprocal fashion, we also condition spaces. Interaction between human beings (with each other and with places) is not an inert experience, it occurs as and in a charged or imbued space. Like weather in the stratospheric encasing, within given spaces people create human atmospheres, they 'make weather', through their emotional communication, broadcasting and telegraphing. This process is self-iterating and unending. Poetically put, we both make weather and weather it. In this regard, all experience takes place as and in an atmosphere. Following this, aesthetic collectives are a special type of atmospheric phenomenon and they offer a unique space for the experience and contemplation of intersubjectivity and the transmission of affect—that is, this natural process is foregrounded. Foam structures, as metaphor and conceptual tool, help to expand on how the intersubjective realities in aesthetic collectives are not singular in any case. When experiencing them, a foam structure emerges as the dominant feature. To experience them is to experience a plurality of participants taking-in, processing and affecting/being affected by the subjectivities of the other participants while negotiating their own subjectivity into a stable totality. The multiplicity of spheres combine to create single macro-entities that shape-shift as the collective performance evolves. This is what audiences and participants are immersed in and experiencing. Ephemeral and transient as a soapy foam.

I also turn to the work of Gernot Böhme[26] and use his aesthetics of atmosphere to expand on this more. Böhme's definition and explanation of atmosphere begins with discussion of how it is a psycho-spatial feature. Using his elaboration of atmosphere as the psycho-emotional tinting of a space, often

16  *Introduction—The* Aesthetic Collective

mixed or conflated with the idea of mood, I discuss aesthetic collectives throughout the second part of the text in terms of affect, emotion and mood. Inspecting further I illustrate how atmosphere is the experience of an-other (any other, living or not) and the affective presence both of the subject themself and the other. In performance, the performers and audience colour and suffuse the encounter with their presence and consequently influenced the phenomenological experience. In a formulaic statement, the atmosphere is the circulating exchange and transmission of affect in given environments. On one level, aesthetic collectives are special cases of atmosphere: the collectives themselves aesthetically conditioned and designed atmospheres in which participants exist. On a second level, that atmospheric conditioning is con-spicuous to the external, but immersed, witnessing audience. On a third level, the collective-audience relationship and the joint space they occupy is its own atmosphere.

In performance, there are a wealth of aesthetic choices. To establish or construct atmosphere also is to design experience and choose affective hap-penings; to structure, create and manipulate affective reality. This expands to features of design and the choreographing of experiencing subject(s) within those designs. Following Brennan, atmospheric conditioning becomes a matter of controlling the sensory environment and its implied emotional re-sonance. The atmospheric artist first and foremost determines and makes choices for the reality of the artistic experience. In a colloquial way, they are reality-constructing. It brings to mind Dee Reynolds' discussion of kinaes-thetic empathy and the experience of watching dance as the 'dance's body'.[27] That while witnessing choreography, the spectator is immersed in the affective experience of the dancer moving *through* a body of choreography and the spectating experience is tinted and toned by other elements, in particular she discusses sound. Reynold's discussion focuses on kinaesthetic empathy as being 'an opportunity to experience a mode of perception [...] producing a virtual dance's body at the interface between performer and spectators, which chal-lenges established frameworks of how we come to know and to move in the world'.[28] Reynolds otherwise phrases this as a focusing and unfocusing of the self to immersion in the affective environment. Such kinaesthetic empathy runs close to what I propose here, but I extend from it a bit, showing that there is no singular or dyadic flow of intersubjectivity in the immersion I discuss. No necessary focusing or unfocusing on *one* thing. Atmospheric analysis will instead show that such plural experiences are field-like, and that everyone and everything are simultaneously emanating fields in which we find ourselves and through which we have access to multiple bodies of experiences simultaneously.

My analysis shows the ontological nature of aesthetic collectives to be complicated. Ontologically speaking, to be entitative is to have object status and perhaps also subject status. Entitativity refers to perceived objects that have a sense of subjectivity or to be perceived like sensate, sentient beings but are in

*Introduction—The* Aesthetic Collective   17

themselves not bounded by a single natural physical container, like a skin. While aesthetic collectives do not have physical containment in this sense, nor do they have centralised or commanding intelligence, they do variously shift between being coalesced entitative wholes and dissipated pieces (individuals) or even collections of smaller groups. Even more troublesome the individual parts, the member people, are themselves subjects.

In this way, they are not easy to discuss or write about. Their nature as perceived things, their non-fixed ontological status and the restrictions of language to address such phenomena mean discussion is continuously constrained by categorisation and relating them to other, more concrete and understood, phenomena. Upon realising this I considered how such analogising and metaphor dominates the text and the conceptualisation of the aesthetic collectives. It is ever-present and pervasive. Consequently, in the precis of Part 2, I draw attention to and unpack such issues and what the process of conceptualisation entails. I apply George Lakoff and Mark Johnson's text *Metaphors We Live By*[29] and many of its key considerations of metaphor to highlight what I consider to be germane processes of thinking. An overarching narrative of metaphor emerges in how we conceptualise aesthetic collectives to understand them. Conceptualisation relates them to objects and specifically containers, something bounded and shaped (things that we *go into* or *stand outside of* or are *around*). As experiences, they relate to entities and substances through ontological metaphors (addressing *them* and *their effect* or the ways *they* are and how *they move/flow/transform*, etc.). We also personify them, graft human characteristics onto them. Such a matrix of metaphor establishes a conceptual coherence for aesthetic collectives, while also foregrounding what complex things they are.

The implications here are elastic and extend into several directions and other disciplines. Since I consider simultaneously scenographic, directorial and spectatorship practices clearly this contributes to the field of performance studies/practices. However, the underlying critical elements concern notions of subjectivity, intersubjectivity, identity and plurality. Philosophical and sociological features are enchained in it. A further application of this work, which exists in further study/discourse, is the consideration of the aesthetic collective as a testing ground for human behavioural sciences, particularly in social or collective psychology. The ways in which aesthetics are used to create atmospheric tactics/techniques and the affective manipulation of groups could be used to explore and map the behavioural scripts by which human beings operate (there relating back to Tomkins). Most germane, though, are those implications of the aesthetic collective and its reception as reflective medium; through artistic form, they offer access to and exposure of phenomenological structures reflective of human existence and being as social creatures who construct social realities and adopt and shift agentic roles. A glimpse is offered into the relational and experiential balance between individuality, sociality, collectivity; all of us reconciling these three while navigating our collective reality.

## 18 *Introduction—The* Aesthetic Collective

# Notes

1 The distinction between which is that 'khoros' will refer specifically to the Greek khoros, whereas 'chorus' can represent a singing chorus, a backup chorus, a musical theatre chorus or the like.

2 Bill Brown, 'Thing Theory', *Critical Inquiry*, 28:1 (2001), 1–22.

3 Tonino Griffero, *Quasi-Things: The Paradigm of Atmospheres,* trans. by Sarah De Sanctis (New York: SUNY Press, 2017).

4 It falls beyond the scope of this monograph to explore these features in detail. For a comprehensive text on the issue, I recommend Peter Wilson's *The Athenian Institution of the Khoregia* (Cambridge: Cambridge University Press, 2000).

5 Donald T. Campbell, 'Common Fate, Similarity, and Other Indices of the Status of Aggregates of Persons as Social Entities', *Behavioral Science*, 3:1 (1958), 14–25.

6 From German, directly translates as clarity/pithiness/succinctness.

7 Edward T. Hall, *The Hidden Dimension* (New York: Anchor Books published by arrangement with Doubleday, a division of Random House, Inc., 1990).

8 David Shearing, 'Intimacy, Immersion and the Desire to Touch: The Voyeur Within', in *Theatre as Voyeurism: The Pleasures of Watching,* ed. by George Rodosthenous (London: Palgrave Macmillan, 2015), p. 71.

9 Euripides, *Medea,* a new version by Rachel Cusk, dir. by Rupert Goold (London: Almeida Theatre, 2015); Euripides, *Bakkhai,* trans. and adapted by Anne Carson, dir. by James Macdonald (London: Almeida Theatre, 2015); Aeschylus, *Oresteia,* adapted by Rory Mullarky, dir. by Adele Thomas (London: Shakespeare's Globe, 2015); Chris Thorpe, *Chorus,* dir. by Elayce Ismail (London: Gate Theatre, 2016).

10 Martin Heidegger discusses this *being* as *dasein* and as a problematic centre of ontology, one that underpins his entire phenomenology as expressed in *Being and Time*. I refer the reader to Martin Heidegger, *Being and Time*, trans. by Joan Stambaugh (Albany: State University of New York Press, 2010). Dasein is also addressed by Alice Rayner in regards to theatrical dualities and their exposing/concealing of reality (and my further comments on aesthetic collectives having a present/absent sense of being or ontology) as a representation or metaphor for being. I direct the reader to Alice Rayner, *Ghosts; Death's Double and the Phenomena of Theatre* (Minneapolis, MN: University of Minnesota Press, 2006)—particularly see pages 146–148.

11 Jean-Luc Nancy, *Being Singular Plural* (Stanford, CA: Stanford University Press, 2000). While essence and being will recur as topics throughout the text, the extent to which I can pursue and define them will be limited and framed, again, in the main through their definition, conceptualisation and use as drawn from studies in entitativity and the literature I present later. To move significantly beyond these is beyond the main purports of this text; however, for further discussion, I suggest comparative reading between Nancy and Heidegger as referenced earlier.

12 Yoshihisa Kashima, 'Culture, Communication, and Entitativity; A Social Psychological Investigation of Social Reality', in *The Psychology of Group Perception; Perceived Variability, Entitativity, and Essentialism,* ed. by Vincent Yzerbyt, Charles M. Judd and Olivier Corneille (New York and Hove: Psychology Press, 2004); Yoshihisa Kashima et al., 'Culture, Essentialism, and Agency: Are Individuals Universally Believed to Be More Real Entities Than Groups?', *European Journal of Social Psychology*, 35 (2005); Yoshihisa Kashima, 'Communication and Essentialism: Grounding the Shared Reality of a Social Category', *Social Cognition*, 28:3 (2010), pp. 306–328; Wolfgang Wagner, Peter Holtz and Yoshihisa Kashima, 'Construction and Deconstruction of Essence in Representing Social Groups: Identity Projects, Stereotyping, and Racism', *Journal for the Theory of Social Behaviour*, 39:3 (2009).

13 Janet Jackson, *Rhythm Nation*, A&M Records (1989), online video clip www.youtube.com published on 16 June 2009, https://www.youtube.com/watch?v=OAwaNWGLM0c [accessed 15 July 2017]; Lady Gaga, *Bad Romance,* Red One & Lady Gaga (2009),

## Introduction—*The* Aesthetic Collective   19

online video clip www.youtube.com published on 24 November 2009, https://www.youtube.com/watch?v=qrO4YZeyl0I [accessed 15 July 2017]; Lady Gaga, *Alejandro*, Red One & Lady Gaga (2009), online video clip www.youtube.com published on 8 June 2010, https://www.youtube.com/watch?v=niqrrmev4mA [accessed 15 July 2017]; Sia, *The Greatest*, Kurstin (2016), online video clip www.toutube.com published on 5 September 2016, https://www.youtube.com/watch?v=GKSRyLdjsPA [accessed 15 July 2017].

14 Philip Auslander, *Liveness: Performance in a Mediatized Culture*, 2nd ed. (London and New York: Routledge, Taylor & Francis Group, 2008).

15 Sigal G. Barsade and Donald E. Gibson, 'Why Does Affect Matter in Organizations?', *Perspectives,* 21:1 (2007), 36–59; Sigal Barsade, 'The Ripple Effect: Emotional Contagion and its Influence on Group Behavior', *Administrative Science Quarterly*, 47:4 (2002), 644–675; Sigal G. Barsade and Andrew P. Knight, 'Group Affect', *Annual Review of Organizational Psychology and Organizational Behaviour*, 2 (2015), 21–46; Sigal G. Barsade, Olivia A. O'Neill, 'What's Love Got to Do with It? A Longitudinal Study of the Culture of Companionate Love and Employee and Client Outcomes in the Long-Term Care Setting', *Administrative Science Quarterly*, 59:4 (2014), 551–598.

16 Theresa Brennan, *The Transmission of Affect* (Ithaca and London: Cornell University Press, 2004).

17 Ben Anderson, *Encountering Affect; Capacities, Apparatuses, Condition* (London: Routledge Taylor and Francis, 2016).

18 See Silvan S. Tomkins, *Affect, Imagery, Consciousness: The Complete Edition* (New York: Springer Publishing Company, 2008); Gilles Deleuze, *Spinoza: Practical Philosophy*, trans. by Robert Hurley (San Francisco: City Lights Books, 1998); Gilles Deleuze, 'Ethology: Spinoza and Us', in *Incorporations*, ed. by Jonathan Crary and Sanford Kwinter (New York: Zone Books, 1992); Gilles Deleuze & Félix Guattari, *A Thousand Plateaus*, trans. by Brian Massumi (Minneapolis: University of Minnesota Press, 1987).

19 Gregory J. Seigworth and Melissa Gregg, 'An Inventory of Shimmers', in *The Affect Theory Reader*, ed. by Gregory J. Seigworth and Melissa Gregg (Durham and London: Duke University Press, 2010), pp. 5–6.

20 Seigworth and Gregg, p. 6.

21 Seigworth and Gregg, p. 6.

22 Peter Sloterdijk, *Terror from the Air*, trans. by Amy Patton and Steve Corcoran (Los Angeles, CA: Semiotext(e), Foreign Agents Series, 2009); Peter Sloterdijk, *Spheres; Volume 2: Globes, Macrospherology*, trans. by Wieland Hoban (South Pasadena, CA: Semiotext(e), 2014); Peter Sloterdijk, *Spheres; Volume 3: Foams; Plural Spherology*, trans. by Wieland Hoban (California: Semiotext(e), 2016).

23 Gareth White, 'On Immersive Theatre', *Theatre Research International*, 37:3 (2012), 221–235.

24 Catherine Buoko, 'Interactivity and Immersion in a Media-Based Performance', *Participations; Journal of Audience and Reception Studies*, 11:1 (May 2014), 254–269.

25 The literature on immersive theatre/performance as a style is expansive and vast. While I do not invest much in discussing such styles of immersivity (although chapter 6 does consider it and associated practices) I have reviewed related literature and direct the reader to the following pivotal research in the bibliography: Susan Bennett, *Theatre Audiences: A Theory of Production and Reception*; Gordon Calleja, *In-Game: From Immersion to Incorporation*; Erika Fischer-Lichte, 'The Art of Spectatorship'; Helen Freshwater, *Theatre & Audience*; Josephine Machon, *Immersive Theatres: Intimacy and Immediacy in Contemporary Performance*.

26 Gernot Böhme, 'Atmosphere as the Fundamental Concept of a New Aesthetics', trans. by David Roberts, *Text Eleven*, 36 (1993), 113–126; Gernot Böhme, *The Aesthetics of Atmosphere*, ed. by Jean-Paul Thibaud (Abingdon, Oxon: Routledge, 2017).

27 Dee Reynolds, 'Kinesthetic Empathy and the Dance's Body: From Emotion to Affect',

20    *Introduction—The* Aesthetic Collective

in *Kinesthetic Empathy in Creative and Cultural Practices*, ed. by Dee Reynolds and Matthew Reason (Bristol: Intellect Ltd, 2012), pp. 123–136.

28 Reynolds, 'Kinesthetic Empathy', p. 133.

29 George Lakoff and Mark Johnson, *Metaphors We Live By* (Chicago and London: University of Chicago Press, 2003).

# Part I

# Precis

The following chapters develop an understanding of the entitativity of aesthetic collectives. Before beginning, it is useful first to break the idea down a bit. As introduced, entitativity is a concept invented by Donald T. Campbell in 1958. Borrowing heavily from gestalt psychology, he coined the term to denote a conceptualising spectrum on which human beings perceive and come to recognise multiple disparate/individual things as groups and those groups as being *entitative, like an entity.* Campbell offers four different natural elements, or means of measuring, entitativity: proximity, prägnanz, similarity and common fate. Either as an external observer or from within the group, this recognition process is grounded in comparison, categorisation and analogic language. We use metaphors to conceptualise them: *they are like* … or *they are as* … . Thus, the conceptualising process and analogic thinking are themselves germane. Metaphors and analogic thinking occur as we conceptualise collectives and masses. We naturally compare and associate sensation in terms of others, or features of others, that are more fully understood and cognitively framed. That is, we use metaphorical substitutes to conceive things better. The language we use and the thought processing it signals lend insight into what our cognition is actively doing. Entitativity thus comes to be an analytic process that sorts our sensation and perception of groups into categories of entities. It is also something that happens without any real awareness or executive intelligence; it happens in the background functions of our brains.

I use Lakoff and Johnson to help outline our conceptualising activity as broken into four key categories:

> *perceptual,* based on the conception of the object by means of our sensory apparatus; *motor activity,* based on the nature of our motor interactions with objects; *functional,* based on our conception of the functions of the object; and *purposive,* based on the uses we can make of an object in a given situation.[1]

This kind of conceptualising activity engages these four considerations simultaneously, not in progression, forming a mosaic of understanding. To avoid confusion, though, I examine them one at a time.

DOI: 10.4324/9781003205661-2

22 *Precis*

Chapter 1 will majorly address perceptual and motor activity categories. I do this while exploring proximity and prägnanz in entitativity as creating feelings of aesthetic collectives as bounded and bodied, *like* objects and containers. As measures they help us objectify and bound groups, conceiving them as something that is contained, whole and continuous. We conceptualise them as a *body,* as in a *body of people together.* Aesthetic collectives are in fact non-bodied entities. They do not have a physically continuous, contained or centralised body and are composed of individual bodies separated and surrounded by measures of space. But, we come to envision them as a *totality, membership, whole, collective, group, gestalt.* As much as possible I use these terms as they imply both a singular one and multiple components.

This body does not actually exist in any physically or materially contained form. There is always some empty space between and around the individuals that create the body. Moreover, that space is plastic or elastic in terms of volume and shape. With any movement of a part, it can increase, decrease, shift, contract and spread. Moreover, bodies like this are physically permeable and can be navigated in, around and through should one wish. Their containment *as a body* is conceptualised out of my perception of their close enough proximity and degrees of prägnanz. As spatially contained bodies they further contrive feelings of being inside or outside, or of observing from inside/outside. The very notion of sides even implies a sort of surface, barrier or walling. This experiential perspective aligns with descriptions of immersion, feeling contained in or surrounded by something. They contain, have containment, and that quantifies. How big is 'it'; where does 'it' begin and end; what kinds of measurement do we apply? Quantification is one of the most important first steps in understanding collectivity, allowing us to grasp collectives and make them object-like, to objectify them.

Aesthetic collectives are also something we interact with, *like* experiential things, and in so doing can change us, we can change it or both. This notion carries over into chapters 2 and 3, where I overview functional and purposive dimensions. In chapter 2, a detailed investigation of similarisation shows how it creates collective function out of individual people. Similarisation is broad in its scope and in a sense means 'making everything the same or close to the same'. I apply the term, in the way most social scientists in this area do, to examine similarisation of physical appearance and of action/behaviour. This includes a perspicacious look at how much choice, freewill or individual expression occurs in groups and how those might be manipulated to increase entitativity. This leads to an involved consideration of agency and how members of collectives have a negotiated, similarised agency and undergo a type of deindividuation. Key questions arise such as: Who makes these manipulations, the self or other? How does it happen? Who/what is in control? What effect does this have on the self/collective?

These ideas carry over to chapter 3 where I scrutinise purposive aspects to aesthetic collectives through an unfolding of the notion of common fate. This involves personification, giving them characteristics *like* people such as goal, purpose, intention, motivation, and in the process make them more relatable to human beings. Purposive dimensions can also detail two smaller types of purpose: What is the purpose of the group and of the individual in the group? This means we categorise and analogise collectives in terms of human psychology and biography. We extend their existence as something moving towards outcomes and thus as something occupying not just space, as above, but time. As temporal entities, common fate draws together individuals beyond physio-spatial limitation, and indeed as something that exists as a virtual entity beyond the duration of performance—we come to think of them as something that might exist before the performance and after its conclusion.

# 1 Proximity and Prägnanz—Space, Order, Touch

In the dark, sonically booming environments of the dance club a natural aesthetic collective emerges in the form of the dancing crowd. We go to these places and attend these events to engage in social and cultural dance. Walk into clubs and a group of pulsing, bobbing, dancing and moving people are one large body. We draw together and move to the music, weaving our own personal, internal narratives together into one chaotic, yet cohesive, public totality. A diametric relation opens between this dancing crowd and the DJ, and/or other artists, formulating the sonically led aesthetic experience. Clubs are aestheticised, performative environments with clear artistic aims, intentions and considerations. Lights, sound, spatial design, dress codes, entertainment acts, stages, food and/or drink, projections, haze and further spectacle elements are variously employed to generate aesthetic experiences. Not all these elements are always used, but these events are designed explicitly for crafting and using planned atmospheres for entertainment, enjoyment and even cathartic purposes.

Unlike gallery installations, theatre events or music videos these experiences are in a way marginally classed as performance as there is perhaps not an artistic object or audience as such, but rather as artistic *experiences* in which roles and properties of participant and audience are blurred. In a club we, the attendants, are explicitly and actively involved, brought into and constitute the aesthetic world. Peripherally or actively watching the dancing or moving to dance ourselves, participants operate as key actors in atmospheric production alongside the designing hands of the DJ and additional technicians and engage as both audience and participant. We do this for at least two purposes: entertainment performance and ritualised transportative (possibly even transformative) behaviour.[2] Once within the aesthetic spaces the crowds fulfil the two roles or audience and participant simultaneously. These two terms indicate very different forms of encounter and immersion in the aesthetic experience. *Audience* tends to imply a receptive role which may involve some participation/interaction with the aesthetic event and some degree of feedback directed at the aesthetic event. *Participant* tends to imply an active role which must involve degrees of participation and interaction with the aesthetic event. A participant in an aesthetic event can have planned participation, as in the case

DOI: 10.4324/9781003205661-3

26    *Precis*

of actors and performers, or unplanned, as in participatory attendants. Club crowds merge the two roles, something the other aesthetic collectives in this book tended to minimise. There is scope for an attendant to a clubbing event to assume fully one role, the other or both. Attendants also typically shift between those roles actively.

All of this is from my own participating and observing perspective and as such reflects a subjective reading of the events. Holding both those roles interchangeably made apparent the psychological and physical shifts that happen when changing between them. Something that immediately became apparent was that it is relatively awkward to be physically within the dancing group but not dancing/participating in its activity and vice versa for dancing outside the collective group in the 'open' space. As a researcher, I also noticed a third role I occupied, when I actively took moments to step to different non-participating vantage points of the event to observe these as whole events. Often this constituted a move to the edges of the rooms or to an upper gallery (in the case of Metropolis). When this was not physically possible, I had to heighten the psychological shift into a non-participant mode of thought, examining my surroundings and experiences from within but with critical distance.[3] This role, however, involved clandestine behaviour, working so as not to disturb or alert people to their being watched in a critical, though non-judgemental, way. My notes also include testimonial evidence drawn from conversations with companions who attended these events with me (often as a mode of comparison to my own experiences).

Clubs, as places slightly outside that of more formalised performance venues (again, galleries, theatres, etc.), stand as a place of social–cultural performance. As such the dancing crowd sits at the limit of my definition of aesthetic collectives. They are potentially problematic when situated alongside other more formalised instances that are more concretely understood as performance. Within these events dancing crowds emerge as aesthetic collectives and the discussion here follows a close study of instances of clubbing events that I attended. In this chapter, I will use these dancing crowds to expand upon the spatialisation that emerges in aesthetic collectives. In isolating and attending to spatialisation in aesthetic collectives, trends occur in how we manipulate space and the arrangement of bodies that contribute to perception of them as entitative. While dancing in these crowds, I noticed that these spatial trends relate the individual people to the collective entity. Spacing, and in particular the regulation of distance and orientation between bodies, directly affects the sense of groupness, of cohesion and collectivity, as conceptualised like a body, a contained object.

While under the heading of entertainment for the attendants, it is an artform for the creators of the experience (DJs, events managers, lighting and sound designers and technicians, special effects coordinators, projectionists and others). Any casual discussion with a DJ, for instance, immediately makes clear that they consider themselves music and experienced artists. They will often quickly make note that they are not musicians in the same way that an

*Proximity and Prägnanz—Space, Order, Touch* 27

instrumentalist or a composer is, but more like collage artists whose medium is sound (unless they actually are a musician or trained as one). Equally, they often comment on the responsive relationship they have with their audience, much like actors or dancers do. These events also are all highly produced, stage-managed and technical experiences for an audience.

I am going to trace a series of visits I made to different clubs or club-like environments as a participant and observer over 18 months from 2014 to 2016. These range different types of clubbing experiences, from large-scale and more explicitly commercially focussed clubs to smaller scale and more 'homegrown' to impromptu, private and non-commercial. These events, except an event in Suffolk which is more like a party/rave, were all self-regulating (i.e. there were no police present, but there were dedicated front-of-house staff, bouncers and licensing). Issues of legality, choice, manipulation, power, consent and the like are assumed to be socially agreed upon entry. Club contexts offer a unique type of experience in which physical interaction and participation become key themes of engagement. This means that my observations of collectivisation will have various personal feelings and inter-pretations associated with other participants. While I can only speak directly to my own experience, I can comment on what I witnessed across the perceived crowd and anecdotal commentary from friends. While these concerns are important and connected to the experience, they lie outside the scope of this text and my arguments. I will thus cut through issues of demographic and stay focussed on common and, as far as possible, objective experience.

Addressing my roles at these events, the choice of role entirely dictated my experience and formed strong associated feelings. The role of critical, re-searching witness for instance created feelings of loneliness, isolation, shame, fear and even anger. This was most obvious at one event, a Guerilla Science ex-periment in clubbing at Carwash in Bond Street, London in December 2015. I attended that event on my own with the intention of watching how a crowd under controlled conditions would behave. I felt it was a ready-made research opportunity. However, being alone and entering with the mindset of ob-servation I felt most comfortable sitting outside the group witnessing their ex-perience. This created a strong sense of outsidership. I felt lonely and found it impossible to put myself in/interact with the dancing crowd. I never really entered or engaged with it. Different to other events, here I was not really a participant, other club experiences I engaged with the dancing crowds and the experience from the outset as an attendant, not a researcher. I also had com-panions at all my other experiences; even when I was a witnessing audience member, I would return to and be brought into/immersed in the dancing crowd by friends.

These encounters and experiences are social in nature. To be faithful to the experience I had to experience it and attending with friends allowed me to access these events fully as a genuine attendee. This notion of immersion or being drawn in relates to the encounter itself. The type of encounter and immersion in these clubbing events are conditioned by this role choice and its

28    *Precis*

manipulation. Even if aware of this feature while attending, only afterwards, in analysis, did I recognise how fully my role choices affected me. The first realisation is that there is an inside and outside to aesthetic collectives. There is, in other words, an orientation to them. My choice to be an audience, a participant or a critical witness situated me inside or outside the dancing crowds. This is not only a physical but also psychological orientation—*feeling* inside or outside the crowd. This immersion conditioned my experiences of clubbing crowds by creating a sense of inclusion or exclusion, insidership or outsidership, a witnessed or experienced event.

## Insides/Outsides, Proxemics and Containment

Physical or spatial insides and outsides to these aesthetic collectives become clear in describing the attendants to a club. To illustrate, I went to the Oslo club in Hackney Central, London in December 2014 and attended a gig by the band Monarchy. There were perhaps 100 dancing people as well as about 25 others not dancing. The venue itself was small, approximately 8 m by 16 m space and then a stage for the band.[4] During that event there was a clear division between the dancing crowd and the rest of the audience. The dancing crowd filled the forward half of the venue and was considerably dense in that area—dense enough that mobility was pretty restricted. At about the halfway point there was a significant thinning of the crowd where dancing, while much more possible, was not happening. Here, people rhythmically swayed and bobbed to the music as well as stood still and listened or watched. This area was about one-fourth of the total space in the middle area of the venue. At the back fourth of the venue, people spread far apart and were simply listening, watching and talking to each other. Theatrical lights illuminated the darkness of the space, the music was strong and most of those present were perceptibly drunk (they became more wildly intoxicated at about 01:00). From the perspective of an off-centre point in the dance space (still within the dancing crowd) the DJ stage could easily be seen and from which many of the lights were directed at the crowd. Everyone danced in small enclaves closing in on themselves, seemingly grouped with friends and companions. The smaller groups either closed in and formed an inward-facing circle or a circle/semi-circle that faced forward, towards the musicians. The edges of these smaller groups, however, were neither clearly nor strictly delineated or maintained; one group easily bled into another. People from groups overlapped. The dancing was rhythmically synchronised with the music and everyone in the dancing crowd was very physically active.

In other clubbing events there is similarly always a densely compacted dancing crowd around which I could perceive a sense of edge. There is a body to the crowd, a containing of dancers 'in the crowd'. Moving concentrically away from that crowd there is a field of surrounding space in which people spread out much more and *sort* of dance (meaning, they were not fully dancing, but more rhythmically moving to the beat of the music). Further out

*Proximity and Prägnanz—Space, Order, Touch* 29

from that space (in smaller venues this means up against the surrounding walls) there is usually a dancing-free space where people tend to listen and watch (to the DJ or musical acts or the dancing crowd). Each of these concentric spaces is radial in geometry and roughly speaking circular, albeit very irregular in its circularity. Each space is a separate *sphere* and is orbital in nature. These spaces are conceptually spherical and press-up against or radiate around each other. Different types of activity, interaction and states of being happening and are allowed in each sphere. The dancing crowd occupies the densest and most active sphere of space. The crowd body may also be identified by their behavioural difference from the more audience-like attendants outside that space. This spheroid geometry follows Peter Sloterdijk's spherological philosophy of space, more of which will come later.

Returning to Oslo I may further detail the dancing crowd from my own perspective within the crowd, as an immersed and interacting participant. The dancing crowd was compact and dense. My own body pressed not only against that of my friend accompanying me to one side but also against the person directly in front of me, the person directly to my other side and the person directly behind me. Our bodies were in near-constant contact. The points of contact, interestingly, were both intimate and not. The hips, buttocks and groins of all of us pressed and moved together. Shoulders, arms, chests and backs were also in contact. This kind of physical contact, particularly of hips and groins, is neither common nor generally acceptable in other non-intimate contexts. When there was no contact there was always the sense that contact would return imminently.

There was also a perceivable edge to the collective space of the dancing crowd. There was a sense of where the dancing crowd ended, and the other spaces began. Where the dancing crowd ended in the middle of the venue was a bar. Earlier in the night while the crowd was assembling and during the warm-up act (before a significant number of the crowd had arrived) we all occupied the space differently; there was no defined collective and thus no collective space. At that time all of us mitigated the space between our bodies. We were evenly spreading through the room—admittedly more densely near the stage at first, wanting to 'have' that space when the act started, and thinning as progressing backward away. We were also constantly adjusting our positions. As the number of attendants grew this adjusting became more nuanced and minor. I felt I had to do this to ensure everyone had a degree of personal space so that we would not touch. However, the crowd eventually reached a capacity at which touch was inevitable and we begrudgingly huddled together. Bumping and knocking into each other was unavoidable. At first there were muttered apologies for such contact, but after about 15 minutes that stopped being necessary. It became assumed contact and ignored. The casual physical interaction made me uncomfortable and I noted the same sentiment in those surrounding me. I masked this discomfort and pretended not to notice. As the main act began, so did the dancing. The movement of dance increased our physical contact and eventually our bodies

30    *Precis*

completely pressed together. We no longer acknowledged, cared about or acted on our discomfort. The experience of the music and the environment was more involving and diminished the discomfort.

There were also intermittent surges in which the crowd would press forward a bit more and our bodies compressed together harder. The first few times this happened I had a sense of worry about it; once I acknowledged its inevitability, and even predict it, it became humorous. The dancing and music were very pervasive and very loud (in fact midway through I had to jam parts of a tissue into my ears to muffle the sound a bit). I could feel the vibrations of the sound through me and the rhythm and coordination of its flow were evident in the movement of the crowd. Especially obvious was the bass beat that vibrated through our bodies and stimulated pulsating movements. The beat of the music was kinaesthetically apparent in the beat of our movement: they were synchronised. Not only did each dancer dance in their own way but also everyone was dancing in the same restricted volume of space with the same restriction of movement. As such we all started to have similar movement. For instance, no one moved their arms above their mid-body or extended them to the sides. This was not possible as it would not only touch the others surrounding but also strike and possibly injure them. This feature became very clear during a few instances when the band shouted to the entire group to 'PUT HANDS IN THE AIR!', which we did. Suddenly, it was very clear we had not been dancing with arms raised. It was also clear that the reason for this was that it was tiring to keep them up and getting them back down required awkward shimmying of the body. For the same reasons, there was also no thrashing or wildly unpredictable movement (I tried, it did not work).

Beyond physical restrictions, our movement was also styled to the texture of the music. The music was mood establishing; our movement had to match that mood and its rhythm and dynamics. The most interesting moments were when the music changed. A clear instance of this happens when an established phrase in the music with a definite beat and pulse that had been playing for a good time suddenly cut out and the crowd was plunged into a steady tone or held sound with no beat or syncopation. Crowd members at first tried to continue moving to the absent pulse and then quickly stopped—or some continued to sway, thrust and pulse to an imagined beat (the internally resounding retention of the beat). People appeared to be searching for one amidst the sound before finally stopping and waiting for the next beat to drop, by which point they seemed completely self-aware. This is a bizarre moment whose oddness is often used as a musical 'trick'. It creates relatively unpredictability; there is no known or determined response in the drone and it is usually embarrassing as you become self-aware of your dancing. What it does is build anticipation and intended withholding. What will come next? Is it just a return of the beat or is this a shift in song? Whatever the case, the moment the beat drops back into the music the crowd always goes wild and bursts into dance again. To have clear rhythmic music is a release and relief.

*Proximity and Prägnanz—Space, Order, Touch* 31

The movement and dance type/style becomes a vocabulary of action. It matches the music and environment and it evolves with the music/environment as it unfolds through the event. Similarly, the way the crowd uses space also evolves. Oslo's crowd was thoroughly compressed by the latter part of the set and our engagement with the environment and mood was more complete. Where at the beginning of the evening we tried to maintain distance and spaces of personal ownership, by the end of the evening connection, physical engagement and the homogenisation of behaviour was fully normal.

Physicality, movement, co-presence and spatial regulation dictate much of the success of dancing crowds. On the most fundamental level, I experienced dancing crowds by their presence and containment. I felt the presence of the crowd and, once participating, the sensation of being co-present with the crowd or even of the subsumption of my presence within the crowd presence. It is a gathering of individuals occupying a limited space. Each member occupied an individual space with their body, a space into which nothing else could enter. Likewise, a collective group occupies a collective space. Within that space the collective is present. Outside that space, they are not present, but their *presence* might still be encountered.

This collective space is similar to the spaces of individuals. If we consider the space of an individual and their distance from others, the study of which is proxemics, there are different imagined spatial spheres surrounding them. These spherical[5] spaces bubble out around the individual in concentric orbs, radiating outwardly into the world. Proxemics details the different types of communication, interaction and affective experience that can occur or are allowed in each of these spaces moving closer to or further away from the individual. Here I will use Edward T. Hall's theory of spaces as outlined in *The Hidden Dimension* to categorise and analyse these spaces.[6] While several decades old, Hall's proxemics and notions of the different categories of spaces and distance regulation in animals, in the main, hold today. I will narrow to his focus on human interactive spaces. He terms the space immediately surrounding a person's body *intimate space* (a space up to about 45-cm radius) and we consider it fully possessed by the individual. Entrance into this space is, by its very name, intimate and as such vulnerable and emotional. Extending slightly further from intimate space (up to about 70-cm radius) we term *personal space*. Still considered possessed or territorialised by the individual but personal space allows a somewhat greater range of interaction, movement and affective scope. These spaces also establish protective barriers between the individual and others. We consider 70-cm to 3.5-m *social space*, the expanse in which most interactions and affective exchange is acceptable and happen. In a post/Covid world, the notion of *social distancing* echoes this and works on two meters as a safe, comfortable distance to socialise. Beyond 3.5 m is the *public space* where mass exchanges may occur and towards its limits others become greatly distant and more object-like. Hall observes how the individual 'has around [them] as extensions of [their] personality the zones described' and that 'they use the senses to distinguish between one space or distance and another.

## 32  *Precis*

The specific distance chosen depends on the transaction; the relationship of the interacting individuals, how they feel and what they are doing'.[7] These different spaces will be elaborated below, but this brief introduction is sufficient for discussion at this point.

The Oslo crowd seemed to me contained in its own space. With this seeming containment I treated the whole group as a *body* of people. It had containment like a human body. As I began to explore its boundaries I noted how I could be in that body or outside of it. Outside of it I felt more like an audience member, dancing outside their space felt awkward and exposing—I was too apparent. Inside space surrounded the membership, closing-off the dancing crowd from outside space, and it also permeated between the members. Unlike an individual body, a collective body is not a singular concrete body; it has empty space in between members. This interpersonal space is also part of the crowd, though. It is also constantly flexible, dynamic and active. The collective possesses and territorialises this in-between space. In terms of aesthetics, we call this *negative space,* a void of space surrounding any foregrounded subject or object. Negative space gives focus to the subject/object and allows the observer enough context by which to understand what they are observing. With a collective the individuals and the negative space are equally active and blur distinction between background and foreground, subject and context.

I could be outside the crowd looking in or inside looking out. At different distances outside the crowd body, though, I could still feel and interact with the collective presence, like expanding spherical spaces just as Hall indicates. Just as each individual body has Hall's intimate, personal, social and public spaces relative to their own bodies, the dancing crowd had similar spaces. I experienced the crowd by its physical presence in and through the spaces that are within it and the outside spaces separating and differentiating it from non-participating audience spaces. As Hall states the space surrounding the dancing crowd was 'extensions of [their] personality'.[8] The closer to the crowd body, the more personal and intimate the sensation of nearness and the more I could feel the personality and mood of the crowd. The further away from it, the less I could sense its personality and mood, but the more able I could perceive it as a whole and thus the more I could objectify it.

At the edges of the dancing crowd, there was a threshold space of about 1–1.5 m where I felt intimately close to it. In that immediately surrounding space, I could feel a need to interact with the dancing crowd at the same energy level or to step in and become a part of it. In that immediately surrounding space, I was very near the crowd and my perception of it was limited to the members that were vicinal to me. I did not linger often in this space as it felt unstable. In it I felt the urge either to be more a part of the collective or more apart from it. Stepping back a bit more (about 1.5–3 m away from the crowd) I felt much more like an audience member and less compelled to participate. In that further space, I could perceive a larger portion of the dancing crowd. The nearer members I could see in detail but could only view

Proximity and Prägnanz—Space, Order, Touch    33

the totality of the group with sweeping glances of the room and observation of it at different depths. In that space, I also still felt that I should move to the music, but definitely at a lower energetic register to the dancing crowd. Further from that I felt very much like an audience member/observer and off in my own place. Minimal movement felt appropriate here, restricted to swaying and bobbing to rhythms. Dancing fully here felt very exposed. Here, I could see the whole of the dancing crowd in one glance. Different to the first and second spaces separate to the dancing crowd here I could fully objectify them. I could see them as one contained object. Additionally, at this distance individual dancers became less distinct and more anonymous. They began to lose individual characteristics and appeared less like individuals and more like members.

Containment operates on further, larger levels. The experience of an aesthetic event itself, in which these dancing crowds exist, takes place within a contained social and/or public space. They are usually within enclosed buildings demarcated and designed to hold and achieve music, lighting and dancing experiences (as with all my instances). On the largest level, these buildings contain the aesthetic event and are fitted to prevent seepage of that experience out into the external world (success here varies from site to site mainly with regards to noise bleed). A large enough space is necessary for attendants to interact and co-experience the events in social and public distances. However, as attendance capacities increase, interaction changes to include experiences between attendees in our personal and even intimate spaces, which I turn to shortly. Reconsidered, the spherical space of the dancing crowd at Oslo was much like a field. It was an expanse of space in which various properties or phenomena occurred. As a field, this space can be non-tangibly sensed and creates a feeling of enclosure and emanation.

## Aesthetic Fields, Collective Domains

Hall's proxemics mainly consider issues of proximity itself and the sociological tensions that occur in distanced spaces; but in the fields of these dancing crowds more than that is happening. To explain how we experience this field differently I turn to a phenomenological perspective through Don Idhe's studies of phenomenologies of sound and sensory perception. In *Listening and Voice; Phenomenologies of Sound,*[9] he expounds on how human perception operates in relation to spaces surrounding and extending from the body, just like with Hall. He explores a notion of sensory field phenomenology. Idhe illustrates human perception as generating a field of understanding with various levels of focus and intensity. Within the sensory field there is sense; beyond the sensory field there is the insensible, the unknown. Key to his illustration of sense is a central focus area surrounded by a less focussed space in which form is more vague. There is still sense of phenomena here, but it is not well determined. Moving further out the focus deteriorates more and sense stimuli are only understood in general ways. Moreover, 'the field [… is] seen

34   *Precis*

to have a spread or expanse that eventuate[s] in a barely noticed, vague, but nonetheless discernible border or limit. This [is] the first meaning of the *horizon* [emphasis added]'.[10] The horizon is that point where sense ends and the insensible begins. Beyond the horizon there is a great nothingness in which anything could be or is happening but is not known to the sensing subject. In most aesthetic events there is a field in the contained space of the event; the horizon here often is physically embodied in the form of walls, ceilings, floors, doorways, barriers, hoarding, ropes, an encircling of natural phenomena (trees, cliffs, the sea and so on). It could be the limit of sensorial reach—the point at which sound dies-off, the extent to which smell can reach—or even at times a psychic membrane. It is an edge where the aesthetic and the non-aesthetic spaces gradate one into the other but are still distinct. The horizon is an acknowledged space, albeit one forgotten once within the aesthetic experience. The aesthetic event must be experienced from within its own field in which the participants and audience coexist and co-perceive.

All of the clubs I visited were self-contained buildings. The aesthetic fields created were bounded by the walls, ceilings, floors and doorways of the respective buildings. The aesthetic horizon was literal in the form of these material edges beyond which a genuine unknown existed. Oslo, for instance, had its stage and dance floor occupying the first floor of the building, separated from the rest of the bar/restaurant by a staircase (see IMAGE 2 in Appendix A). There, the aesthetic field was fully contained on its own floor. Some of the spaces, however, had their aesthetic fields even further contained within the building. Changing out of the context of British (and London in particular) clubbing I visited Morrison's bar in Budapest in November of 2015 where this was the case. Comparatively speaking the experience here was very similar to those in London. The club had a dance space hidden deep within. I entered the whole facility through a stairway to an underground environment. There was at first a bar, a karaoke lounge and some offshoot rooms with tables and chairs. The DJ and dance area was through a further tunnel, set-off in the back-most corner of the space, which was also a tunnel (as illustrated the dark blue space in Image 1, Appendix A). Consequently, the aesthetic field for this experience was contained and sequestered away within the larger space of the entire building. The music from the dance floor did not really permeate into the main bar area which had its own recorded music, although I could sense the reverberations in some of the corridors and more private rooms. The horizon for the aesthetic field here was, in the main, the tunnel walls of the dance floor and the table area just outside of it. Beyond those areas, the aesthetic experience was of a different nature and could not be sensed or known while in the dancing area.

Metropolis did not have this clear differentiation. This is a strip bar in Bethnal Green, London I visited in August of 2015 on a Saturday when it is not used for stripping but is taken over by Sink the Pink hosting a gay club night called Savage. Bar, dance floor and other spaces were all so close together as to create a fully immersive and (nearly) inescapable aesthetic space. The

Proximity and Prägnanz—Space, Order, Touch 35

music and dancing spread over all three floors of the building. There was nowhere I could go to get away from it. The best I could achieve was to withdraw into the dark and remote corners where it was difficult to communicate with people. There was a second-floor bar that was used to 'chill-out'; this place, however, was equally dominated by dancing, just with lower energy music. The aesthetic effect to stimulate dance was successful there and the aesthetic field was tolerable despite its omnipresence.

This was not the case at Debbie in the Resistance Gallery in Bethnal Green (nearly across the street from Metropolis, which I visited in June 2015). Debbie also had complete penetration of the space by the event aesthetics. The entire space was one large rectangular room with a stage at one end and the bar opposite in a corner. The stage was not used when I was there (there were retro pin-up collage films being projected on a drop-screen, however). The aesthetic experience and its overtaking of all the other spaces made the environment feel invasive, oppressive and difficult to do anything but dance. Ordering drinks was very difficult as I had to scream my order to the bartender. Using the toilets was challenging and revolting: a long wait in a densely packed queue followed by a small room that was filthy with a broken toilet, a sink, no soap. I did not want to touch anything. Music was also constantly present at very loud levels. The aesthetic field extended through the whole space and the only place I could escape it was in the garden where the smokers were (it was also raining and not an ideal place to relax). Generally, there was not a good sense of order or plan to the spaces of this event.

Thinking about these spaces, the spread of the aesthetic field had to surround/contain the participants and audience members for the aesthetics of the event to work or apply. Within that field aesthetic collectives like these dancing crowds might occur. From an audience perspective, the perceivable presence of the dancing crowd filled a smaller, concentric amount of space within the buildings. I understood this presence by the physical relation of participants to each other as well as their difference from the non-participant others also in the aesthetic field. All the dancing crowds had noticeable, albeit non-tangible, boundaries. There was always a physical point at which people and I were outside the dancing space watching and, when traversed, within it participating. The dancing crowds maintained sensible and discrete presence within the spaces they possessed. To sense and consequently objectify it, I also had to be at a correct distance from the dancing crowd (in its social or public space).

These dancing crowds carved out a pocket of space nestled within the aesthetic field that operates as its sub-field, a realm or territory they inhabited. Like at Oslo, this was the space of greatest density and activity occupying the forward third to half of the room. I will term this contained space of the collective the *collective domain*. Like an individual's intimate and personal spaces, the collective domain demarcates space occupied and possessed by the collective and is an immediate 'extension of [its] personality'.[11] So, there is a

36   *Precis*

full field of sensible aesthetic experience, inside of which there exists an aesthetic collective which is present within its own sub-space, its collective domain.

Like the aesthetic field, the collective domain also has a few horizons. Beyond it I failed to feel connected with the collective and I inhabited my own subjectivity and felt individual again. I was not connected to the dancing crowd and felt much more like an observer or audience to them. At a far enough or perceptually blocked distance they ceased to exist. In the reverse, looking out from the dancing crowd, those beyond the group were somewhat outside my perception or vaguely at its edges. They appeared disconnected, not participant. For example, when I used the bathroom at Morrison's I was dancing and a part of the dancing crowd, but as soon as I stepped out of the collective domain I noticed that I felt separated from it. I stopped dancing and felt individualised again. There were several people on this side of the collective domain as well. Some were buying drinks at the bar, some standing at a distance watching, none dancing in the same way. They clearly were not part of the dancing crowd. As I went to the toilets (located far away around halls) I felt progressively more individual, until I was entirely alone within a cubicle. As I returned I could experience the entire process of assimilating into the dancing crowd. The closer I came to the horizon of the collective domain the more I felt the impulse to dance. Being at this edge-horizon of the collective domain created this feeling and I believe it is indicative of the relationship between choosing to be a participant or an audience member. Slightly closer, at the edge of the collective domain, I felt discomfort being between roles. I felt an impulse to exist as part of the dancing crowd or to step back away from it. My ambiguous role here was strained and collapsing, compelling me to be either audience or participant. As I noted earlier, this space felt unstable.

### Proximity and Prägnanz

What I am discussing here are two spatial measures of how these dancing crowds become conceptualised like entities, as entitative. These two measures are *proximity* and *prägnanz*, and I am here following Campbell's use of the terms. *Proximity* refers to the nearness or farness of members to each other. Besides a metric of distance between bodies, proximity also indicates what spaces (intimate, personal, social and public) are active or being engaged. At Oslo, our proximity was within a few centimetres of each other, frequently making direct physical contact. Such overlapping/intersecting of personal and intimate spaces charged the available space. To illustrate better, assume the perspective of a participant within that dancing crowd. Our bodies are all quite close together. Unified in our dancing activity we direct our attention 'at' the music performers. The collective domain surrounds and contains all of us within it—a bubble of experience. Like a unified group, the entitativity of the dancing mass is felt within this space. Within this collective domain, each of us

*Proximity and Prägnanz—Space, Order, Touch* 37

is part of the larger entitative collective. Our proximity to each other allows us to feel a part of this group, but not so close as to feel suffocated by it. The space between members is just enough to allow desired dancing movement. This is important. We modify movement and actions to adapt to the available space. If the space collapsed much more our dancing would be too restricted and the experience unsatisfactory.

Moreover, from outside the collective domain, the spatial barrier between dancing crowd and others was only a metre or less. The dancing crowd is compact, the proximity of the members within centimetres of each other—overlapping the close personal and intimate spaces. Close and distant proximity lend interesting behavioural responses, but there was clearly an ideal range of spacing.

In the dancing crowds, I was always acutely aware of extreme near proximity of other dancers to me. When very close or feeling too close, my tolerance would strain. When this happened, the too-close proximity undid my and others' sense of entitativity to the dancing crowds. A lack of space agitated us and I even felt worried about how close everyone was to me. If there were a sudden need to get out, I would not be able to do so easily. I also thought about how in an emergency we might crush together with the need to exit quickly. These thoughts, which I acknowledged as an over-reaction, were nonetheless distressing and heightened my discomfort. I felt myself become more selfish, wanting more space and having everyone back away from me. At the other end of the proximity spectrum, moving out of and away from the collective domain made me feel progressively more disconnected and like an observer. In a (post)covid age I have now witnessed and had to teach socially distanced dance. When dancers are spaced out too far, given more space, they feel and look disconnected from each other. A 2-m 'safe distance' can be aesthetically utilised in dance, but in general it prohibits relationships between dancers and fundamentally alters the nature of the dancing. These experiences have taught me how social dance, of any sort, requires certain nearness, either as a collective or as partners/small groups. Even line dancing, which does work in socially distanced ways, had an altered sense of enjoyment. It also demands much larger, in fact huge, spaces in which to dance and this often prohibits audiences or reduces their numbers considerably. It certainly does not work in clubs. The nature of club dancing is linked to closeness and contact. Our sense of entitativity as a club dancing crowd would spread too thinly. We literally and figuratively would not connect.

In the club crowds, the more pressing issue was about the very nearness of others. The other dancers were close; they were in my personal and intimate space. As it was, the available space restrained my possible dancing actions. If pressed yet closer together not only would I not be able to dance and enjoy the event, but I would begin to be uncomfortable in intolerable ways. This would likely be at the point when movement is entirely restricted. This would induce the feelings of not being able to move or get away—a type of claustrophobia and panic. So, proximity and its contribution to entitativity is a measure of

38    *Precis*

nearness and of farness in a collective and the related feelings each engenders. At either extreme one stops feeling a part of the group and instead, partially or entirely, inhabits their own subjectivity.

The boundary between what is inside and outside the crowd also created a greater sense of containment. The collective body needs to be differentiated from the rest of the aesthetic field; like any individual body it needs edges, boundaries and order. Without this separation it becomes difficult to apprehend its entitative containment. In the language of a gestalt it needs to have closure. The notions of *inside* and *outside*, at the most basic level, imply sides. With Campbell, the differentiation between those sides, the intangible boundary or sense of edge to the crowd, is part of what is called *prägnanz*. This intangible yet perceivable boundary and containment to a crowd emerges from both the placement and ordination of the individual bodies. Prägnanz denotes boundedness but also order to the bodies: their direction, orientation, vertical level, any emergent patterns or choreographic order. These are features of arrangement and they are important to the sensibility and intensity of the entitativity of the collective. The collective domain limits its boundaries and edges, closing off the collective. Taking Campbell's definition further, the relative position, arrangement, and general topography of the bodies of the participants when heightened or reduced will have an equivalent effect on entitativity. Prägnanz measures such order and design, increases in each having equal increases in perception of entitativity to collective bodies.

How we oriented ourselves was important to making the experiences enjoyable. As our intimate and personal spaces were frequently entered or invaded in all four examples of dancing crowds, those intimate-personal spaces surrounding my body had to shift to an amalgam intimate-personal-social space. The activity allowed in my intimate and personal spaces mixed with that of social spaces. In these closer spaces interaction now included what happens in all three spaces of distance. For instance, the conversation between several of us took place despite our faces being literally 4–6 cm apart, normally too close to be talking, certainly too close to maintain eye contact (it strained our eyes to focus at that close a distance, so we looked over each other's shoulders as we talked directly into our ears). At Oslo, Morrisons and Debbie, the music was very loud and this arrangement necessitated conversation to take place with mouth and ear within this 4–5 cm distance. The physical proximity of bodies changed the meaning of my intimate and personal spaces to include this interaction, which normally happens at social distances. Additionally, I consciously managed the orientation and arrangement of our bodies to make the closeness of these interactions tolerable. Face-to-face dancing was far too intimate and awkward, even for my closest companions. Instead, side-by-side, back-to-front, or angled orientations were preferred—something that eliminated direct face-to-face engagement.

I realised I could sensing prägnanz to aesthetic collectives. In Morrisons and Oslo, the dance floors were such that they could differentiate between collective domain and the rest of the aesthetic field. It was possible in those spaces

*Proximity and Prägnanz—Space, Order, Touch* 39

to step out of the domain of the dancing crowd yet remain within the aesthetic field and survey the room, watch the dancing; to experience as an audience member. As such I could recognise and note the prägnanz of those dancing crowds. Their dancing crowds had perceivable space boundaries and senses of shape. In fact, in those places, the boundary was so definite that I could sense it almost within a few centimetres. Standing on the outer perimeter of the collective domain I could lean forward and be 'with' those who were dancing; lean back and be outside and 'without' it.

Metropolis and Debbie were more totally immersive dancing crowds and as such that arrangement challenged the closure to the dancing crowds and the sense of boundary. Their lack of space, the fluidity of and between space types and the ever-presence of music deteriorated the horizon of the collective domains. At times it was hard to establish what or who was the dancing crowds and who were bystanders or non-dancing attendees. Almost anywhere in those two venues, I could start dancing and it would be completely acceptable. In these cases, the presence of the dancing crowds quite literally filled all space, and the collective domain and aesthetic field were one. On all floors at Metropolis, except the ground floor, there was no designated dance floor. Consequently, all spaces became dancing spaces: the stairs, the booths, the stripping rooms, the alcoves to the toilets. As such, the dancing crowd sprawled across all spaces as well. In a way this was enjoyable as any space could be activated as a dancing space and there was no sense of centralised or densest place of 'fun'—thus everywhere seemed 'fun'. At Debbie, however, this was problematic and made the experience less enjoyable. As stated ordering drinks was very difficult, not only because requests needed to be screamed over the omnipresent, very loud music to a person with whom eye contact was not possible due to dim and flashing lights, but also because the queue was composed of tightly compressed bodies, many of whom continued to dance, pulse and grind(!) while waiting—everyone was very keen to get their drinks and move out of that place that they were shoving and pushing to order regardless of any queue. There was no discernible difference between the collective domain where such behaviour should go and this, where more restrained behaviour should happen. The dancing crowd permeated all spaces and, different to Metropolis, this felt aggressive, rude, crude and even infuriating.[12] Besides dancing, this compression of bodies additionally made other activities (talking, standing still, carrying drinks) very difficult.

What made this pervasive dancing crowd manageable and enjoyable in Metropolis but not Debbie was the sheer scale of the space. Having more available space meant that in Metropolis the dancing crowd was not oppressive, that my body temperature could regulate and there were available spaces to which I could move to feel individual or free. Metropolis is perhaps 3 times the size, has a few bar spaces and moves vertically as well as horizontally; Debbie is a compact open rectangle of space, has one small bar and the space spreads only horizontally (there was an upper gallery but that was off-limits). Consequently, in Metropolis, the proximity of me to the other members was

40   *Precis*

malleable. No matter where I went, I was still within the collective domain; however, I could still distance myself from others and occupy, maintain or even protect my intimate and personal space. At Debbie this was not the case. The collective domain was everywhere and I was constantly in the presence of others and almost everywhere physically touched or pressed upon by them. As Hall notes, '[t]he use of intimate distance in public is not considered proper [... and we] have defensive devices which take the real intimacy out of intimate space [... generally] it is taboo to relax and enjoy bodily contact with strangers!'[13] Moreover, this touch was also not sympathetic or followed with kindness, it was often aggressively forceful and careless. I was knocked in the head several times and shoved out of neighbouring spaces by dancers.

Since the collective domain and the aesthetic field in both these examples were the same the proximity of the members being too far apart was not a challenge to the entitativity of the dancing crowd. The closeness of the members, however, did adversely affect the entitativity of the dancing crowd for me. I would often re-inhabit my own subjective awareness. That is, at times the intrusion of others into my space, or through physically making abrupt and strong contact with me, broke my feeling of unity with the dancing crowd and made me feel individual and aware of myself. This experience was not comfortable and had a polarising effect. On the one hand, I felt the urge to unify with the collective; on the other hand, I felt the exact opposite and jarred back into my own self-awareness. This challenge to unifying in fact broke down the collective around me. The dancing crowd at Debbie did not feel very unified and instead I felt competition for space and aggression as we were so close together. This was not only my own observation. A casual survey of several of my companions (eight at Debbie) revealed that this discomfort and consequent inability to relax into the dancing crowd was common. In fact, we had to territorialise a space as 'ours' with the use of coats, bags and positioning of bodies. The management of the event in this capacity made Debbie a less successful event in this regard.

The total occupation of space by the dancing crowds with no peripheral space to which one could extricate from the collective affected their prägnanz. In Metropolis and Debbie, there was no boundary (except the toilets as an excised pocket) and the dancing crowds seemed shapeless and to spill everywhere. With no perceptible boundary, the aesthetic collectives became entirely immersive experiences; I was 'inside' the dancing crowd at all times. It occurred to me that to be 'outside' of it or to position myself as an audience member I consciously had to open my own subjective mental space separate from the collective domain. Without additional physical space to move to and have a personal bubble I instead suddenly could just 'shut down' and stop dancing. Very different to the others, in this state I felt myself inhabit my own disconnected subjectivity while inside the collective. This is in-line with Hall's 'defensive devices' noted earlier. He discusses, as an example, such devices on a crowded subway or elevator, although they are similar tactics to this situation: 'to be as immobile as possible [...] withdraw if possible [...] the muscles in the

Proximity and Prägnanz—Space, Order, Touch    41

[touching] areas are kept tense [...] hands kept at the side or used to steady the body [...] [t]he eyes are fixed on infinity'.[14] Within the highly active context of the clubs such rigidity and avoidance of engagement were not fully necessary; instead, it was a stopping of activity, a contracting of involvement and a refocussing/directing of attention.

This happened to me several times and I witnessed it happen to others as well. It was unavoidable (especially if the individual was relatively sober) or if they used their phone. Checking one's phone became a frequent means of removal from the collective. It was also easy to see as the screen would illuminate faces with a blue tint. At Debbie, this mental removal from the collective, intervals of relief, was often needed. Moreover, the temperature was very hot and the air very humid. I could not fully engage with the mood or atmospheric narrative of the music and environment. The heat produced by such close proximity caused other moments of discontinuity with the collective, like a jolt back into my own physical body. My body was sweating profusely and there was a strong urge or, at points, need to cool off. Almost every 20 or 30 minutes I needed to go into the garden with the smokers. In all the clubbing cases this happened—'taking a moment' out of the collective while in it. In Oslo and Morrison's, where there were spaces outside the collective domain, this would also usually draw me physically out of the collective domain and turn me into a watcher, an audience member.

As mentioned in the introduction, Campbell outlines proximity and prägnanz as key elements of spatial perception connected with perceived entitativity. Both are elements contributing to how we perceive and conceptualise groups like singular entities. For example, in Debbie a survey of the entire space caused me to take in the dancers as one homogenous group. Such extreme closeness of members eliminated their difference. Indeed, during one return from the bar I had difficulty identifying where or who my companions even were, despite looking directly at them. I not only perceived them as a group, but I did not even entirely see them as individuals, more just as *the group*. Here, the proximity of the participants and the small measure of space between them created the perception of them as united or connected. They all drew closer together, reduced the negative space between/surrounding them. This contraction reaches a point at which 'elements close together are more likely to be perceived as parts of the same organization'.[15] Campbell summarises proximity as one of the weaker or 'less "essential"'[16] cues for entitativity, at least from within the collective. However, he indicates how its impact on the visual perception of grouping from outside makes it rather important. 'Perhaps most significant is the employment of proximity to draw group boundaries [...] Certainly boundaries so drawn would confirm most [...] entity diagnoses'.[17] Here Campbell confirms what my experiences suggest, that proximity of members allows the establishment of group boundaries (prägnanz). From the outside looking in the closeness in proximity of the members allowed me to perceive the dancing crowd and recognise a collective domain. From the inside of the dancing crowd the proximity of the other

42   *Precis*

members to me generated a sensation of cohesion and belonging which actively compelled me to immerge with the entitative force of the group.

The role of proximity extends even further 'For [our] groups, face-to-face communication processes made possible by [close] proximity generate[d] similarity and feelings of belongingness which ma[de] coordinated action and hence common fate more likely'.[18] Coordinated action in the dancing crowds was indeed a primary concern. As noted earlier, our dancing had to be similarised in style and limitations of movement. This is both a drive and purpose in group-based dancing like this as well as a necessity imposed by the limited space. Part of dancing in these crowds is the experience of collective motor activity. We attend to dance to common music and common mood. The increase in common fate, a notion explored in chapter 3, is a natural consequence: a feeling of common objective or purpose. While people close together or in relative proximity to each other do not necessarily constitute a group or a collective, their appearance as one and potential for one emerging increase. Likewise, as our group prägnanz increased, i.e. boundedness, closure, substantiality and internal patterns, the concreteness of the group also developed and deepened the relations between us as dancing participants. As we 'form[ed] a part of a spatial organization or pattern, as a line or more complex form, [we] tend[ed] to be perceived as a part of the same unit [...] [it] may be expanded into the notion of closed figure, or completed boundary'.[19] There was a constant shift and flow of where we all were and who was in the crowd (people came and went at various times in all cases), but there was a general sense of territory or ownership of area. We all stayed in similar locations within the group. Our topography in the dancing crowds partially solidified.

Equally, there were patterns to how we oriented our smaller group within the crowd as well as to my individual ordination. These patterns were fluidic and changed as the crowd changed, but they existed in various permutations of a common theme. For example, in Debbie my group of companions and I were always in a somewhat oval shape, almost always facing inwards (no one much cared for the projections at the front of the room, so we did not orient ourselves in that direction as we did for the band at Oslo). The exact shape of our placement and the ordination of our bodies relative to that shape were always changing slightly (e.g. at times the oval became two loosely connected smaller circles; another time it stretched almost into a line; sometimes I faced outwardly; sometimes some of us were more face-to-face than the others and so on). We were too many to maintain a circle (as then we would have too much 'extra' empty space inside the circle). In principle, this general ovaloid shape was a common feature throughout the night. This concerns the sense of composition to the groups.

In theory we could have existed anywhere from the completely random to the hyper-organised. In all the dancing crowds micro-groups always existed somewhere between the two and were frequently trying to organise or compose, but were always influenced by the natural disorganisation that emerged. Proximity and prägnanz operated simultaneously, one influencing the other seamlessly. They categorise well as spatial elements. Both are

Proximity and Prägnanz—Space, Order, Touch   43

measurements of types of physical and spatial arrangement of bodies. They both concern the perception of individual bodies in sets, as grouped together, not as randomly or discretely occupying space. A closer examination of the spatial operation of members in these settings reveals a complex choreography of distance regulation and proxemic manipulation. Until individuals unified into an appreciable unit there was no collective and the experience of the club space was not fulfilling its purpose.

The necessity for unification also emerged as necessary. At Oslo, the warm-up band compelled no collective to form. The opening act and the intermission DJ, GAPS + NINA and David O'Bryan respectively, had no dancing crowd. There was no urge to unify and no impulse to be aestheticised. They were treated quite literally as background. The acts themselves were not fully developed in their composition and environmental control: the music was not fluidly organised and jumped erratically from one mood and style to another, the lighting was not designed impressively enough and was dominated by the house lights being up which repressed any theatricality. Furthermore, the audience had not yet congregated fully during the opening act and were using the intermission point to get drinks or use the toilets—the space was less occupied. As disparate small groups, we were shifting physical locations and attempting to maintain balanced, evenly spread personal spaces. Most of the crowd during these periods were talking (some shouting to be heard over the act) to each other and treating the performance as background ambience. Although some of the groups were watching the gigs, almost everyone was broken apart into separate small groups of friends. No one was engaging with others beyond those they knew—very different to how we would touch and dance in close proximity when the dancing crowd was established.

Again, in Hall's distance regulation being close together (in personal/intimate spaces) creates feelings of personal exchange or intimacy; at these points in these examples there was no underlying reason for such feelings and thus we naturally avoided close proximity. During this period these performers seemed like neglected acts—as warm-up/filler/inter-act entertainment only. As the main performance drew nearer both times we drew nearer in proximity, directed our focus forward and our mood homogenised. We were preparing for a common, shared experience as a crowd ready to dance; again, in Hall's terms, something personal and perhaps even intimate. Everyone was noticeably excited and expectantly still. There was a palpable urge to get closer to the stage and to have a 'good place' in the crowd. Proximity was contracted, the organisation of personal and small group orientation towards the stage happened, bodies were organised so that dance actions were possible, and the collective domain emerged.

## The Discharge

A dichotomous urge accompanied the necessity of unification. In terms of Hall's spatial regulation, we resist too close a contact until close contact is a

44  *Precis*

defining feature of the experience. On the one hand, we resisted the grouping and remained independent and unique. On the other hand, there was an excitement and expectancy to merge and unify with the imminent crowd. I noticed this explicitly at Morrison's as well. I was present in the dance room before the DJ started playing. I stood, alone with my friend, on the periphery of the dance floor as they set up. As we moved closer in time to them playing there was an increase in numbers of others present on the dance floor as well as an intensification in energy. Everyone wanted to dance, and everyone wanted to be in the forward-middle of the dance floor. Of course, in these situations, situations in which one explicitly comes to party and dance, unification is a goal. Resisting the dancing group created isolating and alienating feelings. Thus, the moment of becoming a part of the dancing collective felt welcome. In discussion with participants from the home-made rave in Suffolk in April 2016, this urge was frequently described as a 'release', a 'submitting', a 'giving-over', a 'merging' and even 'being sucked-in'. The semantics here are interesting as they all suggest something being lost or given up as well as a form of movement. The semantics of these phrases also implies a power relationship. All of them indicate a sort of centripetal inward draw of the dancing crowd dominating the individual. The dancing crowd seems to be felt as having a gravity, grasp, or gavelling effect on those nearby or nearly a part. It seems that the closer one is to the collective domain the stronger its pull inward and the greater the urge to penetrate and move within it—to unify with it.

Elias Canetti gives this moment when the individual submits to the draw of a crowd or collective a name: the *discharge*. 'Before [the discharge] the crowd does not actually exist; it is the discharge which creates it. This is the moment when all who belong to the crowd get rid of their differences and feel equal'.[20] It is a transportative moment. It indicates a movement of the self from one state of being into another. This movement is both literal, as in 'into the collective domain', and ontological, as in the 'shift of the self from a singular state to a plural'. In this way, it is similar to Victor Turner's separation phase of ritual in which individuals or groups disconnect from the normative world and engage in 'symbolic behavior signifying the detachment of the individual or group either from an earlier fixed point in the social structure, from a set of cultural conditions (a 'state'), or from both'.[21] Once separated Turner classes participants as equals, in a state of *communitas* where 'the total community [is] seen as undifferentiated'.[22] This moment of discharge, becoming a part (a member) of the collective, is a process of disconnection *through* incorporation and admixture.

Once I could recognise this moment of discharge I consciously witnessed it happen all the time. For example, at Metropolis I arrived with one of my companions. Upon entry to the building, we were confronted with a large platform (its usual purpose being a stripping platform complete with poles that go 10 m into the first-floor ceiling). Gay men were dancing wildly on this platform. Many were shirtless and most appeared to be dancing for the room like performers. It was a very strong image to encounter immediately entering

*Proximity and Prägnanz—Space, Order, Touch*   45

the building. In any case, I indicated I was going to buy a drink and made my way through the crowd (this floor was very busy and crowded), purchased my drink, and turned around to have my friend say, 'let's do this!', jump-up on the stage and begin to dance in a highly theatrical and referential way. Her actions were exaggerated and wild. I interpreted this as a way to gain acceptance into the dancing group of men. They did in fact cheer and welcome her as one of them. They oriented towards her and danced 'with' her for a few moments. She did not leave the platform that night; she spent the entire evening dancing there and the next time I saw her, about half an hour later, she was in her bra and short skirt similarly stripped down like the men around her. That is, she similarised her appearance; more on that in chapter 2.

She consciously enacted this discharge and it was very immediate. This seemed slightly forced to me. It seemed that she had purposely acted this way to gain access to this dancing crowd very quickly. It was effective, though. Elsewhere when observed the discharge often seemed to be a more awkward experience. Standing to the side watching I saw many people experience either an initial reluctance to join in or an exuberant throwing of the self into the dancing, like my friend. In either case, once 'in' there was a period of integration with noticeably self-conscious actions. This involved either an insinuating, a showing that they were members by copying the dance of the group, or, like my friend, they would overtly telegraph their discharge through effusive and exaggerated dancing that signalled they were committed and completely on-board with the group. In both cases, this follows Canetti:

> distinctions are thrown off [so] all [could] feel *equal* [emphasis in the original]. In that density, where there is scarcely any space between, and body presse[d] against body, each [person was] as near the other as [they were] to [them]self; and an immense feeling of relief ensue[d]. It is for the sake of this blessed moment, when no-one is greater or better than another, that people become a crowd.[23]

This initial induction, the discharge, fades. Sometimes very quickly and sometimes after several minutes, but after the discharge they then are part of 'it'—the dancing crowd. With the discharge comes unification, physically with the collective domain and ontologically with the collective entity. My examples were filled with these discharge moments, people constantly trying to become a part of dancing crowds. Once looked for, it is an obvious moment. The discharge is a display of the necessity for unification.

Territoriality and distance regulation changed the roles and interactions permitted with these dancing crowds. People would erect psychological barriers around themselves to shut out the other and safely contain themself. At times people would somehow make it known that spaces, both literal and figurative, around them were 'their space' and that others should stay out in the space of 'everything else'. Returning to Edward T. Hall, humans structure spaces between and around each other at different distances and in those

46  *Precis*

different spacings different things might happen. He asserts that as adults we organise the surrounding space to accommodate for comfort in socialisation, the correlation between comfort and distances structured according to cultural prescription. While comfort with contact varies greatly between people, biographies and cultures, in general human adults tend to regulate inter-personal distance to the social distance or possibly personal, especially with non-intimate others. Hall's theory delineates how 'it is in the nature of ani-mals, including [hu]man[s], to exhibit behaviour which we call territoriality'.[24] Territoriality, he posits, underpins all the distance regulation that humans conduct, maintaining their intimate, personal, social and public distances. While more generally discussing the spaces that are habitually inhabited by humans he explores how we regulate space around our bodies so to engage in socialisation through different activities.

> Territoriality [...] is usually defined as behavior by which [we] character-istically lay claim to an area and defend[] it [...] [it] regulat[es] density. It provides a frame in which things are done [...] thus it co-ordinates the activities of the group and holds the group together. It keeps [us] within communicating distance of each other.[25]

The impulse to act territorially reflects the need to regulate the density of bodies within a space and thus maintain communication and social cohesion.

These four clubbing cases clearly demonstrated how the space of aesthetic events might not be fully territorialised, but within it we exhibited territorial behaviour, sometimes overtly. At Metropolis, there was obvious territorial claim being laid on spaces. Groups would dominate a given space and fill it with their bodies creating a micro-domain and even operate as a sub-collective within that space. Invariably, the placement of bags, coats and garments on chairs, booths, and the floor signalled ownership of space. On several occa-sions, outsiders would sit at a booth with possessions from my own group. This elicited a few responses. The most frequent was a heightened awareness of the space by at least one or two of the group members and a watching of these invaders as though a threat (thieves most likely); but no direct action towards them. At one point, I was one of the only ones around and I felt compelled to watch our possessions carefully. Another common response was a consolidating of the possessions, moving them into a tighter, larger heap. The greater the heap of possessions the more that space seemed fully owned—moving a single coat or a bag is not a big issue for an outsider, but to touch a large heap of many people's possessions seems very invasive and possibly aggressive. I also noticed those who owned the bags and coats completely remove them elsewhere—giving the space up to others. This was frequently coupled with a relocation to another part of the building. On a few occasions, group members would verbally suggest the stranger leave, in-dicating that the booth was 'taken', even though only a few were sitting at it. I only noticed this once in this (Metropolis) venue and once in the Debbie

## Proximity and Prägnanz—Space, Order, Touch    47

venue. I suspect this is probably the least likely response to occur as it requires direct communication with strangers and it might seem hostile. Moreover, at Oslo groups of friends would organise in inward facing circular or semi-circular patterns aimed at the stage. Groups would signal outwardly that the contained space was claimed through the inward directing, literally turning backs to the outside. This established and maintained close proximity with their own people and kept others at a further distance. The smaller groups heightened their prägnanz by bounding themselves, adopting these organised patterns of circles. The presenting of their backs to others is also a generally protective excluding of action. In that environment, people placed bags, coats and other possessions either in the centre of the group or in a centralised floor space immediately near or under their feet.

The closing of proximity between participants signals territorial ownership of space as there is literally no space for an outsider to occupy. If they try, they must very awkwardly press against the occupants. In these situations, prägnanz and boundaries become much more apparent. Everyone avoided others entering their intimate space, where possible. Alternately, sometimes people would move themselves away from others to a greater distance, which had the effect of casting them into the more isolated public space. Hall again notes how 'perception of [our] space[s was] dynamic because it [wa]s related to action—what c[ould] be done in [those] given space[s]'.[26] In these clubbing environments, the action was predominantly atmospheric dance[27] and the available space was limiting the possible dance we could do. Atmospheric dance, which I am claiming as a term to embrace this sort of activity and its pursuit to meld with club (or club-like) experiential situations and environments, creates a homogeneity of aesthetic collective and sensorially designed environment.

As noted, the dance and body motions were limited by the close proximity of members. The most immediate effect of this was our adjustment of the organisation of our bodies and our orientation. The proximity of members and the prägnanz of the group adjust in simultaneity. Interestingly, 'most of th[is] distance sensing process occur[ed] outside awareness. We sense[d] other people as close or distant, but we [could] not always put our finger on what it [wa]s that enable[d] us to characterize them as such'.[28] The orienting and organising of bodies seems equally to be on the fringes of conscious action and with it the resultant prägnanz of the whole. In the next chapter, I will further define this category of low-level awareness as being the remit of the protoself—an element of our processing mind that exists subconsciously with the purpose of scrutinising stimuli and interpreting it before announcing urgent, important or relevant stimuli to our full consciousness. It is a concept drawn from Antonio Damasio's theory of consciousness as presented in *The Feeling of What Happens*[29] where he distinguishes between three levels of consciousness, the other two being core consciousness and extended consciousness.

The protoself is non-conscious (meaning we are not fully aware of its activities) and is a neural pattern linked with homeostasis and physical state.

48    *Precis*

Constantly active, the protoself maps the external experience of the body and mind with their internal effects, connecting various neurological systems so that responses occur. Protoself activity is largely similar between people and operates with common objectives. That is, most responses to stimuli are similar from person to person and generally operate according to a rule of maximise pleasure/minimise pain. However, biographical experiences and memories of individuals vary and with that variation comes variance in what and how protoselves trigger responses. Later discussion of affect with Sylvan Tomkins will show him referring to this as a *script*, defined patterns of behaviour shaped by and repeated out of prior experiential outcomes in similar situations. Thus, some individuals respond to given situations on this level in similar but not congruent ways due to biographical conditioning. It is this deeper, less conscious part of our mind that mitigates and modifies our ordination and positioning relative to shifts in proximal inhabitation. It is an innate action to shift our position in groups as the proximity of others contracts or expands. This theoretical aspect of consciousness recurs throughout this text, but I return to discuss its properties in more detail in chapter 2. Here I reference how awareness that is low-level, just below consciousness or is similarly peripheral, is the activity of the protoself.

Collective motor activity requires our constant low-level vigilance of what is happening around us and consequent adjustments. From an objective distance (outside the collective domain) I noticed how the prägnanz of crowds as wholes also shift and flow. At Oslo and Morrisons, stepping outside the collective domain into an objective position allowed me to perceive the entire collective at work. Patterns in movement type and positional change became obvious and appeared to be reactions to the increasing or decreasing of given space. While there were obvious cause-effect patterns here, the compositional aspect of prägnanz with respect to these dancing crowds seems more random or uncoordinated when compared with designed aesthetic collectives, like the installations of Vanessa Beecroft or theatre events in the next chapters. As a non-formalised group this comparison is expected. Nonetheless, there was order, composition and causality in collective motor activity. Usually, the composition and pattern development organised like organic, amoebic shapes and forms—globular and radiating out in tendrils.

It is apparent that the compositional prägnanz of the groups was shifting in relation to the expansion and contraction of the immediate space surrounding individuals and micro-groups—the sudden movement of others into/out of their personal space.

> [T]hink of [the participants] as surrounded by a series of expanding and contracting *fields* [emphasis added] which provide information of many kinds ... including personality types [...] [and] the simplest form of the situational personality is associated with responses to intimate, personal, social, and public transactions.[30]

*Proximity and Prägnanz—Space, Order, Touch* 49

I emphasise the word *field* here as I consider the spaces that surrounded us to be fields of presence and the spaces surrounding the collective also to be a field of collective presences; a notion that returns in chapter 6, but is highlighted here as a feature of space and its dynamics. Each of these spaces was measurable and allowed for only certain types of activities, as indicated above.

Let me elaborate more on these different categories of space. Beginning in the reverse order the public distance is about 3.5 m from the self to the other at the closest and expands from there. The public distance provides a good spatial arena in which one is outside of a collective domain and can generally observe it with objective clarity. This was possible in Oslo and Morrisons if I stood at the farthest ends of the rooms. At those points while still within the aesthetic field I was not a part of the dancing crowds and could comprehend them in totality. This distance, according to Hall, constitutes the distance 'set around important public figures ... [or] anyone on public occasions'.[31] At this distance people strongly objectify other individuals and at an extreme distance—'when people look like ants—contact with them as human beings fades rapidly'.[32] This objectifying certainly did happen to me at Oslo and Morrisons, but not as much as might happen at arena performances or mass encounters. When removed from the aesthetic collective (again at the farthest corners of the spaces) I noticed myself feeling more like a scientist studying the crowds. Also, I noticed at this distance idiosyncratic behaviour of individuals that up-close had a strong effect on me did not affect me strongly (e.g. irritation, interest, humour, etc.). In Debbie and Metropolis, this was never really the case. I was always within the collective domain and members of the collective body were always closer, within at least the next nearest distance, the social distance.

Social distance was maintained in the events in terms of interaction with bar and staff and often there were barriers to ensure this spacing (such as the actual bar, a desk for coat check or glass panes or plinths for ticketing staff). As an audience member (so standing outside of the collective domain) social distance was difficult to maintain due to very full capacities in all cases, especially as the nights moved into later hours. Similarly, where there was seating it was always positioned in ways that seemed to space people out into social distances, but as the ambiance became louder and more invasive that space was diminished. Social distance ranges from about 1.5 m to 3.5 m in separation of self and other. In this range, Hall notes that physical contact is not very easy, 'nobody touches or expects to touch another person unless there is some special effort'.[33] It is the range at which we conduct most socialisation, hence its name. It is also the distance that marks 'the "limit of domination" [...] [and a] proxemic feature [...] is that it can be used to insulate or screen people from each other'.[34] Social distance is the preferred range at which to converse and conduct business.

Most interactions in these clubbing events, though, occurred within personal distance. Within this distance dancing in congress with other people is possible. It allowed just enough space between each participant for movement and the limbs to bend and gesture aesthetically. I could also maintain personal distance outside the collective domain very easily (again, except at Debbie). The

50   *Precis*

overlapping of personal spaces outside the dancing crowd was noticeably less; an exception, which later seemed obvious, was queuing (for toilets, at the bar, for tickets or coat check). Another exception was the transient intersection of personal spaces in movement through the spaces—for instance, passing someone en route to different locations. Within the collective domain, we all played with and manipulated our overlapping personal spaces and distancing. In fact, it seems that much of the enjoyment of the dancing is this act of involving others in one's personal space and the intersubjective relationships that came about through the expansion and contraction of that space and the activity of communicating in physical-spatial terms. We were not able to communicate verbally very well at these events. The atmospheric elements were too powerful to allow successful transmission of thoughts; the music was too loud to hear voices well, the lighting too dim to see facial expressions, the space too active to gesture properly. Eventually, everyone was shouting or screaming at each other, as above usually right into the ears. Consequently, real communication generally required a couple to contract into a small, displaced space within the domain or to step out of the domain entirely, to a more secluded space. Generally, the space outside the domain was where most verbal communication happened.

This personal distance 'designate[d] the distance consistently separating the members [...] It might be thought of as a small protective sphere of space that an organism maintains between itself and others'.[35] It is as close as 0.5 m and as far as 1.5 m. It demarcates a space filled with strong sensations and engagement with others who are within that distance. 'The kinaesthetic sense of closeness derives in part from the possibilities present in regard to what each participant c[ould] do to the other with [their] extremities. At this distance, [we could] hold or grasp the other person'.[36] This sphere of space was very noticeably 'my' personal spaces, 'my' territory. In this volume of space 'subjects of personal interest and involvement [could] be discussed' by allowing others to enter that space—or more specifically, to allow my personal space to overlap with someone else's.[37] As noted, verbal communication was not very successful anyway (although it did happen), so physical communication was more prominent. As this space allows for physical contact and relates to personal interest and involvement it became a space of vulnerability for all of us. It '[wa]s the limit of physical domination in the very real sense [...] [hence] where people stand in relation to each other signals their relationship, or how they feel toward each other, or both'.[38] We would gather closer to our friends than strangers. As smaller relationships were displayed or evolved individuals would get very close to each other, far closer than with anyone else. This further contracting of space moved these participants into intimate distance or space with each other. In fact, a lot of the dancing engaged our intimate spaces.

## Touch—Known, Unknown; Security, Threat

While dancing I noticed (and experienced) groins, buttocks, breasts, necks, ears, thighs and other sensitive body parts physically connecting with other

Proximity and Prägnanz—Space, Order, Touch 51

people. With aesthetic collectives of the club, it is inevitable that co-occupation of intimate space occurs; there simply was not enough space. Indeed, speaking from historic experience in club-like environments this is one of the main draws. Intimate distance denotes the closest proximity and with it the most vulnerable, exposing interaction possible.

> At intimate distance, the presence of the other person [wa]s unmistakable and [...] at times [...] overwhelming because of the greatly stepped-up sensory inputs. Sight (often distorted), olfaction, heat from the other person's body, sound, smell and feel of the breath all combine[d] to signal unmistakable involvement with another body.[39]

It is pure contact or up to about 0.5 m away (or in the case of sex, one of the most intimate engagements of intimate spaces, penetrative contact). In this environment, all my senses were active in communication. My space of private kinaesthetic experience overlapped with those of others and suddenly intimate communication happened. To experience shared intimate space and be in such proximity to others, particularly non-familiars, was exciting, interesting and alluring.

This close, haptic contact[40] can drive feelings of comfort, security and insulated protection. To return to the observation that groups of friends would compose themselves in inward-facing circles and shut-out the others worked at maximising this contact with familiars and minimising it with strangers. This is difficult to maintain consistently, though. Available space frequently collapses or shifts. Eventually, physical compositions would fail and, as noted with Oslo above, bodies compressed together regardless of grouping. Sometimes familiars would be sharing intimate space with each other, sometimes with non-familiars. All of us within the collective domain, however, seemed to allow and permit sharing of intimate space. There definitely were instances where individuals continued to press into 'our' space, perhaps unhappily in some cases and particularly when men pressed into my female friends' intimate spaces. In those instances, my friends would contract space even further, thus phasing these men (and women at times) out, or my female friends would change positions with one of our male friends or me and thus create a human barrier to that contact and intimate encounter. This issue was undoubtedly more problematic for lone or small groups of women.[41] On the larger level, the full dancing crowd became simultaneously intimate and personal, mainly via the act of physical touch or, at bare minimum, the close experience of a collective motor activity as a gesturing, moving body.

Elias Canetti observes that unknown or unpredicted touch is filled with fear.

> There is nothing that [the hu]man fears more than the touch of the unknown. [One] wants to *see* [emphasis in the original] what is reaching

52  *Precis*

> towards [them], and to be able to recognize or at least classify it [...] All distances which [people] create round themselves are dictated by this fear.[42]

The idea of the touch of the strange/other normally disturbs us, even if in a minor way. The organism withdraws from it, contracts its space inward while telegraphing outward the psychic alarm of having been touched. 'The repugnance of being touched remains with us when we go about among people; the way we move in a busy street, in restaurants, trains or buses, is governed by it [...] we avoid actual contact if we can'.[43] The desire for sufficient and observed barriers is strong. Often these barriers and the behaviours ensuring them are so ingrained, so operationally rehearsed, that they fall into the realm of procedural memory functioning in the background of consciousness. This is another element of the protoself working at the deeper levels of consciousness. This kind of sensory processing and response is usually not so important that it requires our immediate, full attention. We do not even need to think about this.

In these clubbing examples, the manipulation and involvement of these interpersonal spaces always conditioned our coalescing into a crowd. In the early stages, we actively avoided the threat of touch from strangers. As the number of participants increased or we entered the crowd the potential volume for personal space decreased and we began a constant game of adjusting those personal spaces. Friends crowded closer together; groups and individuals shuffled about in their areas; the denser populated spaces were nearer the centre or stage (or the DJ) and then thinned moving towards the perimeters or back wall(s). The adjustments at first were quite large, changing actual locations or moving meters in any one direction to maintain personal space. As density increased these adjustments became slighter, shuffling a step one way or another, adjusting orientation to maintain intimate space, which included the shifting of bags and coats on the floor out of the path of 'outsiders'. The negative space between all of us had to be as equal as possible and there was a sense of 'filling the space'. We also wanted or needed to occupy a decent amount of space to dance. However, when members moved or shifted as they dance, the negative space between us changed. Consequently, there is a constant adaptation to this shifting and changing. We would move in concert with each other, again adapting to the collective motor activity that was occurring. The movement of the members and the way by which they territorialised the space surrounding them is responsive in this way. It changes with the dance actions and with the nature of the topographical changes in prägnanz.

Unintended contact also demanded response. Again, the individual withdraws from it, contracts their barriered space inward, telegraphs outward its psychic disturbance of the event, and then waits, waits for the apology.

The promptness with which apology is offered for an unintended contact,

*Proximity and Prägnanz—Space, Order, Touch* 53

the tension with which it is awaited, our violent and sometimes even physical reaction when it is not forthcoming, the antipathy and hatred we feel for the offender, even when we cannot be certain who it is—the whole knot of shifting and intensely sensitive reactions to an alien touch—proves that we are dealing here with a human propensity as deep-seated as it is alert and insidious; something which never leaves a [person] when [they] have established the boundaries of [their] personality. Even in sleep, when [they] are far more unguarded, [they] can all too easily be disturbed by a touch.[44]

The touch of the other disturbs. As Canetti says we like to see what is touching us, where it is touching, when it will touch, and how it will touch *before* the touch. If we can objectify the touch by sight then when it comes the disturbance is lessened—but not eliminated. Indeed, all the senses unify to scan and coordinate the inward coming other. Our haptic sense engages them as agents to manage this disturbance. 'Help me', says touch, 'or we will feel threat'. The maintenance of the barriers, of the individual space, is crucial; its rupture equates to invasion of the Self. First, through the surface of the skin, then through the vibration of that touch into the underlying tissue. Shock waves emanate through the musculature, the antennae of touch elsewhere in the body immediately seize and direct their attention towards this site of invasion. Like a herd noticing a predator on its fringes all attention aims at this place and point. Unconscious and conscious behaviour are suddenly in-tune; the disturbance has invaded the physical self and now the psychic self begins to feel its own invasion—a response is needed.

When and how is touch permissible then, especially in these highly haptic cases? I can only speak from my personal experience and extrapolate from my observations of behaviour, but it seemed that if touch carried with it excitement and allure or was expected or deemed acceptable the disturbance of this touching seemed allowed or even pleasurable.[45] Here, importantly, the disturbance was also consensual as far as I felt and observed it.[46] If it was anticipatable, the disturbance was mitigated and instead became a given condition of the environment, in which case it was both expected and its impact manageable. This was touch as through a collective crowd. Different to a crowded *area*, where the space of individuals simply reduces and contracts, in these cases a collectivising was enacted. We entered and became *part of the crowd-as-a-body*. 'It is only in a crowd that [I could] become free of this fear of being touched. That is the only situation in which the fear changes into its opposite'.[47] The collectivised crowd turned my fear of the disturbance into its opposite. What is that, the opposite of fear? If fear is *of* something then fear is of something else, something other. Fear was of the relation of other(s) to me, of what this/these other/s could harmfully do to me, or potential threat they could pose to me. So, if fear is *of threat,* then its opposite must be freedom from threat—safety and security. Thus, through the collectivised crowd I felt safe and secure.

## 54    *Precis*

> As soon as [I] surrender[ed my]self to the crowd, [I] cease[d] to fear its touch. Ideally, all [we]re equal there; no distinctions count[ed], not even that of sex. The [person] pressed against [me wa]s the same as [my]self [...] Suddenly it [wa]s as though everything were happening in one and the same body.[48]

Again, the concept of a *body* to these crowds emerges. The others in the collective body became like my own self. By establishing a zone of accepted touch and having a common reason to be together, the crowd generated a type of haven of safety and security for us, the members. The touch of the others within the bodies of these crowds strengthened these feelings and ensured this safety and security interpersonally. As a part of that body, being inside, it was from outside of our collective body that threat could now mainly come.

Membership established a larger and wider space than a single individual could territorially own—the collective domain—which created barriers to what is outside our crowd body. Once crowds establish these collective bodies and became *one*, the threat of the other is outside, beyond *us*. Each crowd sought 'to close in on itself: it want[ed] to rid each individual as completely as possible of the fear of being touched. The more fiercely people press[ed] together, the more certain they fe[lt] that they do not fear each other'.[49] These crowds removed threat, fear, and in the assimilation to the crowd each of us experienced the other members' touch either with indifference or with ready acceptance. Now, the touch of these others, of *members*, also indicates safety and security and a desire to continue and perhaps even increase those feelings. The pressing together of the crowds in Oslo, Metropolis, Morrison's and Debbie were acceptable for me and I usually did not feel a sense of threat from others touching me while we were all part of the same dancing crowd (with the exceptions of too close-proximity as described earlier). When I was simply an audience member in those venues (that is, outside the collective domain and not part of the aesthetic collective, like at the bar ordering drinks) having someone touch me was again a surprising and startling thing.

In the examples of Oslo or Morrison's these urges (to avoid the touch of the other or to embrace it through the homogenising, unifying of a crowd) became the behavioural make-up of the club experience. In both examples, I could see and be in the space before the DJs started and thus before the existence of the dancing crowds. Before the main act in Oslo or the DJ started playing in Morrison's the crowd size did not need to occupy all the space, the touch of the other was avoided and apology-ridden. As noted, we mitigated space to allow for a zone of personal ownership. We worked to avoid occupying others' spaces and prevent others from occupying our own. Once attendance grew, space was more filled and proximity between us began to close-in. The unavoidable touch of the other(s), distances separating bodies and the formation of the group as a perceivable entity (not just a smattering of individuals) all came into relation.

## Proximity and Prägnanz—Space, Order, Touch    55

The primacy of physical nearness as a crowd-making force is evident; once the space no longer allowed full personal spaces we had to accept the touch of the other and a process of acclimating to that touch ensued. There was a phase of 'the whole knot of shifting and intensely sensitive reactions to an alien touch'[50] during which acknowledging and apologising for giving 'alien' touch happened. Then a period during which we unconsciously negotiated spaces and bumped into each other but did not apologise. Then finally a state in which we did not acknowledge, attend to or particularly notice the touch. In retrospect the touch of the other in those dancing crowds was always 'known' to be happening, it just did not matter. The aestheticising process of the artists drew everyone together—figuratively, but more importantly very literally.

However, even as a member of these crowds the touch could still come unexpectedly and thus startle or catch me unaware. After all, it is hard to know from where and when the touch will come. I wanted the crowd touch to be as anticipatable as possible. For me, but I do not think this is restricted just to me, to achieve this the crowd must in some way eliminate unpredictability. Mimicking individuals' immediate response to the unexpected touch of the other, the crowd would at times eliminate the option of the unexpected with one clear action: contracting the space inward and re-establishing all barriers. The crowd condensed the proximity of its member and made clearer the edges and margins that separated it from the other(s)—prägnanz was asserted more. When the crowd consolidated inward and increased the density of bodies the possibility of touch being unexpected reduced. It was very hard to penetrate a dense crowd or touch anyone within it from outside. Again, '[t]he more fiercely people press together, the more certain they feel that they do not fear each other'.[51] At maximum density, where the proximity of bodies was very close, I could expect touch constantly across all my body surface. Moreover, the distinction between our membership and the external other(s) became harsh and clear. Except at the edges, there was little chance of an outside threat, so the membership can relax. The place of most assurance of this was the centre, the densest point, '[t]his goal is the blackest spot where most people are gathered'.[52] This contraction and density, though, were again subject to a limit. Too contracted or dense a crowd and again the threat of the crowd became overbearing, disconnecting and claustrophobic. As in Debbie, the loss of comfort turned the touch of the other members into a threat—one that if exaggerated could potentially carry with it panic.

Moreover, the participants in the examples were always working at managing the space in territorialising ways. All of us 'managed' the space we were in and manipulated our own bodies to make use of those spaces effectively. The crowd somehow instinctually responded to this need for predictability; we naturally decreased the random and chaotic by generating types of regularity. We were working towards an order to the space and how we inhabited it. There are several methods I noted employed in the crowds to achieve this, all of which largely fall under two categories: conformity and uniformity. The more we conformed to movement types and the more we

56    *Precis*

unified in our actions and styles the more predictable the physical engagements. For example, we conformed and unified to rhythm, direction of movements, action types, common need for equal space and so on. As conformity and uniformity increased the similarity and common fate of our crowds also increased. That is, we felt and appeared more similar in action and behaviour and we all seemed to be working towards the same general goal with the experience (the next chapters will elaborate on these features). Through conformity and uniformity, the crowds offered more anticipation for all possible happenings, at least within its bounds. We reduced the chance of chaotic behaviour and with it threats from the external other and of the unexpected internal were minimised. The crowd ensured its cohesion and entitativity by managing its proximity and prägnanz, and with that came, at least as far as I experienced it, an assurance of safety and security within the body of the crowds.

## Communitas and Affect Transmission

A final point about what created a sense of safety and security within these crowds for me was my feeling of equality with the others in the crowd. This was important to allowing me to want to interact or to touch/be touched by others. I wanted to feel like we were all equivalent and there for the same, or relatively the same, reasons. The crowd had to foment a social homogeneity and equality for us to want to be together. Barriers to this could not exist. Otherwise, the touch of the crowd, the press of the membership, would have felt physically and psychically confusing or unwanted. Feelings of inequity would have made the cohabitation of personal and intimate space feel more vulnerable or alarming. To dispel the disturbance of the touch it must be the familiar touch, as though my own touch. To reiterate, '[i]deally, all are equal there; no distinctions count, not even that of sex. The [person] pressed against [them] is the same as [them]self [...] Suddenly it is as though everything were happening in one and the same body'.[53] The membership must become homogenous and similar—ideally as similar as possible. To return to Victor Turner this homogenisation and the temporary, liminal state of being in such a crowd is *communitas*. Entrance into membership, entrance into crowds, is a temporary and liminal experience. The membership in the dancing crowd is something that exists for a temporary period for a specific set of reasons. The collective that offers security and safety from the disturbance of the other is thereby a temporal entity. Turner notes how the communitas established in these crowds is also something of the present. 'Communitas is something of the now; structure is rooted in the past and extends into the future'.[54] Turner is using the word *structure* here to mean the structure of society. Communitas exists outside of that structure; thus, in communitas and its present moment there is none of the hierarchy, difference, inequality or disparity of the external world. The existence of the crowd is bounded by time and at either end of its time (its past or its future) it either does not exist or it necessarily must change

Proximity and Prägnanz—Space, Order, Touch   57

forms and modify. The duration of these dancing collectives was mapped to their function or purpose. As their time came to an end, they ceased to have function or purpose and as such ended the sense of communitas and unity.

Our sense of nearness carried with it another element of communication that we could not control. As dancers within the same space and within the personal and intimate spaces of each other, we were sharing and exchanging more than just space and actions. In the dancing crowd, our proximity to each other was so close that we were literally awash in each other's air-based secretions. There was the presence and smell of our own and others' sweat, breathe, clothing, body oils and so on. Aspects of our bodies were permeating the air. Theresa Brennan asserts that pheromones, not actively carrying a smell themselves, are also filling this shared air-space. In our proximity we share or co-experience affect both through the activity and behaviour we put into the space, but also through these bio-physical pheromones that we secrete into the air. This is an element of atmosphere, which will form the key argument in chapter 6, but weaves its way through the whole text.

In *The Transmission of Affect*,[55] Brennan elaborates that in addition to the co-occupation of space there is a set of deeper biological processes occurring that also facilitate the transmission of affect (and later in chapters 4 and 5, I will extend this to emotion and mood contagion). Her work, in psychiatric facilities in the main, notes how elements of the nervous system, most notably the hormone and pheromone mechanisms, trigger communication of stimuli from individual to individual (or amongst pluralities). Whereas other theorists attribute much of the transmission of affect to the concrete aspects of the senses, particularly sight and hearing, Brennan opens her discourse to delve into more recent findings in science, stating that endocrinology and pheromones are far more participant in the activity. Brennan notes that *entrainment*, 'the process whereby human affective responses are linked and repeated',[56] is an operational system in which the body takes-in external affect inducers, pheromones, that influence and affect the internal hormones and cerebral functions of the body, which in turn trigger further affective responses.

> One detects pheromones by touch or smell, but smell is more common. To smell pheromones is also in a sense to consume them. But the point here is that no direct physical contact is necessary for a transmission to take place. *Pheromones are literally in the air* [emphasis added].[57]

The use of *smell* here is in the greater sense of breathing in, not necessarily detecting them through an aroma (pheromones largely have no aroma). In her detailed study, Brennan asserts that olfactory and tactile communication between people contributes, sometimes quite heavily, to affect reactions and the exchange, spread and assimilation of affect in polyadic environments. 'Research on hormones supports the realization that the environment, especially the environment in the form of other people, changes human endocrinology, not the other way around. It also changes the affects accompanying those hormones'.[58]

58    *Precis*

What can be gained from this is the assertion that the environment induces in the individual a myriad of physio-psychological effects and that other people, as environment, have the same inductive potential. Much of this affect exchange operates in anoesis, which is a state of sensational experience that operates prior to or in advance of cognition or reflexive considering thought. This kind of affect exchange can, although not necessarily, trigger cognitive thought. Likewise, cognitive thinking can also trigger affect responses and produce these pheromonal secretions. The system is circular in this way and caught in a feedback loop, with affects and thought affecting and triggering each other endlessly.

Brennan's text considers other people as part of one's environment. Others are external, environmental factors. Her observation that 'any inquiry into *how* one feels the others' affects, or the 'atmosphere', has to take account of physiology as well as the social, psychological factors that generated the atmosphere in the first place' exposes the notion of the individual's affect state being porous and subject to the external, atmospheric properties of the world inclusive of the social and psychological.[59] 'The transmission of affect [...] is social or psychological in origin. But the transmission is also responsible for bodily changes [... and] alters the biochemistry and neurology of the subject. The 'atmosphere' or the environment literally gets into the individual'.[60] Brennan's statements here imply this is a purely passive process, but she does observe that as much as individuals absorb atmosphere into them and are affected by it, they also project affect outward and contribute to that atmosphere. This reciprocal affective relationship between the external environment and the individual is *atmosphere* at its most simple. Returning to Seigworth and Gregg, 'affect is integral to a body's perpetual *becoming* [...] pulled beyond its seeming surface-boundedness by way of its relation to, indeed its composition through, the forces of encounter'.[61] How that atmosphere moves, spreads and affects others is *contagion*—a term that Brennan observes reaches back to early studies of crowds and social psychology, Gustave Le Bon and William McDougall in particular.[62] Following Brennan, Le Bon and McDougall, I conceptualise the experiences of the clubbing environment and its affective atmosphere, much like an infection, moving through, from and to the experiencing subjects. Through the aesthetics of the experience the atmosphere, far from distinct from all those present, imbricated us with each other and the environment: 'With affect, a body is as much outside itself as in itself—webbed in its relations—until ultimately such firm distinctions cease to matter'.[63] I will foreground and elaborate this concept of contagion as a theme of chapters 4 and 5 and as I work towards the atmospheric properties of the fuller range of aesthetic collectives. It is noteworthy here that the proximity of members in these clubbing crowds allows immersion in such affectively toned spaces.

My focus here has been to examine how the spatialising elements of these clubbing examples of aesthetic collectives operate. These dancing crowds became entitative through ways in which participants were spatially unified

## Proximity and Prägnanz—Space, Order, Touch   59

through their proximity to each other and the boundary establishment that came with experiencing them as a closed unit. Each of the examples involved a constant negotiation of space, ordination of bodies and engagement with the inside/outside orientation of the crowd to come to be a part of it. This recognition comes from both participant and audience perspectives. Individuals in these aestheticised environments come to be conceptualised as a closed and homogenous whole or unit, a dancing crowd. As examples of aesthetic collectives, the principles of proximity and prägnanz here contribute to this conceptualisation of wholes out of groups of individuals. Throughout the rest of this text, this same analysis will apply, and indeed extends to the notion of aesthetic collectives more broadly speaking.

## Notes

1 Lakoff and Johnson, p. 162.
2 *Transportative* and *transformative* are terms used to indicate the type of experience that might be had in/through the arts. I will further explore these terms later in this chapter, particularly regarding their use by Elias Canetti, Victor Turner and Richard Schechner.
3 I direct the reader to other cases where researchers have immersed themselves within their cases, but have maintained a non-interfering perspective: Andrews, 'Tits Out …'; Thurnell-Read, 'What Happens on Tour …'.
4 Please see Image 1 in Appendix A. When discussions get to it, the dotted lines indicate the edge of the collective domain.
5 And when I write *spherical* I mean that in a generally orb-like way. They are obviously not spherical as they are irregular blobs but hold as a key aspect a relatively equal relationship between a centre and the edges like a sphere does. In most daily encounters, we might negotiate the lateral dimensions, but anyone who has stood beneath an Antony Gormley sculpture can attest to how these spaces definitely extend in the vertical as well.
6 Hall, *The Hidden Dimension*.
7 Hall, p. 128.
8 Hall, p. 128.
9 Don Idhe, *Listening and Voice; Phenomenologies of Sound*, 2nd ed. (Albany, New York: State University of New York Press, 2007).
10 Idhe, p. 105.
11 Hall, p. 128.
12 I wonder as well if this kind of experience is gendered. I am a man and find people grind-dancing against me unappealing, but for women this could be a more invasive, overpowering or harassing experience. I suspect so, but am not sure and hold such conversation for another work of investigation.
13 Hall, p. 118. Here, Hall is generalising to Western individuals, he does go on to note how in other cultures (e.g. Arab, middle-eastern Jewish, Japanese and Russian) the reaction is more relaxed with intimate and personal touching and spacing. However, the principle of discomfort in sustained close proximity remains constant as it eventuates in personal territorial negotiation.
14 Hall, p. 118.
15 Campbell, p. 17.
16 Campbell, p. 22.
17 Campbell, p. 22.
18 Campbell, p. 22.
19 Campbell, p. 18.

60    *Precis*

20  Elias Canetti, *Crowds and Power*, trans. by Carol Stewart (New York: Farrar, Straus and Giroux, 1960), p. 17.
21  Victor Turner, *The Ritual Process; Structure and Anti-Structure* (London: Routledge & Kegan Paul, 1969), p. 94.
22  Turner, p. 100.
23  Canetti, p. 18.
24  Hall, p. 128.
25  Hall, pp. 7–8.
26  Hall, p. 115.
27  I coin this term to signal that it is different from other dance in that it is reactive with the environment and the other people occupying the space and it exists solely for self-satisfying entertainment/enjoyment. There are of course outcomes and other 'needs' being satisfied depending on the context (flirting and sex being obvious and frequent). Differently, formalised social dance has societal strictures imposed on it—it satisfies a series of specific socialising objectives. Artistic dance or dance performance, similarly, exists for a designated audience and conveys (usually) specific messages from one group to another. As a term, I am not aware of it elsewhere in the literature and is different from the categorisation/genre of music as *atmospheric dance music*.
28  Hall, p. 115.
29  Antonio Damasio, *The Feeling of What Happens: Body, Emotion and the Making of Consciousness* (London: Vintage Books, 2000).
30  Hall, p. 115.
31  Hall, pp. 124–125.
32  Hall, p. 125.
33  Hall, p. 121.
34  Hall, p. 121 and 123.
35  Hall, p. 119.
36  Hall, p. 119.
37  Hall, p. 120.
38  Hall, p. 120.
39  Hall, p. 116.
40  *Haptic* meaning in relation to touch or the sense of touch.
41  I return to n26 where I first raise these kinds of concerns.
42  Canetti, p. 15.
43  Canetti, p. 15.
44  Canetti, p. 15.
45  As I proceed to analyse touch becoming bearable or pleasurable, I will exclude touch of an unwanted, uninvited or abusive nature—such as groping, frottage or even striking. These acts are in a class lying outside those considered as they are violating and invasive. Moreover, I did not observe or hear about this kind of behaviour in these specific instances; I have in other clubbing experiences and do acknowledge how such behaviour would indeed result in a break in connection with the collective crowd and a loss of security/safety as I go on to discuss it.
46  As noted earlier, non-consensual touch was observed, but none of it resulted in serious situations that required more than a change in position in the room or a comment to stop such touch. There might have been more serious situations of touch occurring, but I did not observe, experience or hear about them in these cases.
47  Canetti, p. 15.
48  Canetti, pp. 15–16.
49  Canetti, p. 16.
50  Canetti, p. 15.
51  Canetti, p. 16.
52  Canetti, p. 16.

53 Canetti, pp. 15–16.
54 Turner.
55 Brennan.
56 Brennan, p. 52.
57 Brennan, p. 69.
58 Brennan, p. 73.
59 Brennan, p. 1.
60 Brennan, p. 1.
61 Seigworth and Gregg, 'An Inventory of Shimmers', p. 3.
62 Gustave Le Bon, *The Crowd; A Study of the Popular Mind* (New York: Cosimo Classics, 2006); William McDougall, *The Group Mind; A Sketch of the Principles of Collective Psychology* (New York: G. P. Putnam's Sons, 1920).
63 Seigworth and Gregg, p. 3.

# 2 Similarity—Authority and Agency

Kanye West is a contentious popular culture figure. Originally a music artist, he has traversed arts disciplines and become someone with multiple industry elements operating at the same time: fashion lines, shoe lines, video games, visual art, reality TV. He is also aspiring to be a political figure. He tried, not very successfully, to run for president of the USA in 2020 and has previously stated that he wants to run for president in 2024. He has an enormous fan-base and a media presence that captures millions of viewers at any given time. He is also excellent at gathering and using artists' talents to create bricolage outputs under his own name. Since 2008 he has particularly been working with Vanessa Beecroft and through his engagement with her has been creating fashion shows and concert elements with aesthetic collectives. Their work reached a milestone on 11 February 2016 when his fashion line *Yeezy Season 3* and album debut for *Life of Pablo* was stage by Beecroft in Madison Square Gardens and displayed his fashion line, Yeezy, as an aesthetic collective. Considering the live and tele-present audiences, the event has been called the most viewed piece of performance art in history with Artnews reporting it viewed by 20 million people.[1] West/Beecroft's stagings are an example of aesthetic collectives as they exist on the popular and mass scale.

This is a use of aesthetic collectivity that has a long, and politically controversial, tradition, especially in the 20th century. We see them used in Olympic Games ceremonies, in US NFL Half-time shows, military parades or mass games (such as those held in North Korea). In political ways, the mass collective is deployed to demonstrate nationalism, state power and authority, social supremacy and political ideology. I will not be veering into those kinds of examples, leaving them for a different project; instead, I will be examining the intersection of popular art and the avant-garde in the work of Vanessa Beecroft and later Kanye West. Through their example, we can observe features of the aesthetic collective and then extrapolate to the larger socio-political 'stage'. Whereas the dancing club crowds of the last chapter presented and considered spatial aspects of aesthetic collectives, how spatial elements contribute to entitative emergence and perception, this chapter discusses similarisation. In so doing entailed issues of agency, power, authority and direction that dominant

DOI: 10.4324/9781003205661-4

*Similarity—Authority and Agency* 63

agencies exert over individuality will surface, revealing a balancing act between individuality and collectivity that plays out in these collectivised situations.

Similarity expands the potential entitativity of aesthetic collectives. It is a relatively obvious thing about aesthetic collectives—that everyone in them appears similar or the same. The making of one member just like any other establishes a homogeneity, the collective becomes equalised throughout. Homogeneity can impress, awe, disquiet or terrify an onlooker. Seeing groups of people acting and looking the same has a force and power to it. The reason? Similarisation of members creates a stronger sense of entitativity to the perceived collective—beyond what proximity and prägnanz alone create. Like with those two elements of entitativity, an increase of entitativity generates a concomitant collective identity. When we look at aesthetic collectives with increased entitativity we begin to ascribe a sense of agency to it—it becomes progressively more like a human or more than human intentional subject. Something, the collective, is 'controlling' the members. Similarisation also situates members into categories. Another way of stating this is that similarisation creates reference. The members become referential of categories whose properties they share in terms of physical, gestural and agentic capacities. Categorisation in this way is a means of understanding the members 'as being like' various other things. They are *like* a group of soldiers; they are *like* a fleet of naked clones; they are *like* mannequins come to life. The transformation of appearance is particularly effective in generating collectivity or the perception of it. We perceive people as highly linked if they are physically more identical. Techniques of appearance such as uniforms, costumes, make-up, body modification, identifying marks all work to contain individuals in progressively smaller and more specific categories and groupings. Even more so if they move, act or behave in similarised ways. Such ordered presentation of the physical body allows us to comprehend the individual as something belonging to categories. Similarisation *draws people together* or *links* them to create a common category and containment. We perceive and conceptualise them, once again, in a container metaphor, this time as contained within categories, not just spaces.

Beyond being referential to various categories of things, each collective becomes itself a singular category. All the members have the properties of their aesthetic collective and thus become members. Individual participants are all categorised within the entity of the collective. We also then identify that collective entity categorically with non-artistic corollary/analogue archetypes that it references. This comparison between types is a conceptualising act. Similarity between categories elaborates one in terms of another. This chapter addresses these notions of internal similarity between the memberships of various examples of aesthetic collectives and how one member is similarised to the other members.

I am going to draw from the realm of avant-garde installation performance art to start. Specifically, I am going to look at the work of Vanessa Beecroft and then expand from the avant-garde to the mass-popular realm in a slightly

64    *Precis*

lesser degree with Kanye West. Vanessa Beecroft's installation performances are very clear instances of aesthetic collectives. Members of her installations quite overtly are similarised to/with each other. This work epitomises an aesthetic collective both through the immediate visual of a coalesced group, but also through the lengths to which Beecroft goes to transform the participants, both in appearance and in action. There is such a strong entitativity to these collectives and their presentation that they create feelings of the uncanny—something familiar, but foreign; something alluring, yet terrifying. This is focussed as visual messages in these works, whether intended by Beecroft or not, relating to power dynamics, gender politics, authoritarianism, slavery and fascistic social structures. All of these echoed further in West's later appropriation. The act of similarising the participants creates a stronger gestalt, whole structure and stronger relationships (perceived or actual) between those members and the collective totalities.

In the following discussion, the entitativity of the performances is more controlled than in the dancing crowds of clubs—specifically, the participants themselves are highly controlled and the audiences are more formalised. Indeed, an interesting aspect of Beecroft's work is her selection of audiences, the dress code and the way she likes to control them alongside her art pieces. There are more than 60 installations, but I will draw on a few specific instances in which she instals collectives of highly similarised members performing durational installations with severely restricted actions. Almost like living statue work, her installations display collectives of severely similarised women (she has worked with men, but the majority of her work is female focused). Audiences watch them endure, fatigue and disintegrate under the strain of the experience of participating in these collectives for long periods of time. We literally watch women struggle to get through the pieces. There is a plethora of polar responses from participants and audiences that reflect on the work as agonising, shameful/shameless, disturbing, sensationalising, scandalous, boring, racist/race-allied, anti-feminist/feminist and so on. Reactions are complicated, but always revolve around feelings of shame, control, resistance, authority and dehumanisation.

Her work illustrates how the similarisation of visible, overt appearance and the behaviour of participants increases perception of them as cohesive, homogenised collectives. Agency becomes a dominating feature in thinking through this similarisation, specifically individual agency versus the collective's. Similarisation of appearance, action or action potential shifts the balance away from strong individual agency towards strong collective agency and a sense of collective 'self'. Towards the end of the chapter, I will address Beecroft's directorial methods, which constrain the possible visual message and range of behaviour allowed—both in visual appearance and lexicon of allowed action. The sense of cohesion, conformity and the production of entitativity itself are here part of the experience of the work of art and its meaning. Participants are an individual-as-member and audiences perceive their integrity within the overall category of the aesthetic collective. Moreover, the individual as an agentic self transforms and shifts into that of the collective. In another sense, what similarisation shows is a process of deindividuation on the physical and agentic levels.

While she now seemingly only works with Kanye West to which mass publics have access either in person or digitally, her prior performance art was an in-person experience and very difficult to gain admission to, usually restricted to invited audiences composed mainly of fashionistas, 'high artists', celebrities and the extremely rich. Even journalists and critics were frequently excluded. Photographic, video, and testimonial evidence and artefacts are what most can see. Some galleries required her to hold a public open exhibition, but public audiences are not Beecroft's favourites and she has voiced that she would rather they not attend (to this I will return). Her recent work with West, on the other hand, has brought her work into the realm of mass commercial and consumable artworks. Like Beecroft, West's self-aggrandising persona and marketing team attempt to create a sense of exclusivity but also one of mass consumption in his wide-ranging work. Beecroft's name exists mainly in the background of his works, but her artistic signature is clearly evident. In any case, discussing Beecroft's work is necessarily informed by secondary sources (photographs, videos, interviews, personal narratives).

For some background context, Beecroft has been developing installation/performance work since 1993. At that time, she began experimenting with the form in her degree finals performance at the Accademia di Brera. Born and raised in Italy she has since produced work internationally. Influenced by the grandmasters of painting she was originally training in scenic design and has stated that her work strives to achieve similar geometric perfection and construction to the masters that she creates 'in terms of numbers and geometrical compositions. The girls are installed based on a planimeter'.[2] Her work is variously described as art installations or performance art as she uses the living bodies of participants in an ensemble set-up; she does not perform in her own work.[3] She transforms participants into largely static aesthetic collectives that inhabit found or chosen spaces. In her earlier work, there was freedom for the participants to choose actions and behave more as themselves; however, she removed such freedoms as her work entered maturity. The participants do not move, do not speak, they *do* nothing. She invites audiences to encounter these pieces as still, un-acting, *just being* collectives that last for somewhere between one and three hours. She arranges the participants throughout her spaces, usually in clear geometric patterns. She also typically transforms the physicality of participants through the use of nudity, body makeup and scant costume to create groups that are highly similar in appearance, at times even clone-like.

What the pieces mean, or are interpreted to mean, is something that is widely debated and I will attend to various opinions.[4] There is a fee paid to participants which allows her team the right to change them physically, including, but not limited to changing skin tone, waxing away body hair, bleaching eyebrows and dying or wigging hair. This agreement has at times, though, been poorly conveyed to many of the participants, especially in earlier

66 *Precis*

work. She manipulates their physical bodies to conform with a desired image. That conformity is usually built-off of one key model, around whom she selects the rest of the models to appear like multiples. I am going to discuss a few key examples: *VB16, VB35, VB45, VB46, VB48*. These cases are entirely female collectives. She denotes each performance by her initials and the order in which it occurs chronologically in her oeuvre.[5]

## *VB16, VB35, VB45, VB46, VB48*

*VB16* (subtitled *Piano Americano-Beige*), commissioned by Jeffrey Deitch to open his 76 Grand St. gallery in New York in January 1996, is one of her earliest successes with similarising the performing models and it is also the first performance that Beecroft admits to employing an established set of rules. Before that, her works were more like open improvisations with visually similarised models/participants. In earlier works, she allowed participants freer rein to act as they pleased. From *VB16* onwards, Beecroft issues very direct instructions to the participants, to which I will turn later. Beecroft describes her reference 'for the wardrobe [as] a Juergen Teller photograph of a model wearing sheer Agent Provocateur underwear, Chanel slippers, and a green dress like a lettuce'.[6] In it we can see her foregrounding the female form itself, putting most of the models into two different toned (one dark, one light) beige shapewear undergarments. There are three notable exceptions: one woman wearing a vibrant green, tulle dress (the 'lettuce') and two others wearing beige knee-length trench coats. Beecroft indicates that another inspirational 'reference was Hanna Schygulla and Irm Hermann in Fassbinder's "The Bitter Tears of Petra von Kant". In contrast to the beige monochrome of the background, the girl in the green dress is posed on the floor'.[7] This piece also similarises the women with platinum wigs worn by all. The use of wigs (and later dying hair) is something she frequently does in subsequent work. At this stage, Beecroft is not heavily modifying the models in terms of their other physical attributes. They are wearing make-up, but their skin tones are mostly natural, and their body hair is not visible, so it falls outside the realm of concern. Roberta Smith reported years later in 1998 in the *New York Times* that the women 'resembled a gang of Cindy Shermans getting ready to suit up for one role or another'.[8]

Beecroft also states that this performance constitutes the first use of an established set of rules where she inserts clear directorial control into the performance by specifying the action choices for the models. To wit they read:

> Do not speak; don't move too slow or too fast; don't act; don't laugh; don't all fall down together; keep the initial position as long as you can; move in the space at your discretion and eventually go back to your initial position; you are a picture; your behavior reflects on the others.[9]

This last statement insinuates a sense of pressure, like peer pressure, in the mind of the participant. Beecroft wants them to think, even if only

Similarity—Authority and Agency 67

subliminally, that there is an implicit weight, expectation or responsibility on them individually that comes from and for 'the others'.

Such similarising controls become more corporeal in *VB35,* and after that piece. Performed at the Guggenheim Museum in 1998, the performance (often subtitled *Show*) had 20 female models stand in a uniform triangular pattern: 5 were naked except for stiletto shoes and 15 wore glitter Gucci bikinis. A notable shift in the two years since *VB16* is that Beecroft takes full control of the prägnanz (the overall sense of unity and topography) of the aesthetic collective she creates. *VB16* allowed participants to move more freely in the space and change their overall composition. In *VB35* she more rigidly contained the membership in a floor pattern, out of which they were directed not to move. They were to maintain their positions in her pattern which established a clear, perceivable collective domain. No one, audiences or staff, entered that domain. She did not specifically mark that space as off-limits to the audience, though. Earlier works do not make these distinctions of spaces and performers would often occupy the same spaces as the audience or migrate from one area to another. As such audiences had a very large range of viewing options, including from within or surrounded by the performing collective. In *VB16* she did choose the viewing perspective for the audience, literally setting them at one side of the gallery room opposite to the collective domain: a front-on setup. *VB35* appears much like a performance installation in the round. Audience could move all around it.

*VB35* decidedly delineates the collective domain without the need for spatial demarcation. The audience could move fully around the installation and even view it from above on the spiral stair of the Guggenheim. The collective domain is generated purely by the cohesive force of the women and their close proximity to each other. The space they occupy appears inhabited, dynamic and charged. Through that space it seems there are non-verbal communications happening between the participants, who are also quite close to each other. To enter that space would be to enter the personal spaces of the women, which would be uncomfortable but also it would mean becoming part of the gestalt image, part of the performance. This was not a space for the audience. Beecroft told the models not to migrate through space, as they could in past works, but rather to inhabit their own personal spaces. Despite this, Roberta Smith (and others) reported that there were a few instances of models taking a few steps about, apparently seen, as she puts it, as a 'disintegration' of the formal rules. As for their physical similarisation, Beecroft body-painted them with a lighter skin tone and then lightly powdered them all over. This made the skin and hair pale, creating a subtle mannequin-like appearance.[10] The work is strong and signals a further turning point in Beecroft's control over her material. From this performance, Beecroft begins to be more daring with elements of control over the prägnanz and the bodies and actions of the models.

*VB45* and *VB46* both demonstrate a more severe and aggressive application of this control, especially the similarisation in appearance of the participants and their possible action. Performed in Vienna in 2001, *VB45* had 41 women

68   *Precis*

transformed from their individual selves into a collective of white, blonde clones dressed only in fetishistic thigh-high black heeled Helmut Newton boots, arranged in a careful grid of rank and file. Beecroft indicates that this performance shows her progression toward 'the formations and arrangement of *objects* in space and in this sense a cube formation [my emphasis]'.[11] Her reference to the women as objects is significant as it marks a conceptual shift away from seeing individuated people towards material objects. Objects, beyond being non-agentic in the main, she can manipulate and use without concern for an affront to agency or individuality. A common feminist issue arises here, that of objectifying women; but Beecroft resolutely moves past that. She directed the women to stand still, be silent, face forward and sit only when needed. She painted their bodies to achieve a uniform pale white complexion; their hair was coloured platinum blonde (not wigged!) as were their eyebrows. There was one fully nude woman who was positioned front and off-centre. The women appear, in Beecroft's own words, like an 'army', a phrase she uses for many of her installation performances. She states that 'most of the time, these women are naked, wearing shoes and make-up only, to appear as if they were stripped and wear a naked uniform, rather than being naturally nude and free'.[12] The participants themselves are now undergoing a detailed transformation of their bodies. Some of the practices to similarise them, waxing and bleaching, for instance, are not immediately reversible. Consequently, the individual themself must agree to allow Beecroft to manipulate their physical body, not just for the performance, but for a duration of time afterwards while the body restores itself. Her fee to participants covers this request. We can see Beecroft shifting to dominating not only the member of the aesthetic collective but also the individual who walks away from the collective.

The visual in *VB45* conjures images of danger, hypersexualisation/pornographic and the sado-masochistic. The participants' harsh, fetishistic appearance creates an image of a potential perpetrator of violence. Their literal and figurative exposure, however, also complicates that image by displaying them for the audience, making them material (objects) for the audience gaze—something over which the audience has at least visual control and objectifying power. There are eerie echoes of Aryanism and conflicted Nazi undertones. Designed for and held in the Vienna Kunsthalle Wien 'she described [...] [the] performance [...] as "Nazi-looking"'.[13] Themes of abuse, terror, strength and judgement pervade the piece. The women have been similarised so far that they can hardly be distinguished one from the other. During the several hour performance, many would sit or even lay on the floor; however, during the beginning, end and perhaps intermittently throughout they stood in their grid (one of the established commands is to begin and end the performance in the same state). Particularly in those moments, the conformity of appearance seems most striking. With their physical appearance made rigidly equal and the women standing nearly identically the collective achieves a highly entitative status. Their proximity and prägnanz clearly establish them as a contained and related group. It is their similarity, however,

*Similarity—Authority and Agency* 69

that is the most overwhelming feature creating a sense of uncanny, terrifying cohesion.

*VB46* is a very similar performance and is a most insightful performance as there is direct testimonial from participants. It was performed at the Gagosian Gallery in Los Angeles on March 17, 2001—only a short time after *VB45*. In many ways, they are twinned performances. Beecroft applied the same body modification techniques, the same fetishistic imaging of women, the same reduction of the participants into a series of (near) identical multiples. However, where there is a direct reference in *VB45* to a 'character' (the Aryan, Nazi, sado-masochistic archetypes) *VB46* works to eliminate character, to reduce identity down to nearly nothing. The women wear no clothing (except for the signature strap stiletto heels). They had all their body hair waxed away and they were fully body-painted pale white. They also had their eyebrows and hair bleached white and coiffed in identical styles or, if the models would not consent to that, wear identical white wigs. Beecroft reduces them as far as possible to identical pink/white frames standing in a cycloramic pattern facing outwards. There are two breaks in this uniformity:

> [T]he high drama of an Asian woman, shod in the same heels but in lavender, with a matching shade of lipstick, and one long-haired redhead, whose pudenda was waxed to a perfect downy red strip. The latter's dreary task was to walk around and around the other women for the entire three hours of the performance.[14]

There is perhaps an implication of outsidership or racial tension here. She is heavily critiqued, as we shall see, for her treatment of race in her material. However, in *VB46*, this may or may not be the case as she does not comment on it. With the performance taking place within a white cube gallery space, the whiteness of the participants made them appear unnatural. It is certainly drawing attention to whiteness, whether that has racial undertones is for the viewer to determine.

Where *VB46* represents a 'white piece' *VB48* could be said to be one of the first in a series of 'black pieces', meant literally and figuratively. Placed in the Sala del Maggiore Consiglio of the Palazzo Ducale, Genoa, Italy, in late 2001 Beecroft created a performance that foregrounds the visual and racial blackness of participants. In her own words, Beecroft explains the performance:

> As part of the celebration of the G8 summit, I was invited to realized [*sic*] a project in the town where I was born: Genoa, Italy. During the location scouting, I was struck by dark immigrant women hiding in the corners of the historical center of Genoa. They were illegal, clandestine noncitizens, who had no face in the light of the city. I decided to show these beautiful women in the Sala del Maggiore Consiglio of the Palazzo Ducale, the same room where the heads of state would have met a few weeks later.[15]

70   *Precis*

The performance was composed of these 'dark immigrant' women, all painted uniformly black (quite black) except for one woman front and off-centre who has somewhat lighter skin, wearing black strips of fabric across their breasts, a black bikini bottom and strapped high heels. All the women wear afro-style wigs, or their hair is styled to resemble an afro; there is one woman, approximately centre, who has no wig and is bald. As with the other performances above, a clear collective domain is present. The women occupy their space and it is not inviting to the audience to enter it. This performance creates heavily divergent and uncomfortable images/readings. On the one hand, the women resemble a strong, beautiful 'army' of black women; on the other, they resemble stereotypes referential of black women in the slave trade or contemporary diaspora immigration.

These performance installations obviously tread the line between artistic capitalisation and exploitative presentation—a feature not lost on the witnessing world. She uses clothing and especially footwear fetishistically and/or in ways deeply suggestive and referential of the fashion world's possessive, sexualised image of women. One of the most prominent elements of *VB45*, for instance, is the use of the fetish boots reminiscent of fascist Germany or its underground sex culture. In fact, Beecroft often uses strapped high heel shoes, referring to them as a platform, pedestal or plinth for the participant.[16] Feminist critique also assails these performances for their use of the female form and portrayals of femininity. During this phase of her work Beecroft routinely constructs situations in which the female form is gazed upon in dress that is part of a general male fantasy or exposed in sexually suggestive ways. It is a matter of interpretive opinion whether these performances indeed betray anti-feminist sentiments or if Beecroft is hijacking these tropes for empowering purposes.

Moreover, from *VB48* onwards, Beecroft will experiment more with race and racial exaggeration. In one performance installation, *VB61 Still Death! Darfur Still Deaf?*, held at the Pescheria di Rialto for the 2007 Venice Biennale, she constructed a mass of 30 black-painted Sudanese women who laid on a large white canvas as if dead. Beecroft then proceeded to splatter them in red paint. It is a strong statement piece on Sudanese war and death. The result here and with her other race-involved work is that it holds potential for being exploitative or racist with prominent black/white racial representations. James Westcott picks up on this writing about how being an audience member at *VB54* had an incredibly exploitative mood. The piece, which was similar to *VB48* in the depiction of black women but here shackled at the ankles with silver chains, seems both to have created an atmosphere of

> cruelty as […] apparently rich, white voyeur[ism] of suffering […] in black tie […] gawk[ing] at people in blackface […] [and of boredom:] It's somehow rewarding to feel guilty about slavery, but feeling guilt at the sight of [that] re-enactment is redundant […] Beecroft's image of human trafficking […] is perversely nostalgic.[17]

Again, the same use of art to capitalise/exploit these issues, the use of the performers or the depiction of weighty issues such as slavery become disturbingly blasé in this context. Such obvious artistic moves/messaging can also create intense feelings of disingenuous treatment of such sensitive content. This is compounded by the reported relationship between Beecroft and the women in *VB61* which was strained in this regard. The models were more assertive in their opinions of being manipulated and painted and the pain of laying on top of each other. "'Is it difficult to work with 30 black women?'" a spectator ask[ed]. "Yes," Beecroft replie[d]. "It is very stressful"'.[18]

Returning to composition, what these performances show is the transformation of participants to become multiplications in a single image. This transformation of the membership of each aesthetic collective is a process of deindividuation. Participants are corporeally reformed into Beecroft's own artistic image. Their identities are trivialised, eroded and discarded. Through such manipulations of their fleshy exterior the membership has their distinctiveness removed, and with it goes degrees of autonomy and agency. Some performances (*VB45, VB46* and *VB48* in particular) illustrate such an extremity of this loss of autonomy that the works look fascist. The effect of which is impressive, alluring and scary or threatening for an audience. Beecroft generates this aesthetic effect first by restraining the individual self through physical similarisation and second through severe instruction that delimits and similarises the possible actions of the memberships. In so doing the entitativity of the aesthetic collectives increases. The appearance of belonging, cohesion, conformity and commonality generates an atmospheric experience. The visuals and testimonial indicate that this is immersive for both the participants as well as the observing audience. Westcott, for example, detailed the pervasiveness of shame, boredom and guilt he experienced in witnessing *VB54*. This engulfing atmosphere further emerges in the testimonial of participants of *VB46,* Heather Cassils and Clover Leary, to come shortly. There is a heightened sense of surrounding spectacle caused by the careful arrangement of bodies (prägnanz) to create aesthetic patterns, compositions, and interactions between the living collective, the audience and the space they inhabit.

The locations in which she positions the participants are in and of themselves extraordinary spaces, something that furthers the sense of spectacle. All are in already aesthetically charged environments: churches, cathedrals, aircraft carriers, warehouses, airports and of course art galleries of all sorts. The spaces are architecturally refined or designed. Beecroft introduces a complementary aestheticisation of the participants. Indeed, she even attempts to aestheticise the audience. She usually instructs audience guests to dress in black tie and haute couture. In fact, she has stated in interviews that she does not like audiences outside of her designed ones and 'would prefer if the regular audience wouldn't come at all'.[19] Her feelings towards audiences are complicated by her attempts at extending of control onto them. She orchestrates the experience of attendance and, as is reported, the experience is one of coming to terms with feelings of shame as an audience member.[20]

72    *Precis*

## Manipulating Agency and Authority

Costumes, make-up and behaviour instruction are all used to create a sense of cohesion, uniformity and belonging. She crafts the bodies of the participants and the actions they perform to sculpt and contribute to a cohesive performance. 'Cohesive' here means that all the elements of the work are similar, seem to operate in the same world and in our terms are categorically the same. There is a containment to the elements of the performance. This cohesiveness and these methods of similarisation are the same in more traditional theatre contexts. In the next chapter, I show these very tools (costume, make-up, movement type, choreography and so on) increasing the cohesiveness and entitativity in examples of Greek khoroi. Here, Beecroft focuses design and direction necessarily to create a contained performance world that makes or can make sense.

Beecroft attempts to manipulate the agency of the participant by manipulating their body and how they may embody actions. For the individual who performs, the physical self becomes present and agentic through their body, through embodiment. Outside of the performance, an unavoidable cultural programming impacts on the agency of the individuals themselves. Their cultural environment codifies and inscribes on the body ways that it might move and behave, and this is something that happens throughout life. Carrie Noland posits this as a theory of *gesture*, which she defines as 'learned techniques of the body [...] by which cultural conditioning is simultaneously embodied and put to the test'.[21] Following this theory, the body is inscribed by cultural practices and ways of being, which translates into behaviours and expectations in the individual who will perform those inscriptions back to the world: the physical self is written upon and writes back. 'Gestures are a type of inscription, a parsing of the body into signifying or operational units; they can thereby be seen to reveal the submission of a shared human anatomy to a set of bodily practices specific to one culture'.[22] In Noland's sense, individual agency is never actually formed out of the self; the self is already caught within the similarising and codifying field of culture. The social culture into which one is born immediately begins designing the agency of the human child. Already present cultural expectations constrain physical and agentic potential. Adopting this view and using the term *gesture*, Beecroft directs and controls the action potential and *gestural* capacity of the animated bodies of her participants.

> [*Gestures* are] neither natural nor inevitable but rather contingent expressions of the kinetic energy they organize [...] a motor phenomenon and therefore part of the natural world; at the same time, a gesture is a unit of significant, visible shape, a quantity of employable force, and therefore part of the cultural world.[23]

By applying increased similarity to the participants, Beecroft generates micro-cultures in her pieces. Each piece of work establishes a contained, artistic

Similarity—Authority and Agency    73

cultural expression. The individual bodies are written upon by Beecroft's micro-cultures and they write into the world of the performance. In this way, we can read the gesturing bodies of the participants, correlate and index them with Beecroft's 'cultures' that contain them.

The conformity of the bodies of the women reveals two things. First, the similarisation of members reduces their individual presence; the more similar each becomes, the less distinct each is but the more distinct the collective is. As individual presence dissipates there is an increase in the presence of the group, in the entitativity of the collective. If I compare *VB35* (and onwards) to *VB16* for instance, we can immediately see the difference in cohesion and collective presence. Both pieces have a definite sense of entitativity to the collective through proximity, prägnanz and similarity. The collective is clear from the proximal relation and nearness of members to each other, there are clear boundaries in a sensible collective domain, there is a pattern to their placement and the members look like they belong in the same group. *VB16* is less entitative, though. It lacks the rigid prägnanz, but more importantly the weaker conformity of appearance and of action allowed in *VB16* leads to it appearing comparatively less entitative as an aesthetic collective. The women are alike in appearance; all seem to be in the same platinum wigs, unflattering shapewear undergarments and white ribbon tie pumps. There are, however, obvious differences: the undergarments are not all the exact same colour; some wear only undergarments, two are in trench coats, one is in the green 'lettuce' tulle dress; while most of the women appear to have the same natural skin tone (white) there is at least one woman who is obviously different as she is black or mixed race. Moreover, their positioning in the space changed over the course of the performance. The women moved about the room, demonstrating that in this earlier performance the participants still exercised improvised, individual action and by extension individual agency. Compared with *VB35* and especially *VB45* five years later, *VB16* as an aesthetic collective has less similarity between and control over members and as such a reduction in entitativity. The aesthetic collective in *VB16* is still a strongly entitative collective, and their considerable similarity contributes to that. However, the aesthetic collectives of *VB35* on, through a more involved and severe similarity of appearance and action, generate and have greater entitativity.

The second revelation looking at all these performances is that the greater the degree of similarity the more present a sense of authority or authorship to a collective. Tracing *VB16* through to *VB35, VB45* and *VB46*, one begins to sense not only that the aesthetic collectives become more entitative but also that achieving such increased similarity entails control.[24] The similarisation of the appearance of participants in these performances not only heightens the coherence and cohesion of the membership but also, through deindividuation, brings into perception the sense or feeling of an authority. In *VB46*, this was so much so the case that the key model, Heather Cassils, worked with her fellow participant Clover Leary and their artistic company member Julia Steinmetz (not a participant, but an audience member) to write a joint paper

74  *Precis*

on their experience.[25] All three were at the time beginning their art collective, the Toxic Titties. Their work centred on feminism, identity, body-based politics and aesthetics of the gendered body. The women participated in the performance at first as a means of infiltration; they wanted to hijack and stage a protest from within the performance. However, through the rehearsal process they lost this directive and instead became, unwillingly, Beecroft's exact objectified material—that which they sought to protest. As an artistic collective with a feminist agenda, they reported their experience as being exploitative and anti-feminist. Detailing the process from casting call through to final performance their paper makes clear how authority saturated and commanded the whole work. They narratively pit themselves (and the other participants) in opposition to Beecroft, identifying her as authoritative, removed and callous. They describe the experience as truly awful and degrading. However, a closer reading of their text suggests that the authority in the performance and its experience was actually something other, something different from Beecroft herself.

The transformation that these women went through had an impact on their psychological or ontological state. The term *control* returns again. Collective entitativity grows through conformity and uniformity. The circumstances of *VB46* show how one can come to feel controlled or act as if that is the case. Each of the women became 'one of the group' by homogenising with the others; equally, that homogeneity telegraphed to the external audience that 'this body, this person belongs with these' and they ceased to be seen as discrete. This process can elicit many emotions in the experience, but for Cassils and Leary, there was a generally negative reaction. The stripping away of uniqueness and difference—perhaps of subjectivity itself—was fairly extreme and was met with a great degree of resistance and critique.

Their descriptions of the performance make clear that the objectifying nature of the performance constraints and the heightened entitativity of the aesthetic collective, not actually Beecroft herself, is what constructed the authority and their concomitant obedience. An affective state to the group held them in control. To quote Leary at length:

> There was an air of scrutiny, assessment. Some people in the audience openly discussed our individual bodies, postures, and appearance with one another as if we couldn't hear them. The gaze of the audience felt both violating and impersonal, but in an intensely objectifying way that I had never experienced. There was a profound separation between the audience and the models. *The unification of the models* [emphasis added] was constituted through *our sameness in appearance* [emphasis added], through the fact that we were *following a set of instructions* [emphasis added], through the pay we would eventually receive, and through the solidarity formed by the ordeal of the previous three days. For me there was a *psychological necessity in feeling part of the group, less visible in my sameness* [emphasis added]. I tried to mentally withdraw as much as possible, yet I was acutely aware of the

*Similarity—Authority and Agency*  75

discomfort and embarrassment of the people I knew ... to break the facade was understandable, but I couldn't imagine letting it crack, to separate from the mass of models behind me. *A departure from the instructions would differentiate me, draw unwanted attention, and force me to inhabit my own subjectivity again; to do this within the context of the performance would be terrifying* [emphasis added].[26]

It is not Beecroft, the artist, that Leary here seems to identify as her authority. Rather, the text implies that the performance itself ('following a set of instructions'), the objectifying presence of the audience (the 'violating and impersonal' 'gaze' of the audience), and the internal pressure of the group to persevere ('solidarity') constructed a scene of conformity. This tripartite of directorial demands, spectators and the internal conformity of the collective here creates the architecture of a system that removes subjectivity and choice. Not Beecroft, but a transmitting affective pressure of lost subjectivity and terror of its return within the performance seems to command and author these participants.

With the removal of their external individuality in appearance and the replacing of it with a similarity unachievable in the natural world, the women were treated as material objects. Again, Beecroft has on record referred to women in her work as objects (as quoted earlier). Cassils echoes this. Her text notes the performance similarity, extreme similarity, produced a severe and terrifying element of the collective's entitativity—an authority that stripped the membership of their very subjectivity. Ghastly similarity and exposure of it before a witnessing audience is, as she says, 'both violating and impersonal [...] in an intensely objectifying way' that could only be soothed by further removal of subjectivity, by retreat within the protection of the group. Interestingly, the same force (membership within the aesthetic collective) that terrifies and violates the participant also protects and shields them. The psychic touch of this crowd, different from the physical touch of those in clubs, terrifies and yet draws the membership ever closer together. Not allowed to draw their proximity closer for security, the collective seems to have had another option to combat threat. Their similarity *anonymised* them. The same loss of individuality took away the threat of the objectification being personal. In the process, this protected them from the unknown psychic touch of the audience by dispersing it across the group.[27]

While Beecroft's later performances show aesthetics that are more tightly controlled, women more austerely instructed and transformed, potential for difference between members greatly reduced, it also shows Beecroft removing and distancing herself from the work; the performance becomes itself a closed entity. She progressively crafts the experience from removed positions, and once begun the work adopts its own authority, one that exists independent of her. It is visually noticeable that as entitativity increases the agency of the aesthetic collective *as a totality* grows in potency as well. The two are linked. This is also true for the early work, *VB16* for instance; but then it appeared

76   *Precis*

that the individual members could, should they want, still drift off, move as they please or even disconnect from the aesthetic container of the work or leave altogether. In the earlier work, participants could still easily exercise their own agency. This does not seem to be the case with the *VB35, VB45* and *VB46* and indeed of other post-*VB35* performances. The later performances seem to have such strong collective agency that acts of individual agency become antithetical. Indeed, participants, such as Cassils and Leary, have described such independent agency as radical and terrifying. From within the collective of *VB46* they clearly indicate, as previously quoted, how such demonstration of personal agency would disconnect them from the collective and force an alienating exhibition of re-embodied subjectivity: suddenly to become a sole objectified subject. Their testimony reveals how obedience to the authority of the collective entity provided safety, whereas deviance and distinction created the anticipation of unwanted exposure. This safety that the collective provides is entirely like that discussed in the previous chapter. In dancing crowds, the safety of the crowd protects one from the alien quality of unexpected or uninvited touch, of contact. In these performance pieces, there is no touching of the participants or of the audience and participants. However, there is a very real psychic touch in the form of the audience gaze. The objectifying gaze of the audience, especially considering the nudity or partial nudity of the participants, 'touches' the participants in a cognitive or intersubjective sense.

Clearly, an atmosphere of authority can create stronger collectives, but how exactly do you achieve this kind of atmosphere? Beecroft shows us performances that immerse the participants in a situation that transforms them physically, directs them in terms of their behaviour and creates a mood of objectifying scrutiny. It is the expectations, overtly or tacitly conveyed, that generate expected compliance for the participants. Beecroft's very indication in her instructions that 'your [the participants'] behaviour reflects on the others'[28] is a direct means of insinuating collective awareness and pressure in and on the participants. Performing in one of these installations immerses them in an atmosphere of expectation and demand. This means that the mood of these performances is both aesthetically constructed but also affectively created through these transformations and expectations.

Is this different, however, from any other performance? Surely all performance carries with it the threat of being seen as the performer, as one's own subject, and suddenly not belonging in the performance world. Breaking from character or out of the performance is generally anathema in performance. Characters and the playing of roles provide that belonging. Beecroft's performances are the same in this regard, but also different. First, the atmosphere or mood of the performance is itself like a character element. Since these are performance art, like visual arts, spectator observation and objectification are foregrounded. The audience is also overtly present. There are no instigations to hide, disguise or anonymise the audience. For example, different to a lot of theatre, there is no dimming or outing of the lights. The aesthetic collectives

Similarity—Authority and Agency 77

here exist with a present and presented audience whom they can see and with whom they interact, if very minimally. There is a mood that creates a pressure on the collective and exposes them to the audience. Second, these performances remove distinct characterisation. One is not *a character*; one is *an anonymous one of many who are together characters*. The authority here nullifies all distinction. All members are simply equal and less than the whole. They create a collective character. The idea of *character* and *role* forms an entire part of chapter four where I examine these differences between role and characterising as performance elements. In these installations, the character role of the participants (as 'Aryan dominatrices' or 'black immigrants' for instance) is not the main utility. Rather, it is their characterisation and how that contributes to the mood-setting and characterising of the experience that is more important.

Examining the role of similarity more perspicaciously shows how it works on two levels: physical appearance and gesture, following Noland. There is both similarisation of the physical appearance of the members of these aesthetic collectives and to similarise their potential action and behaviour. The controlling of the physical manifestation of the member determines much of their belonging, and in the anonymisation of the member also makes that belonging protective. No longer existing in this state just for themself, the member is existing for the collective and what the collective can provide as well. The expression of self through the physical presence of the body shifts and gradates into a physical presence for and of the membership. As Cassils noted earlier, departure from that membership would expose the individual, draw immediate observation and place them in a terrifying inhabitation of subjectivity. The strength of the entitativity of the aesthetic collective was such as to make individuality and subjectivity vulnerable states of being—in which the gaze and psychic touch of the audience becomes invasive. Whereas maintaining the member-self, their collective self, protected them. Being 'property' of the collective protected and hid their own subjecthood from the audience and with it their own affective-felt experience (their shame, fear or anger, for instance). The affective dimensions of this kind of experience cannot be underestimated. If I narrow to *VB46* specifically, the shared experience of the women was emotively very similar. Cassils, Leary and Steinmetz' discussion indicates that the participants all had similar emotional experiences with the performance. Moreover, when compared with the critical reviews of the performance, the audience, while different from the participant experience, had an equally similarised experience of their own; there is a clear transmission and equalising of affect here.

The restrictions in gesture placed on the participants also contributed to the affective impact. There were rules, regulations, and directives for behaviour. The bodies of the women show how they conformed both in flesh and gestural sculpting. 'It is by gesturing that bodies become inscribed with meanings in cultural environments, but it is also by gesturing that these inscribed meanings achieve embodiment and inflection'.[29] Their bodies were made to behave in certain ways which imbued them with cultural belonging, but by behaving in those ways they also embodied and thus projected outward that very belonging.

78    *Precis*

Beecroft's given instructions created a culture for the aesthetic collectives and by performing those instructions the members projected their belonging. By controlling the gestures of the body, a further embedded authority over the living participants made them more material. From these installation performances, and indeed much of Beecroft's work, I may formulate a generalisation: similarisation is a transformation in agency away from individual authority to agency authored by an-other. Similarisation takes agency away from individuals and gives control over to directorialauthority and then to collective authority.

Again, as the creator of the work, Beecroft is 'the author'; however, it seems more the case that the performance, in its act, is almost self-authoring. Given that once begun there is no interfering or interjecting elements beside the presence of the aesthetic collective and the presence of the audience, Beecroft's work is aleatoric. Chance or the unknown defines what will happen. This is different to scripted events (which I consider in the next chapter) or the club-based collectives previously discussed (where the idea of a script exists only in a socio-anthropological sense). In those examples, there are elements that drive the gestural: plot, lines, music, other agentic cast members, a DJ who can change the aesthetic direction and so on. In Beecroft's work, the only operational elements are the agency of the collective and their response to the presence of the audience. As such, the performance here is that *of* aesthetic collectivity, of it *becoming* and the resulting affective responses.

As members of her collectives, the participants must sacrifice their individuality, or at least internalise it away, shielding it from perception. The construction of her collectives relies on the membership being similarised beyond discrete recognition and beyond individuality. The physical transformation is clear—she makes the body appearance conform with and represent the collective. This extreme control and design contribute to the performances' enhanced entitative status. It also contributes to an atmosphere in the aesthetic space often described as uncomfortable and filled with feelings of shame. Returning to Westcott's narration of attending *VB54* he outlines how his experience, Beecroft's own feelings on her work and other critics have pointed to shame as a key affective tone:

> Beecroft has said that her performances are about shame—her shame (Thurman 2003:114). In this one, she was apparently trying to intensify—and share—the guilt [...] Occasional remembrance of the performance downstairs [after guests had gone to the bar] came with a surge of frustration—and shame, again [...] When documentation of the performance [*VB48*] appeared at Jeffrey Deitch, 'this is racist, fascist stuff—shame, shame, shame' (Finch 2002) [...] [*VB54* is a] push-and-pull deadlock of Beecroft's shame game.[30]

We could attribute this to Beecroft's seemingly nonplussed and blasé attitude about subjectivity. Treating people, in her own words, as *material* yet using identity elements of those people, race and gender in particular, as aesthetic costuming is an uncomfortable action. One she is not aware, or acts unaware, she is doing as she reductively focuses instead on aesthetics:

> I plan performances in terms of numbers and geometrical compositions. The girls are installed based on a planimeter and then break the composition the instant that the performance begins; I admire Piero's geometry. I cite Raphael in the sense that his perfection and balance are the elements that create discomfort. That balance is more disturbing than Michelangelo's struggle, because it doesn't allow you to identify the source of doubt that you immediately feel in that perfection.[31]

I will eventually return to these affective atmospheres and their complications, but now I would like to aim attention at her explicit direction and instructions. She achieves her version of this perfection by giving rigid and enigmatic instructions or directions to the performers. Through those instructions, her direction moves beyond her transformation of bodily appearance. She directs attention and composes their very presence.

## Directions/Instructions—Explicit and Implied

First, she controls potential gestures. Second, she controls and eliminates all sense of the embodied self, replacing it with her own constructed image—often some archetypal/stereotypical image of 'woman'. Her instruction/directions to the performers achieve this reduction of action potential. These instructions/directions, just like the performances themselves, have evolved over time. As relayed by Thomas Kellein[32] in her first piece in 1993, her final degree performance at the Accademia di Brera,[33] her instructions were, in completion, 'hang-out'. She was constructing a biographical performance piece based on her eating disorder, bulimia, by inviting several young women to enter a gallery and read her food diary (a carefully constructed book of what Beecroft ate, how much, and when she would vomit), wear her clothing (taken directly from her closet) and just 'hang-out' while an audience watched. Vague, undirected, non-specific, and open to extreme interpretation this instruction caused the performers to behave in a wide variety of ways. To quote Kellein's description at length:

> … after a while the girls were visited by other student friends who wanted to interrupt the event. They chucked magazines onto the floor and brought, as Beecroft tells, all manner of junk into the room. The aim was to disrupt. The *atmosphere* [emphasis added] grew tense. All at once the audience, the girls themselves, became unpredictable. The latter, who had *arranged themselves* [emphasis added] in poses like prostitutes, smoking and standing about in skimpy garments, bright fabrics, nightgowns, underwear and high heels, began *to scream* [emphasis added]. The audience *started to feel afraid* [emphasis added] by their presence and leave the room.[34]

80   *Precis*

Her instruction of 'hang-out' was obviously not enough to control this performance. The lack of instruction and clarity of desired outcome here is not surprising. Beecroft had never worked with live performers, only fine art materials. Thus, she was not prepared or trained in how to direct live participants. Here, the aesthetic collective that emerged was undefined and aesthetically indeterminate. It had entitativity and it had agency, but it was of the sort that disrupts and aggresses the aesthetic conceit. Moreover, the affective dimensions of this piece, noted by my emphasis earlier, were unpredictable and jarring. Even in her later work with instructions and transformative actions, affectively driven atmospheres are occurring from this earliest stage. Beecroft was not pleased with the atmosphere here or the experience and nearly abandoned her performance future then and there. Kellein describes how with the guidance of a teacher, however, an important change in conception happened and Beecroft came to treat subsequent participants as material: '"[t]he girls are my material" or "the girls are my plain material", as she now sees it'.[35] In divorcing the participants from their status as fully agentic people in her mind, by turning them into artistic material like clay or paint, she allowed herself to begin to treat the participants with more command and to distance herself from the effect of her commands.

This differs from other artists who use living participants similarly. Tino Seghal and Spencer Tunick, for instance, both deploy living people to become similarised rule-based collectives. However, Seghal typically produces the rules as a container in which chance, opportunity and restricted choice emerge and become the focus of the performance. *These Associations* in the Tate Modern turbine hall in London, 2012, for instance, demonstrated this clearly. Volunteers from the community could come and become members of an organic collective. There were rules given for the types of behaviour and its execution, but then it was an improvisation. The members of each collective authored their own directions within that and were complicit with the whole engine of performance. There was no instigation of shame or fear in making choices. Present for that performance I can only say that the atmosphere was enjoyable, stimulating and filled with curiosity. I felt intrigued by how the performers achieved their high degree of entitativity while still working within high degrees of improvisation. Moreover, there was a playfulness present in that work. I wanted to interact with, provoke and play with it and when I did the performers responded in kind.

Tunick, closer to Beecroft, creates scenes for photography composed out of naked collectives posed over different landscapes. His works, for instance, in July 2016 installing blue painted residents of Hull over various parts of the city, in June 2012 at Munich's Nationaltheater or his recent 2018 red capes installation in Melbourne atop a Woolworth's carpark all hold very similar visual connections to Beecroft's work. While applying rules like Beecroft's, what distinguishes his work and its effect is that he is not necessarily pursuing rigid similarity, but rather exposing similarity and difference simultaneously. He allows all body types, all body shapes, all body colours. However, through mass presentation of bodies, he exposes commonalities to human form and shape within which we all live. His practice acknowledges the use of the body, its similarisation and its reduction to material in a more sympathetic way. His models are not confronted by issues of deindividuation, harsh and self-referencing objectification or the exposure of subjectivity as control measure. In his work, the reduction to a small part of a very large picture (literally) does not confront the model with intersubjective objectification, indeed the model never confronts or meets the audience directly while a model.

Beecroft, however, pursues control and commodification of the body in front of an audience. Unlike Seghal and Tunick, Beecroft does not show individuality in her work, nor is her commonality and similarity of humanity one that exists in natural or quotidian form. It is something taken from the fiction and harsh modification/objectification of the realms of fashion and fine art and it is only produced through her transformations. She uses the participant material with increasingly containing and controlling instructions. Following her first performance she quickly reformed her instructions/directions to be clearer, more determined and much more rigidly restrictive of the participants. Systematically she introduced and imbued the work with more conformity through confining cages of instruction and rules.

*VB02* introduced the first key instruction, 'don't talk', which silenced the participants, literally taking away their voice. Over the progress of the next dozen performances, Beecroft would continue to remove the figurative voice of the participant, their sense of self and agency, through further restriction in potential acts. As mentioned, it was *VB35* in which she first employed what she calls 'established' rules. There she told the participants more or less what to do: stand still, do not move, look forward, do not talk, sit when needed. By the time *VB40* is performed in 1999 at the Museum of Contemporary Art in Sydney her instructions are fairly direct and mostly comprehensive, to wit:

> Be still. Go at ease. Move naturally. Do not move out of place. Do not move in real time. Use no verbal communication. Be detached. Be remote. Hold position. Look plain, boyish, quiet. Don't let your mood show. Do not laugh. Be compact. If you are bored show it.[36]

The instructions are now specific, confining, and direct. Beecroft is clear that there is to be no movement 'out of place' and 'no verbal communication', no speaking. Without a way to interact and communicate easily and given the durational nature of the work participants begin to lose track of temporal regularity. By doing this, she distances the participants from 'real time' and contextualises them in a performance space that is deeply psychological. Participants now are told to exist in some 'other' time-space to the audience that requires them to be 'detached' and 'remote'. Some of these commands are vague, requiring contemplation and thus, like a play-text, require the participant to invest cognitively as well. 'Look plain, boyish', for instance, requires the participant to make judgements as to what that means (and in the process interpret a gendered

82    *Precis*

statement into a state of being and then somehow embody that). Actors train for this, but participants who may have no experience as a model or actor might struggle here. *VB46* had even more rigid instructions/directions. Whereas before they were but three or four lines, they now are substantially longer:

> Do not talk, do not interact with others, do not whisper, do not laugh, do not move theatrically, do not move too quickly, do not move too slowly, be simple, be detached, be classic, be unapproachable, be tall, be strong, do not be sexy, do not be rigid, do not be casual, assume the state of mind that you prefer (calm, strong, neutral, indifferent, proud, polite, superior), behave as if you were dressed, behave as if no one were in the room, you are like an image, do not establish contact with the outside … alternate resting and attentive positions, if you are tired, sit … interpret the rules naturally, do not break the rules, you are the essential element of the composition, your actions reflect on the group, towards the end you can lie down, just before the end stand straight up.[37]

During some of the rehearsals, these instructions are even read over loud speaker in a slow, even and monotonous voice. This act further removes Beecroft from the participant material and creates a more fascist feeling to the learning of these performance rules. An obvious development in these instructions to those prior is that there is a sense Beecroft wants no communication between the participants. Whereas before her instructions indicated 'use no verbal communication', which leaves the shear possibility of communication itself still active, now they are commanded not to interact at all, with each other or even to make 'contact with the *outside* [emphasis added]'. I emphasise 'outside' to draw attention to the object/container metaphor at work here. Beecroft, in her own terms and words, sees the aesthetic collective as a contained object. Moreover, she conceives it as one that she does not want the membership to make any contact with the 'outside'.

What she might mean here could be twofold: outside the aesthetic collective as a totality or outside the self. Trapping them within the aesthetic collective and their individual experience she commands the participants into a position of communion with only themselves and the entitative collective (not with any of the other individuals, or members, only with the 'composition', the totality). Confusingly, she also suggests that the participants 'assume the state of mind that you prefer'. Referencing Leary and Cassils' descriptions and the photographic evidence suggests that the assumed states of mind in *VB46* were surprisingly homogenous and narrow. All the women appear distant, removed, scared or angry. In fact, within their descriptions they note how Cassils, as the 'lead' model, attempted to embody her emotional response to the dysfunction of the experience:

> My [Cassils'] fists were clenched and stomach taut. I felt like my skin was a force field against the eyes that were drinking me in. I wanted to make

Similarity—Authority and Agency  83

myself menacing and indigestible. In my mind contracted muscles bounced their viewership off of my body like fists in the boxing ring. My jaw was clenched and I was dripping from quiet exertion. The more I stood the more energy built up in me until I started to feel like I was going to explode in my stillness. 'Wow, she's so angry. Wherever did she find her? Really great'. And it was in this moment that I realized that I was powerless in this situation. My silent anger was easily subsumed by the artwork. No one could tell that my anger was my own and not a possible instruction of the artist. Despite my intentions, I had sold my body and my voice.[38]

This quotation is thick with the affective dimension of the experience. Both Cassils as participant and the commenting audience member express the affective. Indeed, the performance archival footage and the accounts in Steinmetz et al. (2006) suggest they were all in the same state of mind. Steinmetz (as audience) comments immediately after this quotation that

members of the audience and reviewers commented on the anger displayed by Cassils, Leary, and several other models [...] The overarching scene of Beecroft brand "bodies for sale" (or, indeed, already sold to the artist) overrode any attempts at individual agency asserted by the models.[39]

There is nothing in the reporting to suggest this was ever something agreed or openly discussed; the participants somehow psychically transformed into that. They seem to have constructed an affective container for themselves as well as the physical and ontological ones. They existed within the same contained range of affect. Undoubtedly, the physical fatigue, discomfort and extreme objectification are registering on the women and perpetuating some of this affective container. The atmosphere produced in the performance clearly reflected these affective states. However, from the statements, it is also something much more reactive to the performance piece itself. By this middle period of her work, the instructions/directions become one of Beecroft's most potent methods of exerting the performance agency over that of the participants' own agency.

Beecroft's instructions create an entitative collective, but they do so both by isolating the individual performer and reminding them of how they reflect on the group, the 'composition'. Beecroft directs her participants to become as isolated as possible—'contained'—to exist within the given aesthetic moment, in her constructed present. Yet this isolating into the self also creates a deindividuated experience. Those same rigid instructions fail to be tethered to any content of expression, though. Indeed, there is no indication of role, emotion, expressive narrative or meaning. Beecroft actively encourages participants to 'assume the state of mind [they] prefer'. All other expressive indicators lead the participant towards a general category of being ('classic', 'detached', 'unapproachable', 'strong') without any substance of meaning: 'classic' in what

84  *Precis*

sense? 'detached' from whom/what? 'unapproachable' for what reason? 'strong' compared to what? This ambiguity of impetus actually lends the practice intrigue.

Carrie Noland examines this kind of situation in her writing about the work of Merce Cunningham. She examines contentless performance instructions. Noland centres on Cunningham's practice as demonstrated in the pieces *Sixteen Dances for Soloist and Company of Three* from 1951, *Suite by Chance* from 1952–1953 and *Solo Suite in Time and Place* from 1953. In these three pieces, Cunningham allowed dancers to create choreographic phrases or sequences from tasks he offered them. Chance led the way these tasks would proceed or, later, the phrases/sequences that would become larger pieces of choreography. This was sometimes entirely chance-led, for instance by coin-toss. In the tasks Cunningham would give movement operations for dancers to execute without indicating anything else in *how* they might perform or behave. These tasks were often done with no given sound and, as reported by the dancers, would require them to 'to find my [the dancers'] phrasing within the sections [...] there is no other impetus, no additional source of inspiration or energy, no aural stimulus [...] There is only movement, learned and rehearsed in silence'.[40] Similar to Beecroft, the tasks are conditioned by rules about how stimuli in the space should be observed and responded to in terms of physical/ spatial reaction and how the dancer should 'be' in themselves. Noland observers how dancers were 'called on *not* to express a particular emotion, or set of emotions, but instead to develop refined coping mechanisms for creating continuity between disarticulated movements while remaining sensitive to their location in space'.[41] This parallels the Beecroft examples, where participants were directly commanded not to feel any particular emotion, but instead to respond to the performance situation. Different to Noland's discussion of Cunningham, Beecroft's instructions, particularly in the later performances, indicated how to respond, usually by negation of options. Also, instead of allowing emotional responses, Beecroft indicates general profiles or 'states of mind' instead. Again, in isolating the participant within a space, time and physical container constructed by rules, Beecroft created a scenario for the participants in which they exist in feedback with themselves, the audience and the performance. Just like Noland's articulation of Cunningham's work Beecroft's performances opened a space and time in which the gestural response of the dancer was entirely responsive to the given circumstance.

Uninspired by any particular or chosen external stimuli it is entirely a practice of kinaesthetic, proprioceptive[42] reaction—a coping or responding mechanism for the given situation. For a Beecroft participant, the sense of time is divorced from its rhythms by the fatigue and lack of active stimuli. She asks the women only to express and modify their immediate 'human situation' at hand. Blindly and proprioceptively knowing what the other participants are 'doing', Beecroft's participants persevere, collectively bonding into a homogenous whole despite their isolating experiences. Without clothing, defined character, or other artifice they are literally and figuratively naked to the audience. There is a strong parallel

*Similarity—Authority and Agency* 85

to Cunningham's dancers, who simultaneously negotiate physical challenges, cognitive understanding of the situation and their own feelings emerging from the affective experience. In Cunningham's work, the dancer constructed the expression live, operating entirely within and to the given moment; in Beecroft, it is the same.

> They must keep time without musical cues; sense the presence of the other dancers on stage; know blindly, proprioceptively, what these other dancers are doing; and adjust the timing and scope of their movements accordingly, thereby "expressing" the "human situation" at hand. (p. 55)

Like Cunningham's dancers, Beecroft thrusts her participants into a state of intransitive expression, expression that has been divorced from an object of expression. The body here is expressing through its gestures the present moment, the suturing of those moments together and in those processes generating a relationship between performer and situation.

> All this work is "expressive"—it belongs to the "category of expression"— insofar as it is demanded by a human situation on a stage and insofar as human situations on stages (or otherwise) constitute an *embodied response to the present moment,* an embodied response to the utterly unique conditions of existence at one given point in time. (p. 55)

The notion of presence here is clear in the idea of the experience of the present moment. The difference between Cunningham and Beecroft arises in the gestural scope that is allowed. Cunningham (here discussing his *Solo Suite,* but also his work more generally) composed his piece with a set of movement options/material so that there was a given gestural vocabulary with which the dancers could use, improvise and explore. By contrast, Beecroft reduces the gestural potential to the point of extreme, severe and austere minimalism. There is little they can do. Nearly imprisoned in their own allotted space and disconnected from a sense of time, their present moment, their 'human situation', is the reduction of the natural, subjective self and the elevation of the aesthetic situation. In *VB45* and *VB46,* this clearly happens as she stripped the women of all external indications of subjectivity and made them exude an unnatural and highly constructed image. They were no longer individuals, but more like replications of an aesthetic prototype. Because of this manipulation the '"higher level" processes of conscious thought, symbolization (language), and feeling [...] [suspend slightly, allowing a] more somatic (and evolutionarily prior) layer of activity' (p. 55). This prior layer of brain activity is the protoself. In the previous chapter, I introduced the notion of the protoself in relation to the background processing common to members of dancing crowds. I illustrated how it is that part of our mind concerned with the monitoring, processing and interpreting of stimuli to the body.

In a Beecroft performance, the participant protoself is actively recording what is happening to the body and mind, correlating that with biographical

86   *Precis*

memories of similar experiences and adjusting the body to adapt and respond to the situation. Consequences of this are physiological (sweating, muscular fatigue, hormone surges, dry mouth and the like) and precipitate psychological effects (emotional states, cognitive associations, dissociation or mind-wandering). With the loss of their recognisable subjectivity, the participants in *VB45* and *VB46* transform into an image. With the conscious aspects of what makes one unique and individuated from others gone (visual cues, behavioural patterns, voice, thought), what the performance footage shows is a deeper search for personhood and an experience of this proto-layer of experience. Following Noland, 'this protoself is related to homeostasis and the fundamental intelligence that discerns the boundary between the subject's body and other bodies; it is thus the corporeal substrate of subjectivity understood as an awareness of being a separate self' (p. 55). One of the fascinations of Beecroft's work is how she exhibits this aspect of people and the fact that she makes evident and clear how human beings negotiate individuality and collectivity under mounting pressures of deindividuation.

Following her work chronologically a systematic increase in such pressures is evident, each performance becoming more severe than the last. Each exposes further the action of the protoself to understand separation of self under progressively more self-less situations. Existing on a deeper, less immediate level of consciousness more commensurate with the sensorimotor processes, 'including visuomotor functions and kinesthetic, proprioceptive, haptic and vestibular systems' (p. 55),[43] the protoself is an intermediary. It is the part of the person that explores the interface of self and other—all others of all sorts. When Beecroft deindividuates and situates her participants in her aesthetic confines their protoselves probe the given situation and respond to it. It is this action circuit that brings the members into communion with the aesthetic collective. The lower level work of the protoself is on display as participants weather situations of being in the collective, being deindividualised and objectified. Immersed in the same situation every member must weather the same objectifying forces. There is a common action of protoselves working in similar ways at the same time. The common, simultaneous action of protoselves here is like a unifying mesh between the participants. In a sense the division and boundary between the self and the other is confused and blurred. The audience observes and experiences this mesh activity, a collective activity working to sense and understand the collective situation and reality. As the audience conceptualises and understands the collective as entitative they observe this transformation of the participant into mimetic reproductions of each other, both in appearance and gestural capacity. The participant relationship with the aesthetic collective is eased, facilitated, and established. Belongingness to it is induced via similarity.

At present Beecroft is working as the artistic doppelganger of Kanye West, as noted at the top. The instruction/directions have advanced. An unpredictable union, she now artistically assists with and (co)directs many of his fashion shows, music videos and spectacle performances. It is not fully clear what her role is, only that they are closely collaborating on most of his work, but we can at least ascertain that she helps stage his live work. The list of instructions given to the participants of the Yeezy Season 3 fashion-show/debut of his new album *The Life of Pablo* were ostensibly from West, but are clearly modelled after Beecroft. West is the only name credited, but whatever the case she must be operating as a ghost-author in some capacity. Her previous work instructions constitute most of what the models were given as direction. They were extensive, rigid and confusing. The list, leaked on Instagram, thrust the models into a state of severe expectation that is coupled with bizarre contradiction:

QUIET PLEASE
NO WHISPER
NO SMILE
NO DANCING
NO SINGING, UNLESS INSTRUCTED
NO EYE CONTACT
NO ACTING
NO FAST MOVEMENTS
NO SLOW MOVEMENTS
NO SHARP MOVES
NATURAL MOVEMENT
SHOW PRIDE
HOLD YOUR POSITION
STAY IN CHARACTER
ALTERNATE BETWEEN ATTENTION AND EASE
NO SITTING DOWN ALL AT THE SAME TIME
DO NOT MAKE THE SAME MOVEMENTS AT THE SAME TIME
IF YOU WANT TO MOVE, YOU CAN SHIFT YOUR WEIGHT
IF YOU ARE TIRED, SIT DOWN OR LYE [*sic*] DOWN
CONCENTRATE, FOCUS
DO NOT LOOK AT CAMERA
HOLD POSITIONS UNTIL THE END OF THE SHOW
DO NOT TAKE OFF YOUR CLOTHES OR SHOES
LOOSEN UP NO STIFFNESS
DO NOT BE CASUAL
STAND STRAIGHT
NO SEXY POSING DO NOT ACT COOL
YOU ARE A PICTURE
BE CALM, BE STRONG, BE NETURAL [*sic*]
BEHAVE AS IF NO ONE WAS IN THE ROOM
DO NOT BREAK THE RULES
KNOW THAT YOUR ACTIONS REFLECT WITHIN THE GROUP
YOUR BEHAVIOR [*sic*] AFFECTS THE CONDUCT OF OTHERS
BE AWARE OF OTHERS AND BE PERCAUTIOS [*sic*]

88 *Precis*

BEFORE THE END OF THE PERFORMANCE GET UP STAND
STRAIGHT AT ATTENTION
KEEP YOUR ASSIGNED POSITION ON THE FLOOR
DO NOT EVER LOOK AT THE JUMBOTRON[44]

The command within the instructions is clear—onform. The process of similarisation and the collective becoming entitative generates an atmosphere or affective state to which the participant may either conform or reject membership. The urge to conform is what is propagated in these works and Beecroft has found an artistic means of producing conforming affects. The element of similarity, when applied in designed contexts like art and performance, is a process of conforming the members to the aesthetic concept of the creator. In the next chapter, I explore the work of Stanley Milgram and the notion of conformity, particularly in reference to his concept of the agentic state, a natural progression from this overview of agency. Here I introduce the notion of conformity and its general definitions as a means of transition.

In psychological research, conformity is:

> [A] *state of mind*, not an action [...] arrived at through complex processes of identification and internalization, which enables the person to believe what [they] believe and act as [they] act under the illusion that [they] do so of [their] own free will and without realizing that the pressures to do so really arise from without rather than from within.[45]

Conformity here hinges on three key elements: it is a state of mind, it is an illusion of free will and that illusion is mistakenly believed by the subject to arise from within themself. As a state of mind, it is then an affective feature arrived at through social and environmental interaction. As an illusion conformity operates with suggestibility or susceptibility and the illusory demands require maintenance.[46] Conformity also demands that the conforming subject believe the pressure to conform is entirely their own, not driven from others. This is an illusion the subject must come to believe; the pressure is coming entirely from the external social environment, but the subject must feel it as their own derived pressure. If they realise the conforming pressure is actually driven from outside their own control, 'if [they] do become aware that [they are] conforming and if [they] continue to believe and act as before, [they] are merely complying'.[47] Compliance is different. It is not an illusion and it is not a state of mind per se, but rather a cognitive agreement. The complying subject decides to comply and can acknowledge the forces asking them to do so.

Comparing Beecroft's work over time it becomes clear she has discovered that '[c]onformity behaviour increases when it is necessary for an individual to rely more heavily on the responses of others in making [their] own adjustment. Attitudes are more easily shifted [in that way]'.[48] In her work, the individual is placed in a physical and psychological position of uncertainty which is objectified before an audience. She then literally removes herself and the sense of directorial authority, leaving the participating subjects as authored subjects. To the audience, their agency appears subordinate to the collective. The participants are still under the belief that they are performing of their own free will (and in one sense, ultimately they are indeed responsible for their own decisions), but their identity is morphed by the scenographic control of Beecroft. The demanding and perplexing instruction given to the participants, disembodied from a director, mainly constructs pressures on those participants to be what the performance needs them to be. In other words, because the performance is so strongly dictated and the construction of a complying collective is a principle element of the performance there is a pervading insistence and pressure to be as instructed. As narrated and analysed in hindsight by Cassils and Leary, pressures come from the collective group and the objectifying perception of the collective audience. These pressures are external. It is not pressure from any other group member or a singular audience member either. It is the entitative presence of the aesthetic collective and the collective of the watching audience. It is an atmosphere of expectation that engulfs the participating subject. Beecroft has, over time, come to practice '[i]ncreasing the difficulty of items, reducing external cues which provide objective information, and increasing the strength of the command in the direction of the compliant behavior all serv[ing] to increase the effectiveness of conformity pressures in shifting a person's response'.[49] They still feel that they are generating the urge to conform. In Cassil and Leary's own retroactive account they identify how the objectifying gaze of the audience and the 'air of scrutiny' in the space caused intense fear and terror pressuring them to conform. Their disgust with the performance is perhaps motivated in part by the realisation that it was easier by far to conform to the entitative agency of the performance than to attempt to assert individual attitudes and agency. Perhaps they feel a sense of defeat and/or weakness in this regard. While I cannot fully defend that they do comment on how they feel they surrendered their own agency[50] and became aware of that in the process. A full reversal from their initial impetus of 'infiltration' and sabotage.

## Notes

1 Nate Freeman, 'The Most-Viewed Work of Performance Art In History: Vanessa Beecroft on Ditching the Art World for Kanye West', *Artnews* (17 February 2016), http://www.artnews.com/2016/02/17/the-most-viewed-work-of-performance-art-in-history-vanessa-beecroft-on-ditching-the-art-world-for-kanye-west/ [accessed 29 September 2018].

2 Vanessa Beecroft, 'Vanessa Beecroft', in interview with David Shapiro, *Museo Magazine* (2008), http://www.museomagazine.com/VANESSA-BEECROFT [accessed 6 May 2016]. *Planimeter* here is being used as a term to suggest the measurement of two-dimensional area and its occupation; the term comes from a tool used to measure two-dimensional areas.

3 With the exception of her wedding and her presence in a documentary film and set of photographs that I discuss much later, but do not relate to discussion here.

4 I will return to this discussion later, but it is worth a brief precis here to note this work is problematic as it draws both praise and critique in terms of feminist interpretation and

90   *Precis*

racial commentary. As I consider issues of agency, identity, gender and its performance, objectification and social conformity these issues will naturally be addressed through the discussion of individuality and collectivity in form. Wider discussion in broadsheet and academic critique will be presented alongside such issues as they arise.

5  See Comment 1 in Appendix C for discussion of her titles.
6  Vanessa Beecroft, 'From the Deitch Archive Notes on *VB16* (1996)', http://www.deitch.com/archive/vb16-piano-americano-beige [accessed 6 May 2016].
7  Beecroft, 'From the Deitch Archive Notes'.
8  Roberta Smith, 'Critic's Notebook; Standing and Staring, Yet Aiming for Empowerment', *The New York Times* (6 May 1998), http://www.nytimes.com/1998/05/06/arts/critic-s-notebook-standing-and-staring-yet-aiming-for-empowerment.html [accessed 19 November 2016].
9  Beecroft, 'From the Deitch Archive Notes'.
10  Smith, 'Critic's Notebook'.
11  Vanessa Beecroft, *Vanessa Beecroft Performances*, ed. by Marcella Beccaria (New York: Rizzoli International Publications, 2003), p. 306.
12  Beecroft, *Vanessa Beecroft*.
13  Bruce Hainley, 'Vanessa Beecroft; Gagosian Gallery', *Artforum*, summer (2001), https://www.artforum.com/print/reviews/200106/vanessa-beecroft-48549 [accessed 12 August 2018], p. 189.
14  Hainley.
15  Vanessa Beecroft, 'The Very Best of Vanessa Beecroft', *The New York Time* (2016), http://www.nytimes.com/slideshow/2016/05/19/t-magazine/the-very-best-of-vanessa-beecroft/s/19tmag-beecroft-slide-7RKB.html [accessed 6 May 2016].
16  Nick Johnstone, 'Dare to Bare', *The Observer* section of *The Guardian* (2005), https://www.theguardian.com/artanddesign/2005/mar/13/art [accessed 29 September 2018].
17  James Westcott, 'Black Tie Vs. Black Face', *The Drama Review*, 49:1 (2005), p. 115.
18  Logan Hill, ''Art Star' Vanessa Beecroft: Slammed at Sundance', *Vulture*, January (2008), http://www.vulture.com/2008/01/vanessa_beecroft_slammed_at_su.html [accessed 25 February 2018].
19  Peter Goddard, 'Artist Exposed in Film', *The Star* (2007), https://www.thestar.com/news/2007/02/21/artist_exposed_in_film.html [accessed 29 September 2018].
20  See Westcott. In this article, James Westcott provides a very insightful description and narration of what it is like to be an audience member to her performances. In it there are both details of how she manages and manipulates audiences and of how power plays multiple roles in the spectatorship of her works.
21  Carrie Noland, *Agency and Embodiment; Performing Gestures/Producing Culture,* (Cambridge, MA: Harvard University Press, 2009), p. 2.
22  Noland, *Agency and Embodiment*, p. 2.
23  Noland, *Agency and Embodiment*, p. 206.
24  A comparison of the photographs in Appendix A again will make this very clear.
25  Julia Steinmetz, Heather Cassils and Clover Leary, 'Behind Enemy Lines: Toxic Titties Infiltrate Vanessa Beecroft', *Signs,* 31:3, New Feminist Theories of Visual Culture (2006), pp. 753–783.
26  Steinmetz et al., p. 772.
27  Anonymity will return as a key feature of power in discussion of Greek khoros.
28  Beecroft, 'From the Deitch Archive Notes'.
29  Noland, *Agency and Embodiment*, p. 206.
30  Westcott, p. 115, 116, 118.
31  Beecroft, 'Vanessa Beecroft'.
32  Thomas Kellein, 'The Secret of Female Intimacy' originally printed in *Vanessa Beecroft: Photographs, Films, Drawings* (Berlin: Hatje Cantz, 2008), www.vanessabeecroft.com [accessed 8 May 2016].

33 For which there was no public video or photographic evidence as the photographer did not show up. A further evolution in Beecroft's work begins here as from then she progressively became her own photo-documentarian. Incidentally, photographs of her latter work easily sell for as much as $50,000 each.

34 Kellein, p. 4.

35 Kellein, p. 4.

36 Kaldor Public Art Projects, http://kaldorartprojects.org.au/projects/project-12-vanessa-beecroft [accessed 8 May 2016].

37 Steinmetz et al., p. 753.

38 Steinmetz et al., pp. 774–775.

39 Steinmetz et al., p. 775.

40 Carrie Noland, 'The Human Situation on Stage: Merce Cunningham, Theodor Adorno, and the Category of Expression', *Dance Research Journal*, 42:1 (2010), p. 54. Here it is Carolyn Brown quoted in conversation with Noland.

41 Noland, 'The Human Situation', p. 55. Subsequent references to this edition will appear parenthetically within the text.

42 *Proprioceptive* indicates one's own sense of physical position and movement activity. It is a processing conducted by the neurology in muscle tissues.

43 *Visuomotor* is a term used to describe the coordination of sight input and motor activity of the body.

44 skylar bergl, skylar bergi Instagram account, www.instagram.com/skylarbergl [accessed 15 May 2016].

45 Milton Rokeach, 'Authority, Authoritarianism, and Conformity', in *Conformity and Deviation*, ed. by Irwin A. Berg and Bernard M. Bass (New York: Harper & Brothers, 1961), p. 250.

46 The psychological elements of suggestibility and susceptibility I expand on as functions of another element of entitativity—common fate, again in the next chapter.

47 Rokeach, p. 250.

48 Robert R. Blake and Jane Srygley Mouton, 'Conformity, Resistance, and Conversion', in *Conformity and Deviation*, ed. by Irwin A. Berg and Bernard M. Bass (New York: Harper & Brothers, 1961), p. 11.

49 Blake, p. 11.

50 Something they quite darkly describe as being motivated by the financial reciprocity of the work. They were, in their own words and generally speaking, poorly funded art students; they needed the money. For an account of this, see footnote 5 in Steinmetz et al.

# 3 Common Fate—Objective, Agency and Essence

> The chorus can give birth to tragedy … Nietzsche calls it the primal dramatic phenomenon … thus consist[ing] in being outside oneself, exceeding the limits of one's individuality, disrupting thereby the order and the lines of family, tradition, and city […] The primal dramatic phenomenon is, in a word, ecstasy.[1]

The khoros is tragedy; it exceeds individuality; it is ecstasy. Greek khoros is an advanced and highly developed aesthetic collective. It is, in my opinion, a crowning artistic achievement of collectives in performance as it is one of the only performance collectives able to demonstrate intellectual and emotional expression equal to (and in some cases exceeding) that of an individual. It operates in highly poetic dimensions and opens a transitional liminal space for audiences to traverse artistic and uncanny worlds. It exists to assist the crossing of limits and bounds for an audience by doing so themself. In transgressing boundaries of selfhood, the fundamental tragedy is explored—which happens when one exceeds their limits and the boundary of 'them-ness'.

> Even though the chorus is the primary site of this phenomenon, it also occurs on the side of the spectators—indeed to such an extent as to efface the very opposition between the spectators and the chorus whose resounding songs could not but draw those spectators into the very ecstasy that they celebrate […] The outcome is an artistic doubling of that very movement of excess, of ecstatic truth, into which the dancing and singing chorus must have entered, a doubling that would produce, not a detached image of a natural original, but only a resounding of an abyss.[2]

This collective opens a door to the great beyond from that seduced, seduces, will seduce humankind to its greatest contemplations and experiences.

Mystery, uncertainty and plasticity make Greek khoros powerful and mystique is a recurrent theme with them: its provenance, its character, its number, its self-identification, its manner and behaviour, its voice. In fact, in regards to almost everything about it. Khoros evades perspicacity. This ability to elude and circumvent certainty and definition make khoros difficult to comprehend as

DOI: 10.4324/9781003205661-5

## Common Fate—Objective, Agency and Essence   93

well as mesmeric, alluring and exotic to consider. Like the abyss, the great unknown, to which it grants access the khoros is always alluding and eluding. Unlike many performance practices there is no true concrete knowledge about its origin or exactly how it was born onto the stage; tracing it back to the crucible of archaic Greece it just *was*, was already *there*; all-ready for politicians and tragedians to take, to mould, to shape into its "perfected" form in the tragedies of classical Athens.[3] There are many theories about how it originated: shepherd circles telling stories round the fire at night; the worshiping religious circle round the altar; the community ritual form used for any assortment of sociological phenomenon stretching back as far as human sentience. It is possible that khoros is as old as our very social communication. A way we express our identity as a social, communicative, and community-reliant species. Human beings just seem driven to sharing, copying and collectively acting things out. We also wrestle with features of this need or necessity of being together, of 'being with' and implications this need suggests: order, obligation, constraint or even the permanence of an inescapable condition of being. Khoros displays common human fates, both literally in the sense of the story in which they find themselves and ontologically as re/presenting human being.

This is the final element contributing towards entitativity—*common fate*—and here discussion moves in a more psychological and qualitative direction. With the elements of proximity, prägnanz and similarity, there was always a manipulation of objective, observable and physical variables (space in proximity, orientation/placement in prägnanz, and material appearance and gestural lexicon in similarity). With common fate the key variables are purpose and time. Common fate is also referred to as *joint destiny*. With both terms there are two immediate features: they both relate to mutuality ('common' and 'joint') and they both are bound temporally ('fate' and 'destiny'). Campbell's simplified definition for the term states that 'elements that move together in the same direction, and otherwise in successive temporal observations share a "common fate" are more likely to be perceived as parts of the same organization'.[4] In other words, if things move towards the same direction or goal at or about the same rate, or if over time they are observed together, they are found to be organised together. The idea of movement here is vague. His article mostly defines movement as physio-spatial, something that can be seen. However, Campbell and others (e.g. Yoshihisa Kashima, Brian Lickel and David L. Hamilton) leave the term open to represent not just physical movement, but also movement of thought, body, affect, purpose and/or characteristic. Take as an example a group of religious celebrants pursuing spiritual fulfilment. In the performance *Bakkhai*, which I detail later, such spiritual fulfilment brings the Dionysos worshiping Bakkhai together, gives them a common purpose for existing together and provides them with a movement to enact. They have a doctrine to understand and execute as a group. Such a group would be very recognisable as a unified social whole connected by this common fate. As an aesthetic collective, even if they were to have very few other similarising features, all the participants at least have the

94 *Precis*

common fate of believing in their purpose and the execution of it via the actions of worship.

This chapter purposefully follows the preceding one as common fate is another facet of similarity. Indeed, Yoshihisa Kashima, a social scientist working on the entitative reality of social groups, argues that all the gestalt principles that have been examined in this text so far are really just types of similarity, as 'expected *similarity* [emphasis in original] between instances of the category'.[5] He goes on to state how each of the principles relates to a type of similarity.

> [C]ommon fate, elements that belong to a putative entity move together in space and time. The similarity of elements [...] is just that, the similarity of appearance. Proximity [...] mean[s] that elements of a putative entity tend to be found closer together in space [...] similarity in motion, appearance, and location.[6]

Whereas in the previous chapter similarity was primarily of physicality and gestural lexicon, common fate is the similarity of members over time in terms of purpose, goal, and the underlying intention of action.

I will use two sub-terms in relation to *common fate*: *essentialism* and *perceived agency*. Both *essentialism* and *perceived agency* are terms that address dimensions of how collectives (not just the discrete members) can be conceptualised and personified like a human character. Both terms relate to qualitative dimensions of a collective that go beyond the superficial levels of spatial proxemics, visible appearance or action potential. As common fate is the movement of a group of individuals in a similar direction or towards a similar objective, it operates in regard to a sense of intention, that the group is intending towards a direction and objective. *Essentialism* will denote the perceiving of an *essence* to the totality, a sense of being, selfhood or subjectivity within it.[7] Whereas *perceived agency* denotes the perception of the totality having agency (over the members and as an intending subject). These terms work on a temporal level as well. They suggest a past and a future which link these individuals together. *Movement*, as a term, ties back to the action potential of the membership explored in the last chapter—again the *gestural* potential of the body within a given set of practices—but also encompasses what those actions signify and through their communicative act what they hope to achieve or convey. Greek khoroi communicate with themselves and their audiences through physical (dance/movement) and verbal (speaking and singing) means.

In this chapter, I will be reviewing theatre-based aesthetic collectives in the form of Greek khoros. Greek khoroi demonstrate aesthetic collectives in one of their more extreme forms. In its ancient form khoros represents a completely similarised membership who operate in close proximity, establish a definite collective domain and perform with elaborate choreographic prägnanz. Their action and movement are codified and rehearsed, their individuality stripped away, anonymised and replaced with a collective social

*Common Fate—Objective, Agency and Essence* 95

identity, their voice designed to be one made of many, and their rôle representative. In terms of dramaturgy, they exist simultaneously in the narrative reality of the tragedy, the present-time reality of the observing audience and in the abstract, contemplative poesy of the cosmic messages they convey. As a representative selection, the examples include the khoroi from the Almeida's 2015 season *Medea* and *Bakkhai*, the khoros from the Shakespeare's Globe 2015 performance of *Oresteia*, and *Chorus* from The Gate Theatre's 2016 *Iphigenia Quartet*.[8] *Bakkhai* and *Oresteia* were performances of translations of the extant scripts; *Medea* and *Chorus* were pieces of new writing modelled/inspired by the extent tragedies. I gathered evidence from them as an attendant at each (*Bakkhai* I saw twice) and through discussion with audience members and other attendants. I saw the performances over the course of one year in London.

Somewhat like some of Beecroft's installations, these khoros cases are examples of aesthetic collectives that are characters, specifically (as I noted above) human characters. However, they are far more formalised as characters and they have voices, literally and figuratively. I do not wish to engage here in a long discussion about what constitutes character in different dramaturgical contexts; I conduct a greater discussion of character in terms of dramatic and post-dramatic readings in the next chapter. Here, I introduce and use a relatively common dramaturgical concept of character—as a role performed by an actor that stands in for a human element. I adopt Elinor Fuchs discussion of the concept:

> Character is the theatrical 'element' (as Aristotle says) that best represents the 'standing in' invitation that endows theater with this double fullness of meaning. By standing in I mean what Bruce Wilshire describes: that in a theatrical event 'an actor must stand in for a character [...] and through this standing in the audience member stands in for this character [...]', to which continuum of involvements I would add playwright and director on the theatrical side of the interface between theater event and world, and the community at large on the other, for which in a sense the spectator 'stands in'. [...] [C]haracter representation [...] constitutes at the same time the manifestation of a change in the larger culture concerning the perception of self and the relations of self and world. 'Character' is a word that stands in for the entire human chain of representation and reception that theater links together.[9]

Characters model and personify human beings and their actions which facilitate the evolution and progression of plots. As 'stand-ins' for human elements, characters have objectives, goals and reasons for existing. Khoroi have a collective character. They represent a demographic of people with objectives, goals and reasons for existing. As characters with these features, they then have a common fate which in turn creates stronger entitativity for them.

96  *Precis*

As movement towards intended outcomes, common fate then enfolds a further dimension of performance that is common to most theories of acting: pursuit of objective or goal. In the western traditions of acting, particularly those following Stanislavski, the performance of a role inculcates actors with a deconstruction of performance into objectives and units of actions that move characters towards their objectives.[10] Characters pursue their objectives and goals—the desires, needs or wants towards which all their performed action moves. With collective characters, several individuals move towards the same objective or goal. Collective characters similarly pursue goals. However, the experience of them doing this differs from singular characters. Notably, the objective or goal they share must be something that applies to all. Objectives or goals that only satisfy one of the members are generally not common fates. For example, the pursuit of a monogamous lover. A collective cannot pursue a lover, it would need to pursue a collective of lovers as one lover would not be meaningful to the collective; the Bakkhai might be an example of how this in a sense applies to all, as they ecstatically pursue connection with Dionysos. He is a god though, so he has the ability to affect all members in a distributed sense. Another element that might differ is the drive for the objective/goal. Revenge, as is the objective/goal of the khoros of *Choēphoroi*, the middle play of *Oresteia*, is a revenge originating from a collective resentment of their enslavement and treatment by the house of Klytemnestra. This differs from the revenge drive in Elektra, who is motivated by injustice, as she sees it, of her father's murder by her mother. Such a personal motivation would not apply to the khoros in the same way. In another performance, it is possible that a member of the khoros might be similarly motivated, but such personal sentiment is not likely to be held by the group.

It is also harder to expose psychological dimensions to collective characters than with singular characters. With singular characters, the dramatic tension caused by the challenge and conflict in attaining their objectives/goals creates easily understood psychological reactions—we witness it as it is expressed emotionally through their body. With a collective, psychological reactions are more delocalised as they are dispersed throughout a larger group. The decentralising of that reaction through many bodies changes the reception of it by an audience. In any case, groups that pursue the same thing have a unifier: the outcome. When a group of individuals holds the same objective or goal we perceive them as a cohesive and similarly motivated group and their entitative state increases. To relate it back to Campbell's phrasing, they move in the same direction in successive temporal observations; they strive towards their objective/goal and all members work towards it collectively.

So, in terms of collective togetherness, all four khoroi examples showed common indications in terms of movement, both in space and time. There was uniformity to their physicality and this was consistent through the durations of the performances. Their action was shaped and rehearsed. It conformed to an understandable and determined lexicon. Second, all four examples operated in relation to an internal pulse or tempo. All four

Common Fate—Objective, Agency and Essence    97

harmonised with the aural ambiance of their performance spaces to ensure cohesion. This was either a musical element, an aural texture/soundscape or a combination of both; in the case of *Bakkhai*, the khoros almost entirely produced this themself. Third, they all spoke the verbal text in some form of unison or in a state of co-narration in which different members of the khoros would interrupt, pick-up or complete phrases. This is overlapping, simultaneous or co-narrative speech. Voice often seemed not to come from any one intelligence, but rather emerged as a gestalt of fractured and piecemeal thoughts. Fourth, as gestalt entities, they had very clear and defined characters; each khoros had a membership composed of highly similarised characters moulded from and reflexive of the collective khoros character. To return to discussion at the end of the last chapter, they all held similarised properties that categorised them within their collectives. I roughly equate all of this to these performance features: choreography and rhythm, dialogue, and character/rôle.

## Choreography and Rhythm

'Choreography' I use inclusive of movement style. Each khoros demonstrated understandable choreography and movement. They physically moved in ways that conformed to an internal style and this similarisation limited the potential action they could perform. What I mean here is that a specific type of movement for each khoros was apparent and in some there was also choreographic dance. Like the Beecroft installations, the action the actors could perform narrowed to a selection of directed choices and similarised amongst the performers. Used in sequence, those actions combined to form phrases which then flowed to become choreography. Choreography is itself, to paraphrase Susan Leigh Foster, an activity of arranging patterns of movement and dance and it is both the actual movement/dancing and the recording of those dance actions.[11] For the purposes of this text *choreography* will cover the arranging of all action, encompassing both dance and general movement that is patterned and/or musical. As choreography is an arranged pattern of action responding to stimuli, its intention or underlying purpose can at times be overlooked.

> Each moment of watching [it] [...] can be read as the product of choices, inherited, invented, or selected, about what kinds of bodies and subjects are being constructed and what kinds of arguments about these bodies and subjects are being put forth.[12]

The bodies of the performers who constitute these khoroi were made to have choices about identity and how that identity is or can be expressed; the different choreography of the khoroi represents a physical output of their identity. 'Not a permanent, structural engagement with representation, but rather a slowly changing constellation of representational conventions [...] offer[ing] potential for agency to be constructed via every body's specific

98  *Precis*

engagement with the parameters governing the realization of [action]'.[13] The obvious difference between the choreographies of these khoroi and the choreography of non-collectivised performance is that in these aesthetic collectives it is operational and uniform across both the gestalt and member levels. A common choreography of the composite collective rules the choreography of the individual members. To understand the choreographies of the khoroi, I first look at the basic level of the actions composing them.

In the *Medea*, there was a dancing khoros of mothers who were, as Dominic Cavendish reported in the *Telegraph*, 'reconceived as Islington-ite yummy mummies—trading gossip, stuck in materialist clichés, jouncing toy babies up and down, coloured shawls over their shoulders in a parody of classicism'[14] characterising the oppressive and ostracising aspects of a mumsnet microculture. Similarised in appearance they all wore differently coloured relaxed home wear. They looked like they were going to a yoga class for mothers: loose form-fitting, stretch tops and balloon trousers. They swayed and semi-balletically moved in unison across the stage speaking their odes in a chatty tone. In the first half of the play, their actions were choreographed and rhythmically set to music. This included swaying as if rocking a baby (they carried imagined or toy infant props), gentle nursing actions, laying the child to sleep on a floor cot, retrieving them and comforting them, dancing with them and so on. All of this they conducted in the style of easy modern dance. This generated a convincing atmosphere of mothering, stress, exhaustion and a desperate attempt to present the image of succeeding at being a mother and being happy with it. The mood they generated also felt layered with tones of postpartum stress and depression—something which heightened the pressure and weight of the usually known fate of Medea's children (she kills them in a revenge tactic against her husband Jason). Khoros' presence in the first half intensified the discomfort and social ill-ease with the stresses of motherhood and the imbalance that it can cause for parents, especially women. Medea, a rebellious character who is both empowered and disempowered by her outsidership, juxtaposed with these women who openly judged and criticised her in their gossiping dialogue. A clear purpose for this khoros was to serve as a backdrop of middle-class parental 'normalcy'—such illustration display a social abnormalcy. The khoros, against whom Medea stands as the ostracised outsider, generated intense atmospheres of guilt and judgement.

This khoros operated with a clear purpose and with designed actions through the first half. They had a recognisable common fate, moving with physical and psychological uniformity. They felt very entitative. They were proxemically cohesive, their choreography established a definite prägnanz which also bounded them within their domain, they were similarised in terms of action and their appearance was similarised to a moderately high level with all adopting the same style and make of clothing and hair. Their choreography expressed an identity in its style and type. The use of gentle modern-dance choreography produced an identity of these being mostly modern and contemporary women. Their occasional ability to execute higher technical dance

## Common Fate—Objective, Agency and Essence   99

feats (leaping or twisting/turning) or lapse into a more balletic phrase was suggestive of 'real world' women who probably took ballet in their youth and as adults casually audit dance classes. Interestingly, this very observation draws-up several other facets of identity, mostly linked to class. Ballet for children and the taking of dance classes as an adult is typical of more affluent social classes. The choreography thus defined them as a khoros of upper middle-class mothers. The choices underlying the choreographic style 'constitute the cultural moment within which [these] bodies circulate',[15] allowing the choreography to 'be conceptualized as a theorization of identity—corporeal, individual, and social'.[16] This aesthetic collective's adherence to their choreographic style projected these identities or 'hidden' choices to the audience.

Through their choreography, they became more entitative, contained and set apart. In comparison, their actions and purpose in the second half of the performance shifted to functional roles, that of ornamental scene-shifters. They returned as mainly non-speaking dancers who worked to transform the stage set. Their dance became highly energetic and a mixture of musical theatre and modern dance styles. They moved here much more to embody and characterise the fearful, climactic energy accumulating. The musical score was commensurately soaring and melodramatic. Finally, they took roles as still and silent spectators present to Medea and Jason's eventualities. Their actions largely reduced to decorative reflections of the mood, but this style in the second half was not fully reflexive of the central tragedy and thus seemed incongruous and meaningless.

Differently, the khoroi of *Oresteia* utilised more sedate choreography, but through that it became equally entitative and achieved a readable identity. They rarely danced; instead, their choreography was more a pattern of affected action. The khoros of *Oresteia* was in fact three khoroi (one for each part of the trilogy): the old men of Argos in *Agamemnon*, the palace slave women of *Choēphoroi*, and the furies of *Eumenides*. In each khoros, the director made gender and age irrelevant. The old men of Argos were older and younger men and women; the slave women were male and female with no defined age; the furies were played by men and women and generally treated as sexless and ageless (although referred to as female and agèd). With the opportunity of three different khoroi, the director used three different types of choreography as well. *Agamemnon*'s khoros moved in rigid, angular and blocky ways. The scope of their action was conservative and careful, suggesting careful characters, much like the aged men of the script. This khoros moved in patterns of position and orientation (i.e. transforming prägnanz) and less a dance; dissolving their collective domain at one part of the stage by scattering individually to reterritorialise it elsewhere. Like a smoky cloud they would appear and disappear through their choreography. Similarly, the slaves of *Choēphoroi*, more downtrodden, worn and vindictive, had a choreography of regimented, nearly soldier-like movement which graduated later in the performance to more desperate and anticipatory actions—actions filled with violent energy commensurate with their vengeful intentions. Lastly, the choreography of the

100    *Precis*

furies of *Eumenides*, the most dance-like of the khoroi, was less realistic, jagged, severe and aggressive. At their first appearance, during their murderous ensnaring of Orestes and during their rage of Athene's verdict they wildly threw themselves against and ricocheted off the pillars and walls of the theatre. This choreography revealed dangerous, unstable and violent characters. All three of these khoroi heightened their entitative state not only by similarising their actions to that of the greater collective, but also by operating within a pattern that orchestrated those actions in direction and time. Just like the khoros of *Medea*, identities of the *Oresteia* khoros shone through their choreography, and with it a type of biography was created that existed within the audience mind.

*Bakkhai* and *Chorus* had similar choreographic choices. In *Bakkhai* the khoros moved much less and in affected ways within patterned layouts on a square stage (vacating to the perimeter of the stage during the episodes); *Chorus* had a khoros that changed positions in a quadrant stage and inhabited the stage in affected ways. The khoros of *Chorus* did not dance at all and the khoros of *Bakkhai* did not dance in any formal sense of the word; there were moments in *Bakkhai* when the activities of the khoros resembled shuddering and swaying dance similar to what one might witness at a religious event or in a very low key nightclub. At no point did their activity propel them to traverse or even move in a way that required dance training during their odes—even though *Bakkhai* is perhaps the most dance-filled, dithyrambic and ecstatic Greek tragedy remaining—a choice that I did not fully understand. Both khoroi, however, were highly entitative through their common movement in space and time. In *Chorus* the khoros changed their positions with regularity and in complete synchronicity; in *Bakkhai* the khoros inhabited and deinhabited the stage during their odes. These khoroi demonstrated a common fate through their choreographed movement, each operating as a unit in direction(s) and speed over time.

All cases had regulated and synchronised choreographic action. They achieved this with common speed and timing. To be a cohesive unit they attuned their activities to a shared time register and velocity. Such coordination required the individual members to concert their inner rhythms—not one to another, but one to the common rhythm of the khoros. Logically moving along, then, rhythm is the next indication of common fate. Rhythm is the metering-out of time in marked intervals. These khoroi needed to order all activity (action, speech, affect shift and so on) so it occurred together or in harmonised execution. They maintained cohesion through coordination to the ambient rhythm of the larger performance. In all cases this was a musical score/soundscape, embedded within each there was a pulse. The khoroi moved to the pulse of the ambient score. This pulse/beat of rhythm ruled their activity, making them move at the same speed. Since the sound/ music was ambient in the whole performance space the audience also felt and heard the beat. Consequently, the audience not only could see the khoroi moving in synch, but also shared the internal metronomics. Layered onto this the choreographies utilised very simple, obvious and anticipatable patterns of

Common Fate—Objective, Agency and Essence    101

action. As an audience we could easily experience the choreography of the different khoroi in an empathic way. Such a 'tuning of self and world sets the precondition for a variety of possible responses [...] enacting the simulation of multiple next responses'.[17] I agree with Foster here; by becoming in-tune with the aesthetics of the performance I (audience) could internally simulate the possible futures that the khoroi would be taking. The plausibility of these internal simulations is increased by connecting the actions to a rhythmic certainty. I could not be certain of what the khoroi would do next, but I was very certain of the regularity of the rhythm. I knew the rhythm was very likely to continue. The sound/music usually also built-in cadences that indicated that a change or finish was approaching as well. Through that rhythm I could anticipate what actions would come next as a matter of choreographic form—what made logical sense in a movement phrase. Experiencing or understanding the khoros' rhythms allowed me, and the audience, to comprehend them as something that has a recognisable future. They had a fate into which each member was jointly progressing and moving. The choreography placed them in composed, complex prägnanz; the rhythm of choreography (and indeed all activity) allowed them to move and transition through their patterns in unity, literally and figuratively in time.

## Dialogue

Dialogue is an indication of common fate that will apply to fewer examples of aesthetic collectives more broadly speaking. The installations of Beecroft, for instance, are nonverbal and the aesthetic collectives of the club, while frequently verbal, are not dialogic in nature, particularly to an observer. Dialogue is more typical of the theatre or other narrative form works in which verbal language is a feature. I will define *dialogue* as the verbalised elements of performance in general. I will not use it to denote verbal exchange between two people specifically, so may include soliloquy, monologue, and polyphony. To return to the cases at hand, khoroi produce sound—they can vocalise, speak, sing, utter. All the examples I survey uttered; the khoroi of *Bakkhai* sang and that of *Oresteia* spoke musically (but not quite singing). Like choreography, dialogue operates to an internal metronome and occurs in unity in a khoros. This unity, however, can manifest and be stylised in any number of ways. While in other aesthetic collectives verbalised soundscapes might be created, there are more pronounced dialogic constants in khoroi. At times they may verbalise in unison, use overlapping speech or co-narration. I will address these three each by example.

The first, verbalising in unison, particularly occurred in *Bakkhai* and *Oresteia* and it is when members of a khoros speak the same thoughts and words at the same time at the same speed. Unison speech creates the effect of the khoros being entirely in-sync, as sharing a mind, so to speak. In *Bakkhai* especially the khoros used a heavy amount of unison speech. There were moments when the entire khoros spoke in unison and there were moments when there were

102    *Precis*

smaller subgroups within the khoros speaking in unison. All the members attuned to each other and to their operational rhythm. Above and beyond the effect of synchronicity, overlapping speech creates the impression that the dialogue, or thoughts contained in it, come from a single subject. It elevates the sense of entitativity by engendering this feeling of singular intellect. The members, as part of a khoros, shared the same thoughts and intentions. To return to container metaphors, they were contained in thought to a singular 'mind' that broadcasts or distributes across and through the many members and their voices. This impression occurs in the other dialogue constants as well. The ability to synchronise, share or complete thoughts through unison, overlapping or co-narrative speech generates this feeling of singular mind, or telepathic happening.

Overlapping speech, the second constant, features containment as well, but as a common narrative fractured into separate voices; each member contributing to the larger thread of continuity. *Chorus* heavily used overlapping speech and the four actors were in constant, rapid speech. Modelled after a trolling Internet public with hyperactive shifting between thoughts, they exhumed every informational aspect and datum of the Iphigenia tragedy should it happen in this technologically modern world. Each member was narrating the same plot, drawn from Euripides' *Iphigenia at Aulis*, but each spoke from their different and solipsistic perspectives. The performance thus displayed how four different people could obsessively witness the family's plight online, recounting the same events at the same moments but from the isolated, personal positions of their computer spaces. This displayed the togetherness of their interest and their deeply personal enjoyment. The effect was humorous at first. Then the story moved into the tragedy and the performance progressively revealed more disturbing behaviour: not sleeping at night because they were too interested, illegally hacking CCTV cameras to see unreleased footage, neglecting their own children to engage in their online addiction, scanning mediatised JPEG images for minute details, having orgasmic responses to characters' emotional decline, tears and so on. In any case, while having unique, personal elements, in overlapping speech the individual dialogue is highly similarised. Each part contributes to a bigger, common picture.

Interruption is also key with overlapping speech. The more adroit the overlap and interrupt the more in-sync the members appear, the more contained within a singular narrative mind. Like unison speech, the ability to remain in constant coordination of thought and to deliver many perspectives coherently within their common overall narrative engenders the impression of a singular intellect. It was rife throughout this example. One member would barely complete a short thought (perhaps one or two sentences) before another would interject and pick up the thread from their own perspective. For example, describing the moment of Iphigenia arriving at the battle camps in Aulis: one member relays the moment of her walking into the camp as seen on CCTV footage—suddenly, another member interrupts to describe and

*Common Fate—Objective, Agency and Essence* 103

critique, à la gossip magazine columns, her dress and choice of garments—this is interrupted by a different member who snatches the voice and explains how a jpeg of her face from the CCTV footage could be enlarged and re-imaged for greater resolution to see and scrutinise the emotions crossing Iphigenia's face—another interrupts to add what Iphigenia's twitter feed and the corresponding reposts are saying about the moment—another interrupts to describe how this moment is making them feel—another interrupts to comment on how the excitement of moments like this prevent her from leaving her bedroom to use the toilet and instead she sometimes urinates into plastic bottles so as not to leave the computer and so on. This interruptive nature grounds the khoros members within a common reality; they are experiencing the same thing, at the same time and are digesting those experiences separately, but similarly.

Co-narration is very similar to overlapping dialogue. Co-narration is the thread of thought presented through several voices in sequence. Like with overlapping dialogue each member of the khoros is joining/interrupting each other, but in this case the joiner/interrupter continues the dialogue thought, finishing the sentence of the person they interrupted. Co-narration is particularly interesting as the vocal expression suggestive of one common intellect here shifts or jumps from one member to another. It frequently occurs in khoroi as it makes an otherwise long series of lines move from person to person, but still create the fantastic impression of parallel, telepathic thought. It can also help enhance or decrease the anonymity of the khoros members. In *Bakkhai* and *Oresteia* the khoroi maintained greater anonymity/redaction of individual member character. It did not really matter who the members were in any meaningful way, so a general homogeneity was desirable. In *Medea* and *Chorus,* the members each had a sense of discrete identity. They were certainly anonymous, also composed of several different and diverse characters or types—those two khoroi suggested an averaging of divergent demographics, not a homogenising. For example, in *Chorus* the four members each represented a different demographic of person: the alternative, young, geeky and computer savvy woman; the older, weird, lonely and average-in-all-ways white guy; the serious, aggressive, professional woman with no social life due to her work-load, the everyman, middle-aged, man with a strained family. The unifying factor for all four was that they each turned to the Internet and its anonymity to satisfy their lacking interaction and social lives, which enabled the growth and expression of disgusting and barbaric impulses in their online behaviour and avatars. In recasting a khoros as the embodiment of Internet trolling culture this text also makes a clear, and in my opinion valid, comment on the dangers of anonymity granted by the Internet.

Anonymity is central to khoros identity. It allows them to become the projection of a social group. Most extant tragedy has khoroi of disenfranchised people, thus creating comment on power dynamics and social responsibility. Usually a protective power, anonymity is flipped in *Chorus,* for example, exposing some individual identity. This creates a dangerous and disturbing

104  *Precis*

revelation of what unknown Internet trolls can be like. *Medea* also made this directorial choice, showing a degree of member identity in the five women, albeit bordering on stereotypes—the dizzy mother, the mother who is probably suffering from postpartum depression that no one will acknowledge, the nervous and passive mother, the alpha mother who somehow does it all and so on. Such penchant for identity might be a contemporary interest. These were two newly written transliterations; whereas *Bakkhai* and *Oresteia*, where this did not occur, were the original texts in translation. *Medea* particularly invites further value in its transliteration as the original text was written by Euripides, a man, but here is reinterpreted by a female playwright who is also a mother. This offers perspectives perhaps more congruous with Medea and/or a critique/reflection on the originally male perspective of this myth and its plot circumstances.

In the original texts, the khoroi have a fluid continuity of thought, so unison speech and co-narration are obvious choices for how to direct such a collective. Whereas overlapping speech is somewhat more consistent with khoroi that are expressing a homogenisation of multiple discrete and individual voices. In any case, as *Bakkhai* and *Oresteia* show, co-narration is effective in establishing khoroi as completely mentally in synchronization and operating with a consciousness that follows one narrative path.

Co-narration is also a very powerful way to create the image of common mentality. Co-narration, in a sense, includes members joining and falling out of a single monologue. When executed well it becomes difficult to assess visually which members are speaking. *Bakkhai* was a very good example of this. That khoros had a voice that bounced and moved from person to person so well that they simply became a visual mass with one non-localisable voice. This was enhanced in that instance with layers of tone and song. The membership often spoke in straight-toned voices (that is voice pitched on the same continuous tone) which gave the effect of a monotony of sound or speech voiced along a continuous chord. Not only were they following the same narrative thought, but a singular tone range emphasised their uniformity. Again, uniformity/conformity contains the voice, which in turn accentuates the container metaphor for the mind. Moreover, during their co-narration members who were non-speaking still vocalised, producing a drone or sing-song underscore for the speech-based members. This was like a musical or atmospheric accompaniment—a back-up group (more on that in chapter 5, when I look at back-up dancers).

Co-narration also involves assimilation, the absorbing or folding of one into the others. A khoros can also simply just assimilate into, commandeer and continue the narrative dialogue of other members. In so doing a khoros becomes vocally liquid like streams and tributaries into a river, flowing, merging and irrigating from one vocal path into another. This vocal feat was demonstrated most in the khoros of *Choēphoroi*. During the first stasimon (in which Elektra, Orestes and the Khoros lament the death of Agamemnon/the injustice of Clytemnestra and Aegisthus remaining monarchs/gathering the

Common Fate—Objective, Agency and Essence 105

vengeful spirit to wreak revenge) the khoros adroitly utilised co-narration and assimilative movement. Again, the impression of a singular collective mind appeared to jump from member to member as each became the speaking member. One would speak, then before the end of the thought another member would pick-up the line and finish it until another member did the same, creating a strong sense of intellectual cohesion. This cohesion in dialogue created the sense of them, as a group, moving from a shared narrative past, through a common narrative present and towards a joint narrative future. The activity of dialogue emerging from these khoroi in these ways (unison, overlapping and co-narrative speech) demonstrated a common fate both on the level of movement in direction (from and towards similar outcomes) and in time (from and towards collective history at an equal and synchronised rate). Dialogue indicates common fate; it both requires cogent vocal practice and is revelatory of a common intellect/mind. The activity of speech and the content spoken show the khoroi producing sound in cogent, cohesive and harmonic ways.

## Rôle/Character

Rôle/character is the last indication of common fate that I have identified in these cases that I wish to discuss. In many ways this is the most obvious and easily observed element of common fate. Khoroi have given, explicit identities that are a combination of the written character and the performer/director choices in characterisation. Collective groups like these share, or can be understood to share, a common history/biography/community. As khoroi have singular characters, a distributive character applies to the members. Each member adopts collective identity and in turn they appear more entitative than instances where members (of khoroi or other collectives) do not share this character element. This is quite like the similarisation of character in the Beecroft installations, where appearing to have the same character made them more entitative. As above, khoroi are supposed to be anonymised (traditionally they wear masks, robes and platform shoes) and are intended to be a multiplication of a singular demographic. All members represent that demographic in a flat, non-deviating way. Their rôle/character is to be the same—in a khoros every member is to be the same rôle/character. They are to be like a hive mind of clones. They not only should share the same character background, but they also re/present that background. Only some of the example performances I survey seriously attempted this dimension of hyper-similarity and then only moderately achieved it.

These elements are not strictly necessary in contemporary performance, but anonymity of khoros members is still a powerful and useful choice to observe. If used well, it can create a stunning and very powerful image through conformity. Most successful were the khoroi of *Eumenides* and *Bakkhai*. In *Eumenides*, the khoros of furies were gothic, wraith-like goddesses (although they were played by both men and women and were largely de-sexed).

106　*Precis*

Dressed all in black with dark, black eye and mouth make-up and distorted contact lensed eyes. Their hared or common character emerged through similarisation in physical appearance, speaking in unison, over-lapping and co-narrative speech and moving in similar coordinated ways the whole appeared like one character. Indeed, this khoros is interesting as in mythology the furies are not encountered or understood in isolation. Like others in Greek mythology—the hours, the moira, the graces, the muses—they are not understood as individuals, but *only* as collective entities.[18] Reflecting back, club collectives anonymise individual dancers and the collective appears as a group of 'anybodies'; Vanessa Beecroft de-individualises her participants so that identity is scrubbed away and a homogenised and aestheticised one is applied.

An asymmetrical relationship occurs where the greater a degree of anonymity, the greater a sense of collective history. Eliminating individual and unique biographic-narrative elements in favour of generalised uniformity focuses the sense of communal biographic-narrative. In foregrounding collective over personal identity, especially when non-specific, the collective grows in digestible character. The khoros of *Eumenides* lacked any sense of autonomy or individuation. They were transformed into similarised creatures, and as such they held a common sense of past and a common fate. The same was true in *Bakkhai*. That khoros was a group of women drawn from many demographic backgrounds (races, ages, sizes, nationalities and general appearances). They removed all these features. During their entrance parodos they even emphasised this by dressing themselves in similarised leather-like garments while acting in very homogenised ways (similar movement types, speeds, intentions). In a latter ode they further augmented this, hastily applying make-up to their faces to resemble masks, appearing even more de-individuated. Despite being different they seemed to share an experiential history; they all seemed to have faced the same treatment and back-story, particularly regarding their gender relationship with men (which is true in the original text). Their performance revealed a shared collective history. As far as rôle/character indicates common fate, khoroi have or suggest a sense of shared history or character profile.

For an audience, seeing common fate, the cognitive and action capacity of khoroi working with common intention, enhances an aesthetic collective's temporal entitativity. The other three elements of entitativity get fixed in the present of the performance. In discussing proximity and prägnanz it is a series of caught moments of spatiality. With similarity it is a discussion of the likeness of components at any given time, but during the performance. While they all change over time, common fate suggests temporal continuity to the group *beyond* the performance. It extends proximity, prägnanz and similarity out of the present to include a past and progressing into a future. Common fate illustrates aesthetic collectives having a lifespan filled with purpose and intention. They each must have a collective reason for being that binds members together, and even a directive or goal towards which they strive. Common fate responds to and resolves the issue of what brings these people together and why they are connected. Even if we consider the simplest form of a collective,

Common Fate—Objective, Agency and Essence   107

a crowd, there is a reason for co-presence. This is their objective or goal (which for ease of reading I bundle them together just under the term objective). All four of these indications of common fate (choreography, rhythm, dialogue, and rôle/character) are demonstrative of motivation and movement towards objective; they are features of its pursuit. They exist for and are employed in the achieving of something. The khoroi exhibited common fate through their choreography, rhythm, dialogue and character as pursuits of their objectives.

As pursuit of objective requires some form of motivation, common fate incorporates a dimension of collective psychology. Collective pursuit of a similar outcome implies common motivation (which again is linked to history or biography). Khoroi, first, become more entitative as we can now read them as internally similarised, contained and unified on deeper, psychological levels (shared history, biography, motivation). Each pursued their singularised outcome and each membership was motivated in internally similar ways. They were contained and uniform in physicality, metronomics, verbalisation and characterisation in their pursuit of their objectives. As characters pursuing these objectives, and how they managed obstacles and conflict, I could read these khoroi as having psychological profiles. 'Every lived experience, every psychic comportment, direct[ed] itself towards something'.[19] Their awareness and perception of the world around them was perception *of* something and the sense of their 'mind' directing itself towards those things. Phenomenologically, this is intentionality—collective intentionality.

In the phenomenological tradition intentionality is the contact between the psychic, internal 'mind' and the external or embodied world and its objects, and it underpins subjectivity. It is the fundamental activity of consciousness itself, a directing of the self towards things, and recognising intentionality in other things reveals them as having an underlying consciousness. As a totality, not as disparate individuals, aesthetic collectives direct themselves towards their surroundings, experiencing and responding to their world as pursuing their objectives. They collectively and uniformly move *towards* and experience, both internally and externally, the same events. As an audience to them, their entitativity becomes the same way as human subjects with common fate. Choreography, rhythm, dialogue and character create this sense of singular mind and intentionality to them. The khoroi responded to their worlds in cohesive, singular ways. I could perceive this intentionality as distributed and replicated across the individual members. As totality entities, the khoroi shared, as Heidegger puts it, 'a structure of lived experiences as such and not a coordination relative to other realities [... The khoroi were] *directing-itself-toward*'[20] their worlds and ultimately towards their common fates. Heidegger's idea here is that there exists the sense of a consciousness when lived experiences are structured through phenomenal perception. Those perceptions construct a reality unique to that space, time and subject. The consciousness, in response, directs itself towards that experience to generate an understanding of it and to exist within it. When these khoroi appeared to have this directed

108   *Precis*

perception of and response to the fictional worlds in which they were cast they seemed like a singular, collective consciousness that distributed across the members. They became a collective that operates in the same way and like a singular subject.

To return to Fuchs comment on the 'standing-in' in regard to characters, in these performances the khoroi stood-in for human elements. They represented a potential collective, demographic human experience and showed how they might experience, understand, exist and respond to their realities just as singular subjects would. The key difference is that their experience, understanding, existence and responses are those of the mass. They show us, the audience, a mass experience of phenomenal reality. In at least these examples they stand-in for a demographic human entity and when we, the audience, stand-in for them we glimpse the experience of a collective, distributed being. Common fate exposes phenomenological reality to aesthetic collectives. When encountered as *the* collective audiences can engage with the spectacle of collective phenomenal experience. Membership sutures a perceived collective intentionality onto and into the individual members. The individual member consciousness directs itself towards experiences of the collective whole; regardless of the placement or state of the member, all members are directing their consciousness towards the focus of the collective object of perception and thought. The act of shifting into membership returns this discussion to the notion of conformity. The membership is under a conforming influence of the collective whole, not only in physical ways, but also in mental and intentional acts. They are conforming and becoming agents of the perceived collective mind or consciousness.

My experience or perception of a collective mind or consciousness establishes an authority and agency to the collective above and beyond the members. It is not the case that one participant leads or commands that authority or agency. Nor are they under the commanded influence of an external character. The collective agency, as in the prior chapter, reasserts itself to articulate subject-like entitativity. The khoroi examples demonstrated entitativity to high levels, their own intentional capacity and each operated like any other agentic character.

Aside from inhabiting the narrative or dramatic plots these aesthetic collectives produced highly charged affective environments which modify and condition the experiences for themselves and the audiences. I will return to this topic in the next chapter, but it is clearly a function of khoros, and by extension many other kinds of aesthetic collectives, to set and augment the environment and crucially, the mood. For instance, *Medea* used its khoros, in the main, to frame the social context of the anti-hero Medea and served as a foil to Medea and Jason's story. They were not working towards a true goal of their own, but their social presence attained a meta-purpose—to heighten the drama and unveil social consequences. They helped establish a moral or ethical mood within which Medea and Jason could be judged. This is a stripping back

Common Fate—Objective, Agency and Essence    109

of some of the functional purposes of khoros, a more post-dramatic purpose.[21] They were characters, but they more functionally worked at producing a mood or *characterisation* to the performance. Indeed, this mood establishing and characterising function of an aesthetic collective shows them generating an affective dimension to performance. Moreso, they were generating atmospheric experiences for that performance.

## Agentic States

How does this happen? In brief, the members must conform to the collective and that requires obedience of different sorts. While *obedience* involves a power dynamic it does not necessarily mean it is coercive, forced or against wills. Those might happen, but they are not correlative. To illustrate, I return to my perception of the khoros' agentic authority over the constituent members. All the members were acting in alignment with the supra-structure of the collective. To do so, the members had to adjust themselves and transition out of total independence and into a conforming role. This transition from a self-acting and independent agent to a conforming and obeying agent for others, requires being in what Stanley Milgram calls the *agentic state*. The agentic state defines a state of mind in which system-directed thoughts and actions override and overwrite self-directed thoughts and actions. The system here being the social one, the collective. In other words,

> the person entering an authority system no longer views [them]self as acting out of [their] own purposes but rather comes to see [them]self as an agent for executing the wishes of another ... [it is] the condition a person is in when [they] see [them]self as an agent for carrying out another['s] wishes.[22]

Here, the individual performer (the independent agent) shifts to being an operative agent for the aesthetic collective (the collective authority). That shift triggers a cascade of transformations. To paraphrase Milgram, the performer-subject's relationship to the collective-authority pervades their entire set of activities and, as is typical, that performer-subject wants to act competently and appear well to the collective-authority.[23] To do that they adjust their actions and mindset. 'Moved into the agentic state, the person becomes something different from [their] former self, with new properties not easily traced to [their] usual personality'.[24] Entry to the agentic state requires a process of psychological alignment, which Milgram refers to as 'tuning'.

Let's examine this through the specific example of khoros. In the first place the authority figure of the khoros must be established in relation to the performer-subject. The khoros as authority figure must have real, or at least a real impression of, power. That power imbues the khoros with authority—they *author* the situation.

110　*Precis*

> By virtue of that position, [the khoros authority] is in the optimal position to bestow benefits or inflict deprivations [...] Because of this, authority tends to be seen as something larger than the individual. The individual often views authority as an impersonal force, whose dictates transcend mere human wish or desire. Those in authority acquire, for some, a suprahuman character.[25]

In the second place the performer-subject must enter into and become a part of that systemic khoros–authority system. 'It is not enough that [they] perceive an authority, [it] must be an authority relevant to [them]'.[26] The khoros authority must be of relevance, which means the system of authority needs to hold meaning to them; there must be a good reason for entering into the system. The performer-subjects must have willingly entered into their khoros systems; although they could have been forced or entered with discomfort, force would create a different, more antagonistic, relationship to the authority and from my observational perspective this was not seen. Agreement to obey was then perceptible in the performer-subjects. They all appeared to be in conformity with the khoroi:

> ... the principal sanctions for disobedience come from within the person. They are not dependent upon coercion, but stem from the individual's sense of commitment to [their] role. In this sense, *there is an internalized basis for his obedience, not merely an external one* [emphasis in the original].[27]

To summarise, the establishing of an agentic state required first that the performer-subjects perceived a legitimate authority figure in their khoros and second that they entered into the authority system of that khoros.

With characters and a sense of mind with no apparent commanding agent above them the entities of the khoroi were the obvious authorities. That authority dilates larger, though. Moving out of the dramatic and narrative contexts, the performers in these aesthetic collectives are framed in two levels of authority concentrated through the khoros: the level of the success of the collective itself and of their professional employment. In the first, the authority is the khoros itself as it relates to the immediate performances and the dramas themselves; in the second there is an added authority generated through employment and professional safety. Each asks performers to engage with authority systems with incentive to comply and obey. Khoros success requires compliance and a unifying from the performers to produce the khoros entity and to be part of the drama at a certain quality. There were pressures on the participants here to adapt their agency and individuality to produce convincing, cogent performance. There is a social pressure from the other performers which creates cohesion between them.

This echoes the Beecroft performances in how participants noted the strength, resilience and safety drawn from a sense of group cohesion. There is also the literal and figurative judgemental gaze of the audience. The desire to do

*Common Fate—Objective, Agency and Essence* 111

well and satisfy their experience adds to this authoritative need. I have myself experienced this kind of demand performing within khoroi and directing. The most obvious and debilitating problem with a khoros is being seen as out of sync with the rest of the group or as an obvious individualised actor. This fractures the believability of performance and exposes the artifice of performance—it makes for poorly executed or 'bad' performance. Appearing anonymous within the khoros, again, can protect its members from, to return to Steinmetz et al, inhabiting their own subjectivity in exposed ways. This level of authority, however, is not necessarily imposed on the khoros performers as it was in the Beecroft examples (I will compare them shortly). It is entirely possible and probable that during the rehearsal processes the actors contributed towards the devising and construction of their work and thus the agentic authority that would later appear to govern much of their performance.

Shifting to the second level of authority is a motivating power relationship between performer-as-employee and employer/director. The financial return of performing as a job personally motivated the performers. They were all paid to perform these roles and were invested in producing 'good' work, or else future work could be compromised. Similarly, again, Heather Cassils noted the obedience she felt from the payment to be in *VB46*. Khoroi, and any paid aesthetic collective, gain an added authority from the employers and stakeholders of the theatres. Without commitment, the collectives deteriorate and the performers would appear poor at their jobs.

Performers in all cases modified themselves and behaved in ways that demonstrated the dynamic of authorities over their own individual agency. The adjustments made constitute a gradual, but certain shift in agency away from independence to being an agent for the authority. While this text is most concerned with, and henceforth dominantly discusses, the first types of authority, those linked to employment still hold importance with forthcoming consideration of subsumption in agentic states.

To elaborate, the khoros of *Chorus* were very noticeably concentrating on each other and on the position of the group within the narrative progress of their speech. Members were not just listening to *each other*, they were focussed on the *entire group* and its rhythm; it was a global focus. The authority of the khoros was attended to and the members were very sensitive to its thought pacing. It would not otherwise be possible to land on cue with overlapping dialogue nor would co-narration be possible without all members being in-tune with the khoros. A key adjustment is their attention and receptivity. They maximised their attention and receptivity to information and commands issuing from the authority—the performers were receptive and responsive to their khoros. The first act of obedience and conformity is in directed focus. Attention was given to the authority with heightened sensitivity.

Tangible acts of obedience and conformity come in performer behaviour and action; they behaved and acted in accordance with what they perceived to be what the khoros-authority needs. As above, during the devising and

112   *Precis*

rehearsing processes the performers may have had great agency in helping construct the khoros authorities and its action. In performance, though, we only see the khoros authority and how it governs the performers. They executed behaviour and actions as defined by the khoros authority. In a sense, the origin or trace of their individualistic contributions was lost in performance, with only the collective agency remaining.[28] In *Bakkhai*, for instance, the members had to appear like a mesmerised, somewhat distant and almost drugged people. They conducted all their actions with the same degree of energy, the same band of vocal pitch and volume, the same emotive character. In fact, this was both a success of that khoros (as they demonstrated uniformity) and its downfall as there were no dynamics—the khoros always seemed to be at relatively the same level and volume and that made them very two-dimensional from an audience perspective. Without a greater range of energy or emotive capacity the odes began to feel very formulaic and unimpactful. Compared to Euripides' text, this is not what is suggested or implicitly directed.

Compared to Beecroft's work, a sharp difference arises in what was expected and what is known to have happened in rehearsal. Whereas the khoroi were asked to perform within very acceptable pretend parameters, Beecroft's aesthetic collectives were asked to enter scenarios of real-time physical pain, humiliation, shame, and at times even degrading states of being. The definition of what is acceptable in terms of expectations is different there. The authority dynamic determines what is acceptable action. Milgram makes an emphatic point that

> [t]here is a propensity for people to accept definitions of action provided by legitimate authority [emphasis in the original]. That is, although the subject performs the action, [they] allow authority to define its meaning. It is this ideological abrogation to the authority that constitutes the principal cognitive basis of obedience.[29]

The khoros authorities constructed realities for the performers with an ideological meaning—and the members (subjects) accepted that. The resulting actions of the performers were valid and coordinated with those specific realities. So, the performers of *Bakkhai* were expected to do pretend ritualistic and altered state of mind behaviour, while the members of *VB46*, for instance, were asked to endure a physically painful, exposing and (as reported by Steinmetz et al.) exploitative and degrading experience. Both collectives, though, were performing their actions as they felt them valid and coordinated with the expectations of their performance situation.

Moreover, in such situations of authority performers will execute actions they might not entirely believe to be their own. In Beecroft's work, Steinmetz et al narrate how they abdicated responsibility for the meaning, image or consequences of their performance to Beecroft and focussed instead on how well

Common Fate—Objective, Agency and Essence    113

they were able to execute the directives. They reported how Beecroft represented an antagonising director who forced them into shameful and degrading positions. In other words, to them Beecroft was the second level of authority. However, as their discussion progresses it is much more the pressure of the performance situation itself (the first level of authority) that they felt compelling them onward. They admit the fee involved (again, a second level incentive) motivated them to suffer through the performance, but throughout they knew they still had the agency/power to withdraw from the performance.

Beyond professional obligations, their reporting clearly illustrates how they coped with the first level of authority—performance success and its audience. Their endurance and compliant actions in fact allowed that performance to be exactly what Beecroft wanted. The adjustment here is that the members shifted responsibility for their actions (and thoughts) to the collective authority; in Milgram's terms this is an agentic shift.

> The most far-reaching consequence of the agentic shift is that a [person] feels responsible *to* the authority directing [them] but feels no responsibility *for* the content of the actions that the authority prescribes [all emphasis in the original]. Morality does not disappear, but acquires a radically different focus: the subordinate person feels shame or pride depending on how adequately [they have] performed the actions called for by authority.[30]

Ownership of actions is removed from the self and displaced to the authority. In this way, the performer, as agent, acquires scope to do things they might never normally do, that they might even define as being beyond their ability or morality.

> For a [person] to feel responsible for [their] actions, [they] must sense that the behaviour has flowed from 'the self' [...] actions performed under command are, from the subject's view point [*sic*], virtually guiltless, however inhumane they [could] be. And it is toward authority that the subject turns for confirmation of [their] worth.[31]

Similarly, in the club. those in the dancing crowds often behaved in radically different ways to what they might normally consider appropriate. Returning to the Metropolis outing there were many members of the night gravitating towards a car on the first floor. The car is there as a carwash fantasy prop/set-piece for the normal stripping nights. On those nights people, I assume men, would sit there while female strippers conduct a carwash striptease fantasy. With no strippers on the Savage night different people would take on that role. In fact, almost everyone I saw walk past the prop had a turn at acting out a striptease on the car (male, female, trans—all types). This was not flattering. In fact, it appeared deeply misogynistic.[32] The actions and behaviour that people attempted revealed a humiliating interpretation of fantasy. Everyone

114 *Precis*

progressed from general 'fun' stripping enactment into the most degrading actions strippers are asked to enact: stereotypical poses, subservient or dominatrix roles, touching/sexualisation of the body/pornographic representations and so on. In other words, a full-on sexualised and base objectification of women. Beyond that area I witnessed many people touching themselves, acting out intercourse and masturbatory scenes, dancing in wild and at times garish ways, and overplaying stereotypical gender roles. It seemed that it was allowed and even expected behaviour based on the setting and its aesthetic design; that environment and crowd were assembled to do these very things—it was a special kind of catharsis. Moreover, as a gay club night there was a subversion of these actions as there was no true 'audience' for it. It was more of a pantomime of such themes (although I have seen similar actions elsewhere in gay culture being done for sexual excitement).

Membership in an aesthetic collective is subsumption in an agentic state. The members (subjects) in all these cases (khoroi, Beecroft installations, clubbing crowds) accepted collective authority, allowed that authority to craft the reality and meaning of their situations and became the collective authority's acting agent. Their worth was determined by their successful enacting of the collective authority's desires or requirements to which they seemed to feel a diminished sense of ownership.

Returning to *Chorus,* the performers were required to be in an agentic state to execute their various collective demands. The dramatic tension had to move in synchronicity; one could not step ahead of the collective affective level. They had to remain contained in the collective. All of this was to ensure that the aesthetic collective be consistent, uniform and, hence, entitative. They had to enter an agentic state and carry out the objectives of the aesthetic collective. The creation of this agentic state followed the same pattern as Milgram outlines: establish a perceivable authority, enter into and become a part of that authority system, attune to commands of the authority, accept the ideological definition of the situation, become an acting agent for the authority. They had to attune to the rhythm, flow, and affective state of the khoros. This was not without errors. They made errors, but only a few. For example, they stumbled over words in pronunciation, performers would interrupt each other too soon or a performer would forget the last word or two of a line. They quickly corrected or moved over these errors so that they did not interrupt or stall the pace and rhythm of the dialogue and action. To interrupt or stall the pace/rhythm would have ruptured them out of containment with the collective. Cohesion would have been broken interrupting the whole performance, and that is far worse for the group. The collective authority and agentic state were reliant on continuous rhythm and pace. It was the heart of what drove that performance. In overhearing and speaking with other audience members afterwards the agentic state was often referred to in different ways: they were 'in the zone', 'flowing', 'in tune', 'streamlined', 'psychic'. In this way, the agentic state of the khoros members was quite clear.

Common Fate—Objective, Agency and Essence   115

The success of the performance, and its technical brilliance, lay in the demand of that specific agentic state. The performers *had* to be in that state and sustain it. They then moved in the same direction at the same rate over time towards their goal. As an agentic body they demonstrated enunciated common fate.

Demonstration of collective agency creates a particularly strong impression of entitativity. In a study on whether 'human individuals [are] universally seen to be more real entities or more entitative than social groups'.[33] Kashima et al. explored how social beings (here, khoroi) are granted higher entitative status when they demonstrate agency or agentic action. 'Agentic social beings are then goal-directed, and therefore can carry out actions in pursuit of the common goals, responsible for their actions, and may potentially be praised or blamed for their actions'.[34] Kashima et al. go on to illustrate how perceived agency generates entitativity: '[a]gentic social beings that exhibit activities directed towards a common goal, that are under a common fate, and that consist of differentiated but interacting parts may be seen to be entitative'.[35] It was certainly the case that each of the khoroi in question were agentic and pursuing common goals, under a common fate. Elsewhere Kashima links entitativity and agency at least at the level of the perception of the collective.

> [G]roup entitativity is determined by the extent to which the group has an internal structure that makes group members interdependent of each other [...] a shared group goal, role differentiation, and coordination and interdependence among group members' activities [...] when a group is seen to be a social agent, it is seen to be entitative.[36]

With heightened entitativity, this khoros, as the other cases, demonstrated another, deeper entitative feature. The khoros of *Chorus* seemed to have some sort of underlying constitutive self from which this agentic authority seemed to originate. As an entity it seemed to have a sense of being, something that went beyond the artifice of it being performance.

This product of deep entitativity is *perceived essence*, following the research of Kashima.[37] In their joint article, Wagner et al. outline in brief the idea of essence and how social groups can be essentialised—attributed an essence.[38] Kashima elsewhere states that *essence* relates to a psychological understanding of realness.[39] He explains how

> a human aggregate [...] regarded as having a real existence or having high entitativity [...] may possess an essence, a set of properties that are unalterable and defining, that makes the social category what it is. To this extent, when a social category is believed to possess an immutable essence, it may be taken as evidence that people believe in its real existence.[40]

I noted earlier this sense of being and realness in *Chorus*. It is an observation of my perception of essence, or better yet, of me regarding it as having essence.

## 116   Precis

My experience of the khoros as imbued with essence is a conceptual elevating of it to/granting it a status of an entity structured and considered like a human being. In other words, I regard the khoros as human/being-like.

Khoroi, and any aesthetic collective, is a cultural product, designed and composed. In watching them, I projected/granted an essence into/onto them. This is above and beyond my recognition of essences in the individual members. The individual members of any khoros clearly have essences, but the khoros entity is something constructed—an artistic object. Moreover, that composite entity, and its perceived essence, has properties of transformation beyond those of individuals—it can be changed and manipulated in ways that we cannot do to an individual performer: by manipulating the individual members the whole can be shaped, dispersed, re-ordered, diffused, compacted, expanded, amplified, silenced. Yet, it still maintains its fundamental properties, entitativity and essence. In performance this is how the khoroi were treated, capitalising on the fact that they can cover different areas of the stage simultaneously, that their voice can come from multiple directions and with differing tones, timbres and textures at different times, that it can appear and disappear at will and that it can shape-shift between all sorts of characters and things. Individuals cannot do this (at least not without technological mediation). They and their essence are concretely localised and bound to their body and are not capable of such expansive transformative effects. Essence granting to a khoros allows projection of individual human features onto something that is not *a* human being. But where does this essence get placed or projected? It is not into any single performer; it is into all of them; but it is also into the collective space they occupy and charge in their performance. This discussion, and essentialisation more directly, form a large part of the next chapter. In the second half of this text, I will return to each of these types of aesthetic collectives, club crowds, Beecroft installations, khoroi, and draw out the notion of character and characterisation more. Now that a full picture of entitativity is crafted, I can begin to frame how collective entities, by nature of their many discrete and physically separated pieces, first include the space they occupy and the expansion of their effect about and around them. Second, that this makes them an atmospheric entity—something affective and more aeriform in nature.

## Notes

1 John Sallis, *Crossings; Nietzsche and the Space of Tragedy* (Chicago: The University of Chicago Press, 1991), pp. 89–90.
2 Sallis, p. 90.
3 Again, see Wilson (2000) for a comprehensive review.
4 Campbell, pp. 17–18.
5 Kashima, 'Culture, Communication', p. 266.
6 Kashima, 'Culture, Communication', p. 266.
7 Here I would refer the reader back to my comments on *essence* in the introduction, where I define the term within the framework of the literature on entitativity, which will be addressed later.

## Common Fate—Objective, Agency and Essence 117

8 Euripides, *Medea*; Euripides, *Bakkhai,* trans. and adapted by Anne Carson; Aeschylus, *Oresteia*; Thorpe, *Chorus*.

9 Elinor Fuchs, *The Death of Character; Perspectives on Theater After Modernism* (Bloomington and Indianapolis: Indiana University Press, 1996), p. 8.

10 Constantin Stanislavski is cited as the founder of western actor training in which the above description of acting is adopted. His method, which seeks believability in performance, asks performers to break characters down into psychological motivations, which come in a nesting of small to large steps, which he called units and objectives. See Stanislavski, *An Actor Prepares*.

11 Susan Leigh Foster, *Choreographing Empathy; Kinesthesia in Performance* (London and New York: Routledge, Taylor & Francis Group, 2011), p. 16.

12 Foster, p. 4.

13 Foster, p. 5.

14 Dominic Cavendish, '*Medea,* Almeida Theatre, Review: 'Fiercely Intelligent and at Times Ferocious" *The Telegraph* (1 October 2015), https://www.telegraph.co.uk/theatre/what-to-see/medea-almeida-theatre-review/[accessed on 16 August 2018].

15 Foster, p. 5.

16 Foster, p. 4.

17 Foster, p. 166.

18 This idea of entities that can *only* exist in their collective form certain merits further research. However, while linking very nicely with the core of this text, it is a slightly different project and thus lies outside the scope here.

19 Martin Heidegger, *History of the Concept of Time: Prolegomena,* trans. By Theodore Kisiel, in *The Phenomenology Reader,* ed. by Dermot Moran and Timothy Mooney (London and New York: Routledge, Taylor and Francis Group, 2002), p. 258.

20 Heidegger, *History of the Concept of Time,* p. 258.

21 By *post-dramatic,* I am referring to performance as theorised by Hans-Thies Lehmann in which theatre and drama in post-1960s work allow for a shift away from linear or narrative focussed performance towards performance in which the experience and effect of performance on an audience is foregrounded and the more crucial concern. See Lehmann, *Postdramatic Theatre*.

22 Stanley Milgram, *Obedience to Authority; An Experimental View* (London: Harper Perennial, 2009), p. 133.

23 Milgram, p. 143.

24 Milgram, p. 143.

25 Milgram, p. 144.

26 Milgram, p. 140.

27 Milgram, p. 141.

28 Here a parallel to deconstructionist thinking might be made, linking such erased origins to Jacques Derrida's concept of the trace. To follow such thinking, which is beyond my discussion here, I suggest referencing the following texts: Derrida, *Of Grammatology*; Derrida, *Writing and Difference*.

29 Milgram, p. 145.

30 Milgram, pp. 145–146.

31 Milgram, pp. 146–147.

32 See Comment 3 in Appendix C.

33 Kashima et al., 'Culture, Essentialism', p. 165.

34 Kashima et al., 'Culture, Essentialism', p. 150.

35 Kashima et al., 'Culture, Essentialism', p. 150.

36 Kashima, 'Culture, Communication', p. 267, here referencing the work of Hamilton and Sherman (1996); Lickel et al. (2000).

37 Essence as a concept has a large and voluminous theoretical literature. This spans many disciplines, such as (but by no means restricted to) psychology, phenomenology,

118  *Precis*

sociology, affect theory, performativity. Here I am working to frame my discussion firmly within definitions and uses of the term as drawn from the stated and cited primary literature on entitativity.

38 See again Wagner et al., 'Construction and Deconstruction'.
39 See Kashima, 'Culture, Essentialism'; Kashima, 'Communication and Essentialism'.
40 Kashima, 'Culture, Communication', pp. 265–266.

# Part II

# Precis

I return to Lakoff and Johnson's *Metaphors We Live By*[1] to address directly what has been drawn out through a reckoning of entitativity. Entitativity is a sensory-cognitive process. We ascribe entitativity to groups of things to make sense of them as contained and entity-like. The literature on it implies, sometimes just states, that we are better at understanding singular, individuated things; groups are more complex given their multiple parts and potentially dynamic movement. In its process, we conceptualise and then experience a group as being *like* a singular entity. This means there are underlying phenomenological and cognitive processes elaborating through metaphor here. It is not that we just ascribe entitativity as something novel to each instance of it, constantly repeating the same sensory-cognitive process in full. Instead, we ascribe it to groups by comparison to other things, other entities, with which we have existing understanding. We model them in our mind as being *as* or *like* something else so as to comprehend them in terms of something already known.

Initially, we can get at this through an examination of the language used to discuss aesthetic collectives. Lakoff and Johnson explore the underlying metaphors with which we conceptualise our world and our experiences. Through a close examination of the language we use to think and converse about things they note how we can understand the ways we think about, categorise and experience them. In observing how we structure thought in our language, underlying principles of conceptualisation and how we understand and categorise our existence emerge. While true of any sort, I am obviously focussing on human collectives. I borrow from them to demonstrate how collectives become treated as contained entities.

In chapter 1, for instance, I discussed the collective domain. While not a container in any real, concrete or physical sense, I conceptualised the domain as a container inside of which these aesthetic collectives are and outside of which they are not. Outside that container one can only perceive and objectify them. In my observations, I also noted and drew attention to how there is a perceptual field of sorts constituting these aesthetic collectives and their perceived boundaries. I intimated that this is demonstrative of how they are conceptualised like entitative objects and, through an analysis of entitativity, *like* human beings. Lakoff and Johnson detail that this is a general feature of

DOI: 10.4324/9781003205661-6

120   *Precis*

how we project our own sense of containment onto external things to mark them as separate and contained *like* ourselves:

> We are physical beings, bounded and set off from the rest of the world by the surface of our skins, and we experience the rest of the world as outside us. Each of us is a container, with a bounding surface and an in-out orientation. We project our own in-out orientation onto other physical objects that are bounded by surfaces. Thus we also view them as containers with an inside and an outside [...] even where there is no natural physical boundary that can be viewed as defining a container, we impose boundaries—marking off territory so that it has an inside and a bounding surface [...] There are few human instincts more basic than territoriality. And such defining of a territory, putting a boundary around it, is an act of quantification.[2]

The element of prägnanz assumes this entire line of thinking under its purview.

First, we metaphorically address these aesthetic collectives like objects, with boundaries and limits and conceive them as contained entities with insides and outsides. As I observed at the beginning of chapter 1 there are four natural dimensions to our categorisation for objects: *perceptual, motor activity, functional,* and *purposive.* In that chapter, I observed *motor activity* and *perceptual* dimensions. In terms of motor activity, I worked through how we can move around, about or within dancing crowds and that our physical relations to them contribute to how we conceptualise them. My physical placement relative to these dancing crowds could change my role (as participant within or audience without) and my ability to perceive them. Standing outside of them I was able to objectify them and perceive their edges; within them I could experience them in immersive capacities and thus feel engulfed in the experience of them. These physical relationships altered my perception of them. In and of itself the perceptual dimension was influenced by the different ways my sensory system was called upon to experience these events and those aesthetic collectives.

The notion of the collective domain itself illustrates how we like boundary edges and the ability to assess (quantify) contained volume. For Lakoff and Johnson this is a *container metaphor.* Container metaphors allow us to conceptualise things as containers with insides and outsides, with a surface whether real or imagined. Unbeknownst to me as I made them, I had an impulse or instinct to know *how much of them* (dancing crowds) I was perceiving and how they *stood different to others* present. Without such spatialising them I recognise, first, a difficulty in conceptualising them as some sort of thing, and second, to understand relationships between them and others. Once I could quantify these aesthetic collectives I could address other features of them.

Following this container metaphor, I observe how aesthetic collectives are some sort of thing that people are *inside of.* As containers they *contain* and *hold.* Thus, people become either members of the collective/penetrating audiences,

*Precis*  121

or they are outside of it and are not members/external audiences. Obviously, the aesthetic collective 'holds' the membership, but beyond the bodies of participants other 'things' exist within their limits. I reiterate that as performance the aesthetic collectives are encounters and events. Thus, they are also holding the event, the actions/activities of the collective and the products of its event, actions and activities.

> Activities in general are viewed metaphorically as SUBSTANCES and therefore as CONTAINERS [...] Thus, activities are viewed as containers for the actions and other activities that make them up. They are also viewed as containers for the energy and materials required for them and for their by-products, which may be viewed as *in* them or as *emerging from* them [all emphasis in the original].[3]

Examining language and thinking about proximity and prägnanz reveals these aesthetic collectives are conceptualised as containers. However, since indefinite in form and also as events, the encounter, activities and actions are also conceptualised within these metaphors of object-substances.

Second, beyond containers we treat aesthetic collectives *like* people. The language I used to refer to and address the aesthetic collective is *like* that for singular human agents, and it carried aspects of personality—recall Hall referring to the space surrounding them as filling with their 'personality'. Beyond spatialising them, beyond understanding them as some sort of object or thing, these aesthetic collectives are also *personified like* human beings. Personification is an effort to understand things through our own lens of existence. This point will become an elaborated feature of the following chapters, but so far, the conceptual dimension of similarity illustrates these points.

> [Discussion] involves [our] being able to superimpose the multidimensional structure of part of [one] concept [...] upon [a] corresponding structure [in our case, upon the structure aesthetic collectives]. Such multidimensional structures characterize *experiential gestalts*, which are ways of organizing experiences into *structured wholes* [...] Structuring our experiences in terms of such multidimensional gestalts is what makes our experience *coherent* [...] Understanding such multidimensional gestalts and the correlations between them is the key to understanding coherence in our experience [all emphasis in the original].[4]

Beecroft's work demonstrated this kind of categorical reference—e.g. fashion models, Aryan tropes in *VB45,* immigrant women in *VB48*. If we review *VB45,* the appearance of the participants created reference to Nazis, the Aryan image, mannequins, the synthetic and sexualised/dominatrices and so on. This moved beyond the physical into the gestural as well: stillness, contemplative, isolated, fatigued, strong and so on. This gets at how the members are *objectively similar*. Beecroft creates similarity between members' tangible properties

122    *Precis*

with objective similarisation: of the body, of its presentation, of its gestural capacity or potential, even of the perceived state of mind in the participants. Her artistic outcomes and processes work to create and display properties in the members that make them objectively the same.

Lakoff and Johnson state that this kind of similarity observes parallels between properties of the cases. 'Briefly, an objectivist would say that objects have the properties they have independently of anyone who experiences them; the objects are *objectively similar* [emphasis in the original] if they share those properties'.[5] The Beecroft installations create similarity between the properties of the participants within the aesthetic collectives. Mainly physical, gestural and agentic, she makes the properties between the members the same and shared. In this way, or on this level, she objectifies the women. The treatment of the members here as objects is entirely in keeping with Beecroft's own outlook on the work: 'the girls are my material'. Her work creates objectively similar objects out of the members. Zooming to the large scale, they then objectively similarise as a whole to her larger reference(s). This gestalt similarity is the strongest effect in her work. To behold her installations is to behold the collective effect—the category to which they all belong.

Confronting these kinds of images, though, complicates the validity of this objectivist perspective. As these aesthetic collectives emerge through perceptual processes they are experiential phenomena (there is no 'actual' or tangible subject in these aesthetic collectives, only one constructed in the mind). We can only conceive of 'the aesthetic collective' in her work through the recognition of members' similarity to the constructed entity of the aesthetic collective and through correlations we draw. In other words, through the experience of these works of art we create similarities through processes of metaphor.

This is at ends with the objectivist perspective.

> To an objectivist it would make no sense to speak of metaphors as '*creating* similarities [emphasis in original]', since that would require metaphors to be able to change the nature of the external world, bringing into existence objective similarities that did not previously exist.[6]

While we understand one member as being like another by experience of their similarised properties, we must experience the physical, gestural and agentic equalising that results in the collective to comprehend it, even if only through archival footage. Beecroft indeed creates types of objective similarity through, for instance, make-up, hair, costume and so on. However, these objective similarities do not entirely explain the category to which this relates, the entity of the aesthetic collective, which is a mental, metaphoric construction. Beecroft's works create interesting types of experiences as they foreground the similarisation process on the levels of both experiential reality and metaphoric concept. It is through experience of these installations that the conceptual structure of the entitative whole emerges and presents itself to us. Lakoff and

Johnson refer to this as *experiential similarity* and that it is different to objective similarity: 'things in the world do play a role in constraining our conceptual system. But they play this role *only through our experience of them* [emphasis in the original]'.[7] Beecroft's installations work with objective similarity, but the collectives are only real in a conceptual sense conditioned by metaphor, thus they require experiential similarity. '[T]he only similarities relevant to metaphor are *similarities as experienced by people* [emphasis in the original]'.[8] The experience of the membership creates experiential correlations between them and the conceptual whole of the collective—and these correlations are conditioned.

Continuing with Lakoff and Johnson:

> Our experiences will (1) differ from culture to culture and (2) may depend on our understanding one kind of experience in terms of another, that is, our experiences may be metaphorical in nature. Such experiences determine the categories of our conceptual system. And properties and similarities, we maintain, exist and can be experienced only relative to a conceptual system.[9]

This *experiential similarity*, for example, is seen in *VB45* correlating to the categories of S&M fetishism, the dominatrix and Aryanism/Nazis. Thus, viewing *VB45* and its enacted power dynamics, rigid conformity, harsh transformation of self and durational effort/effect casts experiential similarity on the membership, as being similar to those same dimensions of experience of the Aryan Nazi or dominatrix. *VB45* is experientially similar to a dominatrix experience—not identical to or congruent with, only similar. To be clear, my own language has drawn similarity between experiences to help define, categorise and relate those experiences naturally. I have not intentionally designed my language and comparative description to illustrate these similarities or force my point.

Chapters 1 and 2 established *perceptual* and *motor* dimensions of categorisation and metaphor. I have established how with groups we imagine them as bounded and contained, and thus treat them like objects or substances.

> Once we can identify our experiences as entities or substances, we can refer to them, categorize them, group them, and quantify them—and, by this means, reason about them [...] Human purposes typically require us to impose artificial boundaries that make physical phenomena discrete just as we are: entities bounded by a surface.[10]

The *functional* and *purposive* dimensions of categorisation are followed in chapter 3 Audiences to khoros illustrated examples of aesthetic collectives drawn from theatre contexts and their 'real world' references, but indeed also experience those references as aspects of theatrical characters with ontological

## 124   *Precis*

grounding. The functional and purposive, which will feature again in the next chapters, emerged through detailing of common fate. We recognise common fate by ascribing character and granting essence, by projecting human features onto something non-human, at least not an individual. This is *personification*. Lakoff and Johnson note this is as a type of ontological metaphor.

Ontological metaphor compares experiences and phenomena to entities so as to make them easier to understand as something like a being with some sort of living existence beyond simple matter. Personification is yet another step in a process of understanding these instances of aesthetic collectives, constituting a move in conceptualising them as object or substance entities as also entities like humans. '[W]here the physical object is further specified as being a person. This allows us to comprehend a wide variety of experiences with nonhuman entities in terms of human motivations, characteristics, and activities'.[11] It might seem obvious that this is the case since there are human beings composing a khoros (or any aesthetic collective), but a khoros personifies human dimensions in its collective presence and behaviour. Khoroi, and more generally aesthetic collectives, are not *a* human being. Neither are they just the sum of the human parts that make them. They are a thing above and beyond those parts.

Khoroi demonstrate motivation in their actions and, as established earlier, this indicates a psychological dimension to them. This just as easily applies to clubbing crowds and Beecroft installations, just in different ways. We conceptualise in them intellect of some sort, motivations, agency and impulses. These are not things that apply to non-living and especially non-human entities. We are personifying them. The personification of an aesthetic collective will allow us two very important conceptualisations. 'It not only gives us a very specific way of thinking about [them] but also a way of acting toward [them]'.[12] Through personification the audience to aesthetic collectives can make the conceptual move necessary to understand them in our own human terms—'to make sense of phenomena in the world in human terms—terms that we can understand on the basis of our own motivations, goals, actions and characteristics'.[13] Personification structures ontological thought about them in our own terms.

I have been discussing the cases in terms of being *like* objects or *like* subjects or even *like* things. The entitative structures of these examples of aesthetic collectives are conceptualised in human terms, with human properties and as having the ontological status of human beings. As performance works, they are also very much experiences. Moving forward these ontological issues will become a primary, yet underlying, concern in the second part of this text. Having detailed in these three chapters how entitativity is established, perceived and granted to aesthetic collectives through these sampled cases my observations and analysis will now move more towards ontological concerns.

I have examined the *perceptual* and *motor activity* dimensions; next, I will address the *functional* and *purposive* dimensions fully. So,

*Precis*  125

[o]ur categories for kinds of objects [*perceptual, motor activity, functional, purposive*] are thus gestalts with at least these natural dimensions [...] Similarly, there are natural dimensions in terms of which we categorize events, activities, and other experiences as structured wholes [...] these natural dimensions include *participants, parts, stages, linear sequence, purpose,* and *causation.*[14]

At this point, it is worth stopping to reflect on how elements of discussion fall within these categoric dimensions.

Moreover, we do not just encounter and acknowledge entitativity in and of itself. Entitativity carries with it an effect on us. Encountering an entitative collective creates questions, feelings and reactions. We question what we are perceiving, whether it poses threat and we have affective reactions to it. Encountering an aesthetic collective, its agency and its effect (both on those involved and those watching) I will move to outline as something inter-subjective, affective and behaves more like a gaseous thing than the solid bodies of those who make it up. The next chapters will consider these dimensions and progress to consider how encounters and experiences with aesthetic collectives are atmospheric in nature—that is, they are affective experiences of co-presence with space and others. Indeed, the entitativity of aesthetic collectives will come to equate to atmosphere.

# 4 Character and Contagion

Aesthetic collectives have two overt *functional* and *purposive* dimensions: that of character and that of mood. They are personified as characters and they characterise the performance experience—and by characterise, I mean they transmit and share mood and affect via a process of contagion. They spread moods; and moods are a kind of collective affect. To discuss this I will call on affect theory which has a very expansive and multi-dimensional literature. However, for the purposes here I am specifically interested in the collective experience of affect and the transmission of affect in groups in aesthetic contexts. While very interesting, I will not be addressing the physiological or internal manifestations of affect nor using much of the research on specific affects. Restrained to aesthetic contexts, I largely adhere to discussions of mood, affect transmission and the affective toning of experiences as it happens within a theory of atmospheres.

*Contagion,* similarly, has a rich history and literature and is a thrilling notion. I am drawing and extending it as a term from Brennan, who, as discussed in chapter 1, defines it out of older notions of crowd psychology and behaviour as contagious, largely following Gustave Le Bon, William McDougall, Sigmund Freud and Wilfred Bion. As started in chapter 1, when considering moods, affects and how they move and spread through contagion I see them as a field property, something connate with atmosphere. They are like substances or gases that move betwixt and between people, through the air separating us. Once encountered, affective substances converge us on affective paths—moving from us to others, or from others to us.

These affective paths might otherwise be denoted by their *character* or *characterising*. Aesthetic collectives exist in both noun and verb form of character. As a noun or property, *character* serves narrative functions, such as dramatic roles, narrators and commentators as noted most obviously with khoroi. In verb form, aesthetic collectives function to give character to performance experiences, to *characterise* it. Like the environment or scenography, aesthetic collectives characterise experiences through moods, feelings and emotional contexts. At times, they even become scenery or background. They embody both types of character, as role as well as characterising the experience. I am going to explore these two notions further in this chapter and move through

DOI: 10.4324/9781003205661-7

128    *Precis*

four entailed key ideas: character as role and dramatis personae; essence and essentialisation; characterisation, characterising, mood; contagion. To begin, I examine character role and return to the khoroi examples to illustrate.

## *Character* as Roles and Dramatis Personae

*Character* as a role or dramatis personae is the personification of a human element on stage modelled after the human being with psychological and social background. The khoros examples most clearly demonstrate this kind of character. Khoroi are often narrators or role-based characters within the dramas they occupy (scripted or implied). This is especially the case with theatre wherein a scripted narrative often takes place.

There are two different dramaturgical notions of character which I want to differentiate clearly before addressing. *Character* notes the Aristotelian sense of character, the human perspectival element within a performance. These characters stand-in, to return to Elinor Fuchs, for a lived human perspective within the situation of the performance. The khoros of *Medea* stood in as representatives of 'Islington-ite yummy mummies—trading gossip, stuck in materialist clichés, jouncing toy babies up and down, coloured shawls over their shoulders in a parody of classicism'.[15] Through a close selection of attributes and a paring down to essential elements they became a theatrical analogue of this social figure. They offered a perspective from, and on, a recognisable human element. In other words, they represented human beings, not abstractions of human features or thoughts. On-stage, this notion of character offers a human being experiencing and moving through the action and circumstances, even if in a distorted reality or fantasy setting.

Differently, in the second act, they functioned as characterising elements. They became dancing illustrations of the mood of the performance, as abstractions of a human experience or thought. They broke from the figurative form, 'yummy mummies', into an element *of* human experience, not *the* human element. This is the second notion of character. No longer tied to a recognisable human role, in the second half of the performance they became representations of human feelings. They departed from the concrete or realistic human beings to be an illustrative depiction of a human experience. In this sense, we break from 'the idea of autonomous character […] [where] something else, some other "element" […] occup[ies] the dramaturgical center and carr[ies] the burden of narrative […] that lift[s] the spectator's focus from character to the relationship between levels of dramaturgy'.[16] With their shift from characters-as-roles to characters-as–illustrative-elements they became something hybrid between Aristotle's notions of character and spectacle, and possibly even thought. '[N]o longer in a theater of character, the human figure is no longer the single, perspectival 'point' of stage performance'.[17] This khoros became an intersection of elements of drama. As the performance moved towards its conclusion they became so moved away from a recognisable human element that they turned entirely into dancing abstractions,

*Character and Contagion*  129

only personifying the emotion of the narrative/music and no longer holding any semblance of their earlier character roles. This second notion of character is *characterisation*, which I separately address later.

Khoroi have collective characters (as roles); collective identities that signal recognisable human elements. Khoroi often also have moments when the individual voices of actors are more pronounced. That is, the audience is shown separate individual characters within and composing the khoroi. In *Medea* this happened in their first ode, when the women broke out of their collective state and began to gossip as individuals. Each revealed more personal experiences of motherhood: one overly tired, one like an automaton Stepford wife, one like the popular community ring-leader, all were afraid to admit their own parental struggles. In *Oresteia* this happened in the first ode of *Agamemnon* when they discussed their experience of the long war with Troy; during the second ode of *Choëphori* it happened when they contemplated their revenge strategy, each inputting their own thoughts and feelings. In *Bakkhai* it happened during a middle ode when each bacchant dreamed of the joys of being back in the sacred woods, pining for their different types of joy there. *Chorus* fluctuated in and out of a sense of its members being very collective in their voyeuristic drive while very individual and unique in their biographical profiles. In that production this fluctuation was constant. These performances all used khoros to show the audience both recognisable human beings thinking, feeling and acting, and they were showing a collective body, a demographic. I want to draw attention to how this notion of character is present in aesthetic collectives. I do not intend to review all the various transformations and theoretical perspectives of character here. Indeed Fuchs adroitly traces a developmental history of the notion in classical tragedy, Elizabethan drama, Romanticism and the late 19th century, the modern and postmodern eras.

The nestling of individual characters within a khoros' totality is a feature that occurs consistently through extant Greek tragedy. It is a directorial and textual element. Textually, khoroi typically have a moment in an ode when the collective character (old men, slave women, ocean nymphs, possessed women and so on) shifts to reveal the multiplicity of individual character voices creating the collective. Like considering the khoros as a rope, during these moments the audience focuses on its compositional cords and threads. One of the most stunning and emotionally moving examples of this is in Euripides' *Hecuba*.[18] Made of the surviving women of Troy gathered together on the days after the fall of Troy this khoros is now war slaves of the victorious Greek army sailing away to Greece. The women come from many different walks of life in Troy. Some palace servants, some slaves, some married to free men of the city and so on. They represent the full range of what constituted 'woman' in Troy. None are royal women—those are the named, individualised characters in the episodes. The khoros operates as one firm collective voice and character, but during the third stasimon ode they retell the night of the horse and sacking of Troy.

130    *Precis*

The ode begins with the khoros speaking in singular first person: 'O Ilium! O my country [...] O Ilium,/whose ways I shall not walk again!'[19] Then, they break into several potential first-person points of view, separating themselves into individual voices recounting their separate personal experiences that night:

> Midnight my ruin began.
> Supper was over, sweet sleep drifting down,
> after songs and dances and sacrifice
> my husband lay in our chamber,
> his spear on its peg.
> He was not watching
> for Greek sailors
> to come walking into Troy.
> I was doing my hair,
> I was binding my hair,
> staring down into the bottomless lake of my mirror
> before I fell into bed—
> a scream cut the town,
> a roar swept the street:
> [...]
> I left my bed in just a robe
> like a Spartan girl
> to supplicate holy Artemis. Useless! Sorrow!
> I saw my husband killed.
> They drove me down
> to the salt sea.
> Then I looked back as the ship set sail,
> pulling me further and further from Troy
> and I fainted away.[20]

This could be read and performed as a continued single voice, but the narrative thread suggests plural and differing tales ('my husband' and 'I fell into bed' suggest isolated people). All the women would not be conducting the same actions in the night at the same time but would have variant activities. In any case, I read it as narrowing to the individual level, offering an emotional and voyeuristic glimpse into the quiet and intimate bedrooms of individuals in the last few moments before 'a scream' and 'a roar' initiate their armageddon.

As characters within the ongoing drama, the khoros here exhibits personal identity and a fractal voice connected to the thematic woe of the play. The ode may be performed as one collective voice, but it more suits a staggered co-narration of individual voices. That offers a chance to make the khoros more relatable and recognisable. In other words, by exposing the individual character warp and weft of the khoros it foregrounds the social body, with a common fate, that the khoros emblemises. In narrating individual experiences, the khoros opens to the audience a deeply intimate, albeit brief and finite,

*Character and Contagion*   131

glimpse into their plots and backstories. Still, though, as anonymous voices that could represent or be that of any of their number. Consequently, both microcosmic and macrocosmic pathos are created for the audience through these human elements.

Khoroi also serve as specific character roles against or with whom the individualised, episodic actors can act. In performance, khoroi operate in the same dramaturgical world, and thus style, as the episodic characters, but they also exist in other styles not shared by those characters. They depart into their own dramatic realities. For instance, the Bakkhai of *Bakkhai* sang, moved, and behaved with self-generated music like entranced, ecstatic and ritualistic celebrants; the furies of *The Eumenides* became preternatural entities complete with jerky, dubstep-dance-like movements and ghastly visual appearance. These khoroi had character roles in the episodes, but during their odes also moved in and out of those roles or even in-between.

Aesthetic collectives also move to a different literary level to the drama: they become narrators. As narrators they relay, account and comment on the performance and communicate directly with audiences. *Chorus*, for example, was entirely a four-person narration. The story of the episodic characters was taking place elsewhere, unseen. The khoros, though, recounted their experience of that story as gleaned from the internet. They narrated their internet trolling, investigation and voyeurism of Agamemnon, Klytemnestra and Iphigenia. The whole performance was in effect a large voyeuristic narration. *Bakkhai* had a similar type of narration. The khoros odes slipped between commenting on/reacting to what was happening in the episodes around them and narrating mythos stories of Dionysos. For example, in their parados (entrance ode) the khoros narrated over several stanzas the twice birth of Dionysos, giving clear contextual history to the audience of who Dionysos is and how he is special as a god:

> Bromios
> the one whose
> mother shimmered into fire
> at the moment of his birth
> when Zeus' lightning bolt blew her apart
> And Zeus sewed the infant into his own thigh
> with golden stitches,
> secret and safe
> until the appointed time.
> Then he was born
> a god
> with horns on his head
> and snakes in his hair –
> that's why
> the Bakkhai
> like to play with wild things even now.[21]

132    *Precis*

Coupling the immediate action of their entering the town, they necessarily tell this story to explain to the audience Dionysos' origins. An ancient Athenian audience would know this expository information, as well as other versions. In narrating this information, the khoros defines the background context for the play, and introduces and sets the performance tone. They later also narrate to comment upon other characters and actors within the same performance. After Pentheus jails Dionysos the khoros (who, under the trance of Dionysos, see as a priest) openly summarises what is happening before imploring their god to help.[22] They narrate what is happening, pray to god and comment on/judge Pentheus.

This occurs throughout Euripides' text as well as in odes in other performances. Reviewing the performances and their texts further finds khoroi slipping in and out of the continuities of the dramas as well and directly addressing the audience. In addressing the audience, they exist as another type of character role, something between audience and performance. They even become audiences themselves. Indeed, in this capacity a unique doubling occurs on-stage, where khoroi stand-in for the witnessing audience members themselves. As an audience to the tragedy, they mimic the audience, creating a reflective relationship. This happens throughout *Bakkhai*, but nowhere more comprehensively (or chillingly) as in the final lines. At that point, the khoros is watching the final moments of each named character. They witness their suffering and Dionysos' apotheosis. They duplicate the audience on-stage. Then, in an eerie conflation of all their character roles the khoros not only directly addresses the audience, but further unveil themselves as a theatrical device by breaking the fourth wall and becoming an audience narrator:

> Many are the forms of the *daimonic*
> and many the surprises wrought by gods.
> What seemed likely did not happen.
> But for the unexpected a god found a way.
> That's how this went
> today.[23]

Translators variously interpret this final statement. In William Arrowsmith's translation, the final line is 'So ends the play'.[24] Even more memorable is Colin Teevan's translation in which the khoros simply says, 'Turn out the lights'.[25] Such statements not only display their role changing between character, narrator and audience, but here they even step one further role away, becoming the production crew, the voice of a director/stage manager or even, in ancient Athens, the institution of the khoregia itself.[26]

This pluri-use of khoroi sees them able to operate plastically as first, second and third person narrators depending on authorial and directorial hands. They can even change between these different voices within the performance with no need to explain, which frequently happens in extant Greek tragedies. Capable of breaking from the relationship of audience and performance, they change the nature of the performance experience out of a dyadic structure into a multi-modal one. Using related or emotively similar scenes drawn from mythos, khoroi create a backdrop to the direct action of the play, as in the above recounting of the birth of Dionysos in the *Bakkhai*. The khoroi will lapse into direct address to the audience, pose questions of ethics and morality or offer ruminations on human or divine experiences. As such, they open up the drama beyond the plot of the episodes and take the audience into a realm of narrative on par with philosophical or spiritual thought—as a seminar of ethics/morals.

Beyond plot-based/character roles aesthetic collectives also stand in as static or background elements—as the watchful eyes of society or the ever-present power of a god. In a separate example, I attended *As You Like It* at the National Theatre in London in October 2015.[27] In that performance there were several aesthetic collectives on-stage. In the second through fifth acts they largely operated as two separate collectives: an ambient sound producing collective suspended above the stage in swings as well as in opera boxes above and to the sides of the stage; and as a large collective of woodland creatures—most notably as a highly comedic flock of sheep that ambled about the stage during the shepherds' scenes. These collectives served purely scenographic purposes, creating scenery and ambient soundscape. Their impact was strong. They were easily the most impressive and entrancing element on the stage and, at least as the sheep, stole the show. As Susannah Clapp wrote in The Guardian,

> That thicket is not empty. Actors and singers perch in it, their mouths and hands the instruments for Carolyn Downing's nature soundscape. They whir, whistle, flap and chudder. Orlando Gough's music is a melancholy swell. This is one of the best uses of sound that I have ever heard in the theatre. Not merely atmospheric but informative [...] Even his flock is given a glorious moment. The cast crawl on to the stage in Aran sweaters, nudging and nuzzling, ruminating like philosophers, butting like lovers, earning themselves a place at the curtain call.[28]

The audience reaction to the soundscape and their laughter during that particular sheep scene were palpably two of the three strongest reactions to the entire performance.[29] Particularly when they started in act two and at the final moments before the interval when, as a flock of birds, they absconded in a flurry. Mimicking fauna in the wild, these collectives were effective enough to suggest the idea of what they were embodying, but not so realistic as to lose track of the fact that they were human beings. I would argue this was why the sheep were so funny; they were recognisably people in woolly jumpers ridiculously acting like sheep.

134    *Precis*

In Aristotelian terms their role as scenery or aspects of the environment made them elements of spectacle or thought (in the sense of thought being interpreted like theme or tone). I have witnessed this use of aesthetic collectives in several performances. In such cases, they are frequently silent and still backdrops for and to whom the drama plays. This straddles the two notions of character that I am working. They worked as a surrounding element that directed focus to the central drama and created situational circumstance for that drama in their presence. They are characters, but not human characters. Moreover, the function here is neither to stand in for a human element nor to give a human perspectival point (although as an audience we do personify human features to them). Rather, they were atmospheric elements. Still grounded in a recognisable set of characters, they are, however, working as background, scenery, something illustrative or suggestive. This hybridisation shifts between inhabiting character roles that stand in for human elements and being a spectacle element that contributes to the circumstances, environment or felt theme of a performance.

To summarise, the notion of character as roles allows audiences to conceive of aesthetic collectives like human entities. We personify them with human qualities and that allows an intersubjective experience with them. Return to the example of the khoros of ghastly furies from *Eumenides*. That collective had a singular character with singular objectives, an identity and various capacities like a subject: a sense of agency, seeming intentionality, choice-making capacity, even a sense of consciousness and thought. Considering them as *a* totality and with *a* character means they can be understood and addressed in singular terms. Ipso facto they may be conceptualised with entity status like a human being and thus with subject-like status. Recall, collectives are not a subject as such, these properties of subjectivity are *perceived*, not actual or concrete. Character roles and personification exudes underlying properties that suggest subjectivity that audiences understand or assume as being there. This is suggestive of another dimension to these examples that supersedes their physical properties, some sense of a motivating force that exists independent of the individual members. This goes beyond just agency to subjectivity.

This conceptual creation of a collective subjectivity is a belief that something like a conscious subject is there. The collective subjectivity distributes to the component members. On some level the totality is the active subject, influencing or controlling its members. This sense of active subject I frame as a collective character *essence*. In encountering them, my intersubjective experience is with their *essence*. To analyse this, the encounter of *essence* and what it denotes, I return to the literature on entitativity and extend a notion introduced but not fully pursued in the last part of chapter 3, that of *essentialisation*.

## Essence and Essentialisation

Essentialisation, the thought-based granting of an essence to an entity, completes the entitativity process by allowing conceptualisation of these totalities

*Character and Contagion*  135

like human subjects, which in turn allows us an intersubjective experience. If we take the example of the khoros of *Eumenides* we, the audience, treated that totality as a character having fundamental drives, motivations, perspectives, feelings and agency. They were driven to pursue and exact revenge on Orestes for murdering his mother Klytemnestra. Injustice and a primal hatred motivated them. We as an audience conceptualised them, a subject-like group, as having these properties and being like a subject. Their drives, motivations, perspectives, feelings and agency, though, came from some deep and internal part of this perceived subjectivity. Ontologically, these are part of the metaphysical core of an entity—their being or self.[30] This part of a subject is their *essence*. We treat social entities *as though* they have an essence. I emphasise these points to draw attention to how they are noematic—that is they are an object of thought, not of tangible actuality.[31] At the end of Part 1, discussion introduced work conducted (collaboratively, in part or in whole) by social scientist Yoshihisa Kashima. Here I will draw on research Kashima has co/authored to explain how essentialisation happens, some of its limits and the consequences it has.

Audiences to and members of aesthetic collectives personify the collectives. Personification, as explored, results in the notion of character-as-role, a standing-in for a human element. In some instances that personification was quite humanising. Personifications 'are extensions of ontological metaphors and [...] they allow us to make sense of phenomena in the world in human terms—terms that we can understand on the basis of our own motivations, goals, actions, and characteristics'.[32] In other cases, personifying is far more skeletal and does not fully form characters as roles. We instead imbue totalities with human properties. Here, we can think of the clubbing crowds that 'acted' with 'drives', 'impulses' or 'characteristics'. They had human-like properties that both the collectives and their audiences experienced, but they did not stand in for any human element. Their collective presence, however, indicated an *interiority* from which this presence came and emanated. Their presence established in space a sense of inhabitation or affective life. In encountering them, a distributed presence to the collectives felt alive and co-present. This was not the presence of the individual participants themselves. Personification is the activity that allows us to grant human properties to the totalities, which were supra-human things.

The personifying of the *Eumenides'* khoros in emotional (angry, vengeful, cruel, cold, unrelenting), cognitive (they could think and reason) and psychological ways (they could be flattered, appeased, they had feelings and they could be affected by other characters) created strong human characteristics. The totality was inhabiting space and emanating presence. This is *essence*—an inner reality and seat of the self in a living thing. Gestalt phenomena, though, neither have an inner psycho-cognitive centre for this essence nor are composites of the essences of the members. There is a sense of a *singular being* or *singular essence* here that extends/distributes over the component members.

136   *Precis*

We, audience and participants, grant the totality an understood essence and, entailed with that process, the potential for an intersubjective experience.

The essence of the *Eumenides* khoros was supported by tangible elements of identity that were performed. These included things such as dress type, hairstyle, make-up, specialised movement and action, vocal style, speech patterns, objectives and intentions. In general, tangible things that we perceive or actions/behaviour we witness. These identity elements distinguished them as unique or discrete. They develop the image of their character and promote the sense of essence motivating and driving them. Wagner et al. detail how this is a process called an *identity project*.[33] They assert essence is not graspable, only apprehended through externally communicated aspects of the subject. In other words, essence is hidden away within the private, internal world of the subject and recognised through tangible, perceivable or concrete external projections. Those external projections we identify, composite and conceptualise into a larger whole that we call *identity*. It is through perception of the Erinyes' identity that I could acknowledge and gradually understand their essence. While we can perceive it is, however, their essence that we *feel* in encountering them, as their presence.

Taking the khoros of *Agamemnon*, their identity was characterised by many tangible features: their sex (male and female), gender (neutered male/female), sexuality (asexual), race (Argive Greek), religion (ancient Greek), nationality (Argive), political stance (conservative and wary), hair colour (dark, grey), education (educated and wise) and so on. Many were visible and chosen by the costume and make-up/hair designers. Some of them were implicit in the text. Some emerged from their performed behaviour or disposition. For instance, the nationality of the khoros was one of their key identity characteristics. They are the old men of Argos (in the performance they were de-gendered men and women combined). Their identity as older Argives defines them within the context of the text. They are too old to have fought in the Trojan war and thus sat out the most heroic and awful war of Greek mythos. This defines them and is crucial to their identity. It colours their experience of the war and their political/ personal position to it. Feeling cheated of the honour of the war they were also embittered by its cost (financial and of life) and are conflicted about the cause of the war. All these identity features contribute to a sense of their essence, but none *were* their essence. As they performed, they revealed further identity elements. For example, their dispositions and general mood became clear: dour, despondent, tired, fatigued and politically worn out by the length of the war. They were also distrusting of their Queen, Klytemnestra, ruling in Agamemnon's absence. All this identity was performatively grasped. All of it helps draw a larger picture of them as a character and what is motivating and driving them as well as their needs, wants and desires. The work of identity here helped us, as audience, conceptualise their character essence.

Furthermore, our belief in their essence only existed if the members of the khoros were willing to undergo the work involved in creating and maintaining their identity in aesthetically convincing and consistent ways. The khoros' essence had to be maintained through this identity work or the experience would have ruptured and grounded us and the performers back in the reality of the auditorium. Wagner et al. imply that the identity project is performed by the membership as an *active* piece of work. They outline that '[s]ocial groups [like these collectives] exist as long as there are members willing to engage in the labour of identity construction and identity confirmation'.[34] As labour there must be members constructing that identity, confirming it and maintaining the work involved. What constitutes that work depends on the identity attribute(s) in play. So, for the khoros, part of the work included conscious manipulation of their performance. Labour in their appearance and physical movement, for instance, had to fit the category of 'Argive elder' and the aesthetic dictated by the production team. In this production that included visuals dominated by grey colours, references to 40s and 50s business fashion, and props that accompany city workers (suitcases, umbrellas, newspapers). They also had to move in a more rigid, stiff fashion. To be an Argive, they needed to craft and maintain this appearance and this type of movement in a collectively cohesive way—they needed to work at it.

The performers succeeded in part as they were all working at the same professional level to achieve their performance. If they had not had equal dedication they would have appeared broken, non-cohesive or not well characterised. While I cannot speak to the effect this had on those performers, we can look at the testimony from Heather Cassils and Julia Steinmetz from their work in *VB46* for confirmation. Their description of everyone working equally hard at that performance is pervaded by feelings they outlined as fatigue from the strain of the work. Once performing for audience they were also highly bonded and drawn together by the work involved in constructing the identity prescribed for them.

Such labour has consequences for participants.

> Constructing and enacting identity has the implicit purpose of strengthening the bonds between a group's members as well as to let the group appear as an entity with a reason to exist, an ideology, an agenda, and a series of distinguishing attributes.[35]

In *VB46* there was an assumed imperative to remain hard-working in order to feel protection within the group. Their collectivity, as I stated in chapter 2, shielded them from personalised attention and objectification. Working at these identity performative elements formulated the group as having strong common fate and a real sense of essence to their collective. To echo Wagner et al., the activity of their identity project drew the members together and had consequences of unifying the internal membership as well as projecting external images of cohesion. The identity of *VB46* projected outward to the external world and its construction signalled at least the *sense* of an essence to the totality.

Audiences and performers have different access to the essences of these aesthetic collectives. The testimonial from the members of *VB46* shows them

138    *Precis*

believing themselves to be something different to what the audience perceived. Both felt similar emotional tones (angry, powerful, strong), but the experience of the audience reads differently, not least because the audiences were contemplating meaning in the work. Participating performers differently access the essence of their aesthetic collective by living or enacting it. They feel the group essence but also feel it as their essence—they are entangled with it. This can lead to differentials between what they believe themselves to be and what the outside audience believes them to be.

The work of identity projects also requires internal interaction and communication—the members need to be harmonised through practice. *VB46* included a severe rehearsal practice lasting two full days, physical transformation of the bodies and extremely specific yet contentless instructions for the task of the work. Similarly, the khoroi had costumes, movement tasks, dance tasks, voice and song tasks, and a variety of practices to keep themselves in unison and at the same tempo. The clubbing crowds had dance-based activities that involved them adopting and assimilating the rhythms, styles and moods of the music so that they could achieve collective motor activity. In each the groups generated specific and recognisable patterns; the way they interacted became unique to their group. They necessarily developed internal systems of communication, and audiences perceive this, reading it as synchronicity and internal harmony. Highlighting research by Liu and Hilton, Wagner et al. note how

> [g]roups are maintained as a social unit by group specific interaction patterns [...] These interaction and communication patterns as well as occasional rituals reflect group specific representations that frequently take the form of an ideological foundation of the group's reason of existence (Liu & Hilton, 2005).[36]

The collectives became entitative and cohesive units through their collaborative labour directed at tasks and their contingent interaction and communication. This in turn led to more successful identity projects and thus a stronger sense of essence.

> The purpose is to appeal to a certain notion of essence: their standing as a group is bolstered if they are successful in creating the impression of a shared group-specific essence [...] the result of identity projects is the same for members and non-members: representing the group as an intended entity with a sense of unity and a shared background to oneself and to others.[37]

On the other hand, not working at the identity project of a collective can lead to isolation and individuation. The Carwash in clubbing experience in 2015 (chapter 1) is a good instance where I did not work at the labour of the identity project. The consequence of this for me was deep alienation and

*Character and Contagion* 139

isolation. The participants were encouraged to dress and adorn themselves with disco paraphernalia and general fancy dress props. They were also tasked with dancing and having 'fun'. They were working at being members of that dancing crowd in these ways. I was not. I felt absolutely separate and differentiated from them, and consequently I could not motivate myself to enter that dancing crowd or participate. I could not even motivate myself to be physically within their collective domain. Refusal to work at that identity project prevented me from engaging with the essence of that aesthetic collective and it became an obstacle for me engaging with it or even fully encountering it except from a scrutinising remove. I was distant from this group and its essence, was not interacting and could not communicate with the other attendants in any meaningful way and it felt terrible. They had developed a set of dance practices, in-jokes, ways of behaving and knowledge of each other to which I had no access nor any ability to express.

This internal interaction and communication with aesthetic collectives is also critical to their success. Specific interactions and communication practices allow them to perform cohesively. Some are tacit and covert, some obvious and overt. How well the members can coordinate, orientate and unify contributes directly to the relative success of the performance. In *Oresteia,* one khoros member would lead or initiate the khoroi in the action/behaviour for each ode of each play. This was not overt, however, and that leading role switched from ode to ode. In that way, it was not clear to the audience that the khoros was being led or that there was a method to how they coordinated themselves. In some of the other cases these practices were more explicit. *Chorus* required clear cueing mechanism to establish rhythm, pattern and consistency in their dialogue and physical movements. I noticed, for instance, that when one member dropped a line the rest allowed not more than one second before the next speaker interjected and continued the flow (this happened only a few times). Also, their movements from one quadrant to the other had a pattern. They always moved to the same side of each other and in the same order so that they did not collide. It brought to mind Samuel Beckett's *Quad* in which four performers walk the sides and cross-diagonals of a square simultaneously. The task being perfect cohesion and creating a thrilling moment crossing the centre where a collision looks probably, but is always narrowly avoided. In both plays, this pattern is exposed to the audience. In *Chorus* there were clear signals and indications of when the performers were ready and how quickly they should move. This gave the impression that they were working/attending to each other and consequently that the performance was like a machine that ran itself. Differently, in the Beecroft installations the aesthetic collectives were explicitly commanded not to communicate. As isolated and silent members, their interaction was in and of itself a form of communication. Maintaining their silence and sense of isolation required an active refusal of the others. However, as Cassils noted in her reporting, they made and exchanged signals between each other, most of them in terms of spatial awareness, attitude, and dis/awareness of time. She also indicates how a

140   *Precis*

sense of solidarity and pressure in their deindividualised fugue state emerged and that this was felt between the members. The interaction and communication within groups emerges as something that reveals how cohesive the aesthetic collectives feel. In general, the degree or quality of work invested influences the success of the collective.

In personifying and granting aesthetic collectives essence we move them into a more human class of entities. Consequently, we can understand them in human terms and engaged with them like subjects. In *Medea* the audience granted them an essence, which earlier I defined as being a parody of middle-class, 'yummy-mummy', 'gossipy' and judgemental women. The khoros was supposed to be a theatricalisation of mumsnet, the comforts and threats of postpartum socialisation. While these characteristics are not themselves the essence of the group they are identity attributes pointing towards it. They became a character in part due to their emergent sense of essence. Following analysis in Wagner et al. a bit further:

> Extending these considerations to social categories, it follows that the social group that an essentialized social category refers to is maximally differentiated from other groups and individuals by its well-defined boundary, its members are homogenized, its members' behaviour is explained and predicted by their underlying essence, and therefore any treatment of its members—thoughts, feelings, and actions directed toward them—justified on the basis of their underlying essence is legitimized as natural. Thus, in a single stroke, essentialization of a social category can serve an epistemic function to simplify and to make complex social phenomena comprehensible in cognition and communication, and a moral function to justify and legitimize resolute thoughts, feelings and actions directed towards it. In other words, it 'enhances' a social representation's epistemic and pragmatic function in crafting a social world (Jovehelovitch, 2007; Moscovici & Hewstone, 1983; Wagner & Hayes, 2003) by sharpening its contours and permitting quick inference and 'adequate' reaction in social encounters.[38]

In essentialising an aesthetic collective, I gain *comprehension in cognition and communication* with the group and can then *justify and legitimize* responses to it. As with an individual the collective is understood and interacted *with* (not just acted upon). Through essentialisation an audience gains the ability to comprehend them better, understand how to communicate with and about it and can thus justify and legitimise thoughts, feelings and actions that they feel and direct at it. Wagner et al. summarise their discussion with a further statement indicating that 'group homogeneity is a desired outcome of identity work by and through essence construction and its enactment in practice, and not the causal effect of some pre-existing identity'.[39] Essence is constructed and practiced—especially if it follows from a pre-existing identity.

## Characterisation, Characterising, Mood

The second notion of character moves beyond the character-as-role into the characterising of the experience. In a more postdramatic sense, aesthetic collectives characterise or give character to the experience of the performance. This is a further layer to their presence. In this sense, the examples are not standing-in for any human element in a narrative or plot, but instead stand-in for an element of human experience itself. William Butler Yeats refers to this character as

> no longer loved for its own sake, or as an expression of the general bustle of life, [but now] merely the mask for some *mood or passion* [...] little of individual men and women, but rather of great types, great symbols of *passion and mood* ... [emphasis given]'.[40]

In this sense, *character* moves beyond its dramatic function into a theatrical element, something that does the roles of thought and spectacle. In this capacity they convey the theme or mood of the work (thought) through their presence as more conceptual, environmental elements (spectacle). They 'emerg[e as] dramaturgical and performance strategies that deliberately undermine the illusion of autonomous character'.[41] Whereas with character-as-role there is a contained and substantiated identity, in this notion they are no longer a container for an identity or substantiated concepts of self. Character-as-characterisation

> comes to the stage partly de-substantiated [...] [in a] kind of layering that breaks apart the integrated image of human identity. The burden of signification [...] begins to shift from the unfolding of character and plot to the more abstract interest of the play of ontological and ideological levels.[42]

In this section, I examine more closely the ways in which the engagement and encounter between aesthetic collectives and their audiences are imbued with character by the collectives. Beyond them having a character-as-a-role within some drama of the performance, they create a character or characterisation for the experience. This notion of characterisation of the experience is a tinting and toning of the experience through affective elaboration, mood-making.

While solely physical performances, the Beecroft performers depicted suggestions of character roles, but their presence characterised the experience with an affective, mood element. The combination of Beecroft's physical 'costuming' of the members and the contextualisation within the spaces produces a character palate for audiences. In *VB45* the mood conjured Aryan and S&M themes, for example. While non-narrative in nature the performance allowed the audience to see these women within a fluid narrative of their own mental construction. Transformed into objects, the audience could

142   *Precis*

fantasise and impose any narrative in which these women–objects *could* become characters. As a work of art, *VB45* produced a potential world which audiences associate and develop in their own minds. As Jeffrey Deitch says of her work,

> [t]he image was just so arresting, because it was a new kind of reality that she had developed. It was not a painting or a sculpture, it was not a normal photograph, it was not just people sitting there in real life. It was something in between.[43]

The women could be anything the audience sees them as, almost like a Rorschach painting—a form is given to the viewer, but their mind completes the work through interpretation.[44] The work also moves beyond dramatic or fictional context and engages the audience with the members' actual experience—notably their fatigue and their confrontation with objectification. Like dance or mime, the performers' physical performance and presence were performatively narrative of their internal experiences. The reduction of potential action also meant that small, barely noticeable actions that usually attract no attention became far more dramatic in this context. The live experience of their weathering of the performance betrays moment for moment what they experience. Through them, the audience may experience their fatigue, boredom, pain, fantasy, anger, dislocation from time and so on.

Characterisation here drives the whole event. It is not necessarily the unravelling of action and thought of a human element within a plot.

> [T]he […] figures must not be mistaken [only] for autonomous characters with psychological interiority. They are more like characterological objects in a field […] [that] draw[] on a perceptual faculty not unlike that developed by ecology, a systems-awareness that moves sharply away from the ethos of competitive individualism toward a vision of the whole …[45]

The khoroi did this as well, as noted when I discussed them. They had instances of breaking from their character roles and becoming scenery, abstract expressions of emotion or mass presences that instilled the scene with mood.

Similarly, although with more creative elasticity, dancers in the clubbing examples would adopt and reciprocate behaviour and characterisation commensurate with the mood of the environment. As the DJs progressed through their sets the dancers would pick up the mood created by the music and scenographic environment. Their actions and behavioural tone/inflection would adjust to fit it, dance moves followed a characterisation drawn from the club environment. At Debbie, contemporary charts and pop music was the dominant genre. The actions of the dancers reflected the characteristics of that style of music. They moved in energetic, excited, bouncy and silly ways. As a specific example, at one point the song 'Fifth Harmony' by Worth It featuring

*Character and Contagion* 143

Kid Ink played. This song was a big hit in 2015 and the video for it released only a few months prior to that night. When the song played, I saw dance moves taken directly from the video, and everyone danced in similarly exuberant and jumpy ways.[46] There was a lot of deep squat style moves to the bass beat of the song. In contrast, at Oslo electronic and IDM (intelligent dance music) genres pervaded. There the dancing was more nuanced, less jumpy and had a more fluidic, swaying appearance and feel to it. The action shared characteristics with the music and its thematic tone. The dancing and performed actions of club dancers adopted mood-based characterisations; it was as if they were becoming characters within an unscripted narrative or adopting the mood of the music into their bodies, actions and dancing.

In club dancing in general each crowd has these collective fantasies or enacted micro-narratives. Dancers adopt and share moods and in turn a mimetic phenomenon occurs. In constant shift and flux dancers pick up behaviour and action from each other, copying it. I have previously linked this with a collective motor activity. This mimetic behaviour reflects a deeper aspect at work in dancing crowds: mood contagion. Instead of becoming distinct characters a convergence of characterisation through mood happens. In my experiences, without transposing into an actual, embodied and identity-constituted character there was a noticeable character to behaviours and moods. Dancers did not become specific human characters, but they did adopt and embody characteristics. I perceived these characterisations or characteristics as a general or diffused attitude, tone or mood (mood being the term I will adopt and use more frequently from here forward).

To illustrate these mood elements, I will walk through a rave example that I introduced in chapter 1 (the Suffolk rave). This was a homemade rave and it did not take place in licensed and commercial spaces like the other clubbing examples. As such it sits in a similar but not congruent category of aesthetic events, something covered more by the term *party*. It was a weekend wedding party hosted on a secluded converted barn/event space in Suffolk in March 2016 over the course of a three-day-long weekend. The event included approximately 55 attendees at any given time (some were there the whole weekend, some only for certain days), about a third of whom were friends of mine and of which at least three are semi-professional DJs. One of the spaces was transformed into a dance and party space, with a very powerful DJ table, speakers and theatrical lighting, haze and projections. I will focus on the final night, which was fancy dress.

The night had a reciprocal relationship of music, lighting and our dancing. The DJs responded to the activity of us as dancers just as we were responding to our enjoyment of the choices of the DJs. The DJs were setting the tone for the dancing crowd, but there were instances in which the dancing group dictated what they wanted in terms of music. The most obvious way this happened was the absence or presence of dancers. If the dancing group was not 'feeling' the mood set by the DJ the dancers would literally exit the room, sometimes en masse. A subtler response was when the group would stop dancing, look like

144    *Precis*

they were not enjoying the music, were bored and/or talk to each other. The mood in these instances was simply not powerful enough to command and inspire dancing and partying. The DJs, reading this as a critique of the music, would quickly change the music or shift tones. Dancers would even shout or scream at the DJ that the music should change.

As a constructed aesthetic environment this rave example shows how the affective dimension of the event *was* the experience. The DJs were attempting to generate an affectively stimulating environment characterised by dancing, jubilance and partying. The dancers were in turn signalling to the DJs their effectiveness either by adopting those characteristics and dancing, or not. Shifts in characterisations triggered consequent choices for the DJ. Indeed, one DJ left the table and commented on how the group just did not feel what he was playing. As a diverse group, there were a number of different music genres that people wanted. So, the moods the dancers found stimulating shifted and changed frequently and were not easy to anticipate. There were at least two attempts by one DJ to use dark house music, which uses bass and electronic music to promote moods tinted with fear/terror, anger/rage or distress/anguish. It tends to have creepy, tense and contemplative moods, hence *dark*. In the context of this party those moods failed. The dancing collective shouted at the DJ during these occasions to change the music. They did not want to engage in those moods; it was just the wrong setting for that type of event. The DJ responded quickly and shifted to something the group did want (which happened to be UK garage music, something I knew was nostalgic to the group—something he knew they would like).

In this example, the DJ and the aesthetic collective of the dancers actively pursued experiences characterised by moods. As a participant, when entering the mood of the room I felt an immense pressure to adopt whatever emotional timbre was present, to become a part of it. I would act out emotional states commensurate with the group simply to feel like I was a part of the group. I did this whether I felt that way or not. I noticed this and consciously experimented with it to see what would happen if I did not do it. On occasions, I simply did not feel the mood set by the room, but still danced albeit emotionally vacant and somewhat automaton-like. As a result, I was ignored by everyone around me. To return to an earlier point, I was not working at the identity of the group and thus was marginalised from its essence. As a contrast I also over-emphasised the mood set, to appear exuberantly involved. When I did this the group responded, encouraged and positively endorsed my presence. They shouted (positively) at me, orientated themselves at me, danced with me or matched my energy and dance style. This had a lifespan, though. I noticed that after a period of positive response, usually lasting about twenty seconds and at the very maximum a minute. Then they would one by one resume their own self-interests or return to the activities of their sub-groups. I also discovered that attention only sustained if I remained novel in my performance. To keep attention or cohesion between us I had to vary my dance moves or attitude every twenty seconds or so, but still maintain the same level

## Character and Contagion    145

of high intensity. This was exhausting, and I could only sustain it for the duration of one song at most. This undoubtedly is different for other people—I am not a natural extrovert and do not like this attention. I imagine individuals who are more extroverted and do like attention might sustain this for longer.

Those present became infused with the characterisation and mood of the event. We generated an affective experience through our sharing and co-experiencing of the experience. The purpose of this conduction between members was to experience a collective feeling and emotion. This movement towards common, collective feeling is *affective convergence* and an environment of it is called an *emotional (affective) culture*. Returning to my introductory comments, Sigal Barsade and Andrew Knight use these terms, *affective convergence* and *emotional (affective) culture*, to reflect a group that has made internal movement to solidify their purposeful existence.[47] Collectives in general experience affective convergence, defined as '[a]ffect that is shared, or held in common, by the members of a group or team',[48] and leads towards a more defined emotional (affective) culture (hereafter I will simply refer to this as *emotional culture*). In this rave example, the group of dancers was sharing a common affect or affective range. It changed each time the DJs changed; but the group was constantly similarised in terms of affect. They were very excited, very celebratory, nostalgic and so on, and manifested these affects through their socialisation and dancing.

As the night moved on in time the affective tones progressed and changed. Late in the night, the general affect of the group was more sluggish, uncoordinated and messy. While alcohol and drugs had numbed many participants' cognitive functions, the underlying affective dimension had not changed. Everyone was still operating with motivations of excitement, celebration and nostalgia. In fact, the nostalgia increased as the night turned into morning. There was far more use of music drawn from or referential of the collective biography of the group or of sub-groups, like an opportunity to relive past experiences. This had a sense of sadness to it as well; a tone of commencement.[49] There was a micro-culture here that existed to promote higher and more productive function in/of the group. The *emotional culture* also included

> [b]ehavioural norms, artifacts, and underlying values and assumptions reflecting the actual expression or suppression of the discrete emotions comprising the culture and the degree of perceived appropriateness of these emotions, transmitted through feeling and normative mechanisms within [the] group.[50]

This party/rave was designed to create and exhibit these very attributes.

Viewed alongside entitativity affective convergence is another facet of similarisation. As a group, we similarised our affective states, feelings, emotions and/or moods. This move towards greater similarity in an emotional culture is

146  *Precis*

also a move towards greater common fate. The central model of a couple being married here literally embodied the concept of common fate, but all of us were entailed with their common fate on some level. This culture further defined the character(istics) and objective of the group.

In different ways and on different levels all the clubbing experiences proved this to be at work. The affective convergence and production of the emotional cultures at each event created a cohesion or coherence in the common fate of the dancing crowds, despite the events' short durations. Furthermore, these emotional cultures were reliant on the immersion of the participants within the dancing crowd or within the expanse of its affect. I could feel and experience the mood of the dancing if near it even if not participating (although being outside the group had a lesser intensity). The Beecroft and khoroi examples showed this as well; an emotional culture defined each, and again, this may only have existed for the duration of the performances. Nonetheless, part of their similarity, common fate and subsequent senses of cohesion and coherence as aesthetic collectives relied on this convergence and their emotional cultures. This is true for the affective convergence both for the performers and their audiences. The events all intended their audiences to be moved in some way. In other words, they intended for those present to feel what the aesthetic collectives were feeling or to have concomitant, reciprocal feelings.

The khoros of *Bakkhai* provides an interesting case in which this was both successful and not. This khoros was successful in establishing an emotional culture and mood for its audience, but the mood-making that they undertook was directorially at odds with the text itself. The mood of the performance was relatively flat and still. There was very little in the way of emotional variation and their performance was generally always within the same distant, vague and austere emotional range. Speaking in terms of affect, they always seemed like they were peering out into the audience or at the action in the episodes with something like drugged interest, stunned attention and mild joy or distress. The fourth ode was more ecstatic, but even this only reached a moderately heightened degree of energy and incorporated more sadistic enjoyment into their affect range. The overall mood of the performance was sedate and always perpetuated the same in the actions and machinations of the characters. I read the scenes with the same degree of intensity that they set for me.

This, however, is not quite in keeping with the text. Euripides' text is the most dithyrambic of the extant tragedies—dithyrambic meaning wild, frenzied, irregular. The khoros should ecstatically and wildly dance and sing throughout at least three of its odes. The affect range should be vacillating perpetually between high intensities of several feelings and emotions in the cast and the audience. If we take the third ode as an example the khoros moves through a huge range of emotions as the khoros at first sings an exultation paean to the birth of Dionysos, then castigates Pentheus for his hybris, then supplicate for help before God in an attacking song (of Pentheus). This alone requires several high energy and varied emotions. Then, they dialogue in a type of stichomythia with Dionysos, each alternating line becoming

Character and Contagion 147

progressively more frantic. The stage direction actually indicates '*Thunder and lightning. The earth trembles. The Chorus is crazed with fear*'.[51] They then build towards a climax moment in which the palace is flared by lightning and a burst of fire erupts from Dionysos' mother's tomb. In the Almeida production this was performed with some higher singing registers, some shuddering movement, banging of sticks on the ground and Dionysos emptying a bag of black confetti over the khoros. There was a degree of humour about it, but unfortunately the directorial choices were not adequate to the content of the text or its instruction (implied or stated). The mood set was not frenzied or crazed fear; neither extreme enough nor set in the heightened register instructed in the text or in the prosodic formation of the ode. Personally, I did not find fear or excitement genuinely established. Fear is necessary in Greek tragedy and, according to Aristotle, is the essential emotive tool in establishing the route to pathos that will come with the climax of the tragedy. In terms of classical poetics, this khoros was not very successful.[52]

Inhabiting the stage for nearly the whole performance this khoros was responsible for establishing and maintaining the emotional culture for the whole performance. As they shifted between foreground and background elements (between characters-as-roles and characterisers of the performance) they perpetuated a mood for the performance. In this ode that was supposed to be a crazed mood of fear. The audience and cast should have those emotions 'transmitted through feeling and normative mechanisms'.[53] *Normative mechanisms* represent the behaviour and emotional display norms/expression allowed. 'Emotional display norms constitute one manifestation of emotional culture, and the intersection of an individual's emotional experiences and expressions with emotion norms prescribed by the group resonate strongly in the field'.[54] Audience members take their emotional cues from those they watch. The ever-present khoros duplicates and amplifies the emotional cueing by the scale of its repetition across and through their many bodies. In *Bakkhai* they chose emotional cues that were not strong enough. Contagion of their mood to the audience happened, but the performance suffered because of its low intensity. The restricted normative mechanisms of this khoros prevented the audience from witnessing or themselves feeling crazed fear.

## Contagion

The last element I introduce here is the actual movement of characterisation and mood of these experiences through performers and audiences. This idea will flow into the next chapter where it is developed more fully. The transmission of affect and the sharing of the mood of these experiences occur in a variety of ways and through different mechanisms. This movement is a type of contagion. Contagion, by definition, notes how things spread, transmit, communicate. In aesthetic collectives, there are tangible things that move via contagion (actions, vocal tonality, behaviour and affectations) and there are intangible things (moods, affect, feelings). Both are relevant.

148    *Precis*

In the aesthetic collectives of the dance club, for instance, I observed dancers adopting the behaviour and dance moves of others around them and making them their own. There were an overwhelming number of instances of this happening. Body movement and activity mimetically passed about from individual to individual. Actions were transmitting and were contagious. Moves enacted by one dancer would later be enacted by a neighbouring dancer—sometimes by dancers far across the space. It was not only the action but also the emotive intention beneath it: they performed it in similar emotional ways. When I purposefully looked for this and waited for it to happen, I noticed its ubiquity. I am not sure dancers were even aware they were doing it. The absorption and reproduction seemed to happen without any conscious or perceptual awareness. There were, however, instances I noticed where mimicry and duplication was intentional and planned. I saw dancers actively watching each other and copying what each other were doing. In some instances, they even pointed to someone on the dance floor and then a duplication of what they watched.

This also occurred in dyad relations for sexual or courting purposes. Frequently, I observed individuals becoming intimate with each other and they would synchronise their dancing. First, they would close their proximity to be within each other's personal and intimate spaces. Second, they would mirror each other very closely and perform duplicate or complementary movements to the other; make themselves physically compatible. These movements were usually themselves mimetic of the actions, rhythm or tone of intercourse—a lot of hip thrusting and grinding, lots of very sexually suggestive orientations and positioning of the body. In these instances, the couple would usually become exclusive and somewhat closed-off from the rest of the group.

I believe that group adoption of dance movement is an attempt to commit to the collective and its identity (in courting, to commit to the micro-group of two). This promotes a greater sense of similarity, cohesion, unification and belonging and in turn a stronger, more successful emotional culture. As such this contagious behaviour allows participants to feel convergent affects and enjoy the activity of membership in the collective. In fact, the greater the commitment to the group the greater the enjoyment to follow. Barsade and Knight report this in other research areas.

> Totterdell et al. (1998) found that team members who were more committed to their team and perceived their team environment more positively had greater affective convergence [...] In addition, Tanghe et al. (2010) found in two studies, one survey based another scenario based, that group identification is positively related to the convergence of group member affect.[55]

Commitment to the group and greater positive perception of the group leads to greater affective convergence and group identification. In these aesthetic

*Character and Contagion* 149

experiences that usually means a greater degree of pleasure in the experience. This spreading, adoption and enacting of similarised affective and mood states is *contagion*. Like the catching of a virus or bacteria the affective dimension of the group spreads through its members in a process called transmission of affect. When we speak of collective affective experiences, we generally use terms like *mood*.

*Mood* is like an affective blanket that covers the entire group. Everyone is under this blanket, but everyone interprets the feeling of it in slightly different ways—in individualised affective responses. Additionally, the affective responses of my neighbours or of others near me will impact on my own affective responses. Everyone has the same blanket encounter of mood, but that encounter precipitates affective experiences, feelings, within individuals that are themselves influenced by and influential to those around them. In dancing crowds the gestalt of aesthetic elements and the co-presence of proximally close dancers established a mood. That mood would shift and change along a spectrum. The dancers and the DJs worked in tandem to allow themselves to absorb and behave within that mood. In this way, the dancing crowd has an affective experience driven by aesthetic manipulations. As a pervading element distributed to everyone similarly, the mood provokes affective experiences in the individuals. It is through a collective experience that these dancing crowds achieved their personal affective goals—to feel something.

This seems clear as a result in group experiences like club dancing where the audience is also participant and performer and there is clear physical immersion in the aesthetic design. This equally applies to more passive audience scenarios too, like witnessing a Beecroft installation or sitting in a theatre with khoroi. Physically distanced, outside and witnessing the aesthetic collective, audience members are still immersed in and affected by the presence of those aesthetic collectives. The performing collectives disclose their experience by transmitting it outwardly as a performed element for the audience. The audience is present with and immersed in that affective field. They can thereby psychologically cast themselves in, or as Fuchs would say stand-in for the aesthetic collective, and thus conceptualise that experience as their own. The collectives' characterising of their experience transmits to the audience who then may stand in for the collectives and adopt that experience as their own.

To use the blanket analogy again, collectives establish and cast a mood over the whole of themselves and their audiences. The audience is caught under and within this blanket mood and this precipitates individual feelings. These responses in turn will affect/be affected by the experiences of neighbouring attendees or even of members within the collectives. This coverage, movement and actions of affecting/being affect by are referred to as emotional contagion, mood contagion or affect contagion. It is the physio-psychological way that affect transmits between people. It has been under analysis for the better part of 120 years. Theresa Brennan, introduced in chapter 1, gives a very fine literature review in chapter 3 of *The Transmission of Affect*[56] and I do not want to duplicate such effort here. Instead, I highlight two principles she

150    *Precis*

illustrates in her review as central to how crowds operate in a psychology of images, by which they are moved and to which they will respond: *suggestibility* and *contagion*. Gustave Le Bon[57] and William McDougall[58] explicitly use the terms to explain how crowds are moved emotively and to action. The relative suggestibility of a group, that is how likely they are to subscribe emotionally to and follow an image, controls their impetus to act. Suggestibility of a group makes an idea and its related sentiments more likely to transmit through the group. Put simply, if a crowd group is suggested an image, it and the sentiment towards it will spread through and infect the group via contagion.

Largely discounted in much of the 20th century as 'non-scientific', principles of transmission have more recently been supported and in part confirmed by research on affective transfer processes, emotional contagion, and the means of emotional contagion.[59] Barsade and Knight, for instance, build on the extensive research in the area to assert that mimicry is the primary vehicle by which contagion occurs: '[e]motional contagion occurs through automatic mimicry of the facial expressions, voice, and body movements of others [...] This mimicry then leads the perceiver to actually feel the emotion, effectively catching the emotion of the other person'.[60] This automatic behaviour occurs out of conscious control, as one of the subsystems of the brain. These kinds of reactions just outside of conscious control are likely a product of automatic response generated by the protoself, discussed earlier. To follow the viral metaphor, the mood and affective dimensions of the work infect the audiences who are then moved on affective and emotional levels. Contagion for audiences in the aesthetic collectives I have so far examined occurred through immersion in the presence of the aesthetic collectives—literally being contained or caught within their affective fields. The next chapter unpacks these ideas in more detail, offering a greater overview of affective dimensions and how these processes of affective or mood convergence occur and how they relate to feelings and emotions.

To conclude, I would like to return to the terms *convergence* and *contagion* and the metaphor at work in their use. As I continue applying Lakoff and Johnson's thinking, it occurs that these examples demonstrate lived metaphors. As Lakoff and Johnson state:

> [o]ur ordinary conceptual system, in terms of which we both think and act, is fundamentally metaphorical in nature [...] Our conceptual system thus plays a central role in defining our everyday realities [...] the way we think, what we experience, and what we do every day is very much a matter of metaphor.[61]

They expand on this claim through a large number of examples that demonstrate how to understand the world and our experiences in them, we compare and frame our understanding and experiences in terms of each other. The way we conceptualise our reality is not just an issue of language or intellect, but an issue of how we experience, engage with and understand these encounters.

> But our conceptual system is not something we are normally aware of. In most of the little things we do every day, we simply think and act more or less automatically along certain lines. Just what these lines are is by no means obvious.[62]

In offering various perspectives of how I encountered these aesthetic collectives or how they were commented on/reported by others, descriptions of experiences begin informing us on and of their content. '[Another] way to find out is by looking at language. Since communication is based on the same conceptual system that we use in thinking and acting, language is an important source of evidence for what that system is like'.[63]

Probing the language and use of the terms *convergence* and *contagion* divulges a metaphoric structuring of complex and difficult to understand affective processes in terms of more familiar concepts. Here, in terms of paths and viral infection respectively. When we discuss the convergence of affect in groups we are framing affects as substances that move along different paths until those paths unify and the substances combine. To experience, describe and analyse affect in terms of convergence betrays two underlying conceptual assumptions: affects are like substances, affects move like substances. They travel along paths which can allow them to combine, integrate, unify or merge. In the next chapters, this will become fundamental and very important with discussion of atmospheres. Affect paths may merge, as in a fork merging two paths into one, or run in parallel yet distinct paths. The idea of a path here is also not exclusive to a physical path. *Path*, as an idea, includes the paths of common objective, goal or a path of time—all of which common fate engenders.

This basic conceptualisation of affect also allows for the second metaphor, viral infection. If affects are like substances that means that they can enter the self, be imbibed/inhaled in different ways or seep and emerge from the self outwardly. The movement of affect here is conceptualised as something both native and foreign. It enters the self from the outside world or can rupture out of the self. The container can be filled, leak or issue. Like something viral, I can also be infected with affect from the external world either through direct contact or through a conduit or conductor between our bodies: usually the gaseous space between us. On the other hand, my affects can be spread to others, again either through contact or the gaseous conduit space between us. This conceptualisation of affect, like substances and viruses, indicates a connection, even if tenuously, to an origin point. Affects are not fully recognised as their own thing; they come from somewhere, and more commonly someone. If I catch and feel an affect, it infects me and I am then moved along a course that will combine, integrate, unify or merge with the path of that affect and whomever or whatever from which it came. Affects both affect me and take me on a path and allow me to affect and bring others on my path.

152    *Precis*

# Notes

1 Lakoff and Johnson.
2 Lakoff and Johnson, p. 29.
3 Lakoff and Johnson, p. 31.
4 Lakoff and Johnson, p. 81.
5 Lakoff and Johnson, p. 154.
6 Lakoff and Johnson, p. 154.
7 Lakoff and Johnson, p. 154.
8 Lakoff and Johnson, p. 154.
9 Lakoff and Johnson, p. 154.
10 Lakoff and Johnson, p. 25.
11 Lakoff and Johnson, p. 33.
12 Lakoff and Johnson, p. 34.
13 Lakoff and Johnson, p. 34.
14 Lakoff and Johnson, p. 162.
15 Cavendish.
16 Fuchs, p. 10.
17 Fuchs, p. 12.
18 A very similar ode is also in the second stasimon of his *Women of Troy*, a similar play.
19 Euripides, 'The Trojan Women', in *The Complete Greek Tragedies, Euripides III*, trans. by Richard Lattimore (Chicago: The University of Chicago Press, 1958), p. 48, lines 905, 912–913.
20 Euripides, 'Hekabe', in *Grief Lessons, Four Plays by Euripides*, trans. by Anne Carson (New York: New York Review Books, 2006), pp. 140–142, lines 874–916.
21 Euripides, *Bakkhai, A New Version by Anne Carson*, trans. by Anne Carson (London: Oberon Books Ltd., 2015), p. 16. This version offers no line counting.
22 That ode may also be found in Appendix B.2.
23 Euripides, *Bakkhai*, p. 71.
24 Euripides, 'The Bacchae', in *The Complete Greek Tragedies: Euripides V*, trans. by William Arrowsmith, ed. by David Greene and Richmond Lattimore (Chicago and London: The University of Chicago Press, 1968), p. 220, lines 1387–1394.
25 Euripides, *Bacchae: After The Bacchae of Euripides*, trans. by Colin Teevan (London and New York: Oberon Books Ltd, 2001).
26 For a thoroughly detailed and forensic examination of the institution of the Khoregia, I recommend reading Wilson, *The Athenian Institution*, as indicated in the introduction.
27 William Shakespeare, *As You Like It*, dir. by Polly Pindlay (London: The National Theatre, 2015).
28 Susannah Clapp, 'As You Like It Review—Out with Merriment, in with Humour', *The Observer* in The Guardian 2015, [accessed 22 August 2018].
29 The third being the act one set of office desks, chairs and lamps being hoisted into the air by cables, becoming an angular forest of trees.
30 Here I would refer the reader back to the introduction where I make comments on the essence and being and how I am framing and delimiting my discussion in terms of the concept as defined by the literature on entitativity, already reviewed and as reviewed later.
31 The term *noematic* arrives from phenomenology, particularly as stemming from Edmund Husserl (see Edmund Husserl, *Ideas Pertaining*, particularly pages 211–235).
32 Lakoff and Johnson, p. 34.
33 See again Wagner et al.
34 Wagner et al., p. 369.
35 Wagner et al., pp. 369–370.
36 Wagner et al., p. 369; see also Liu and Hilton, 'How the Past'.
37 Wagner et al., p. 370.

*Character and Contagion* 153

38 Wagner et al., p. 367; see also Jovchelovitch, *Knowledge in Context*; Moscovici and Hewstone, 'Social Representations'; Wagner and Hayes, *Everyday Discourse*.

39 Wagner et al., p. 370.

40 William Butler Yeats, *Uncollected Prose*, as cited in Fuchs, p. 30.

41 Fuchs, p. 31.

42 Fuchs, p. 35.

43 Jeffrey Deitch as quoted in Johnstone, 'Dare to Bare'.

44 Rorschach paintings, widely known as inkblot tests, are psychological tests of subjective interpretation of abstract inkblots; they are named after Hermann Rorschach who invented them in 1921.

45 Fuchs, p. 102 and 107.

46 Worth It featuring Kid Ink, *Fifth Harmony,* online video clip, www.youtube.com, published 28 March 2015, https://www.youtube.com/watch?v=YBHQbu5rbdQ [accessed 20 July 2018].

47 Barsade and Knight.

48 Barsade and Knight, p. 24.

49 It is worth noting that *nostalgia* is a term derived from the Greek *nóstos*, the return home, and characterises a yearning for the past or a return to the past.

50 Barsade and Knight, p. 24.

51 Euripides, *The Bacchae,* p. 179. I use this translation here and not Anne Carson's as Carson chose to remove all stage direction except entrances and exits from her copy.

52 See Comment 4 in Appendix C for additional information.

53 Barsade and O'Neill, 'What's Love', p. 558.

54 Barsade and Knight, p. 26, here indicating research by Blake Ashforth and Ronald Humphrey: see also Ashforth and Humphrey, 'Emotion in the Workplace'.

55 Barsade and Knight, p. 30; see also Totterdall and others, 'Evidence of Mood'; Tanghe et al., 'The Formation of Group'.

56 Brennan (2004).

57 Le Bon, *The Crowd*.

58 McDougall, *The Group Mind*.

59 For such research, see Elfenbein, 'The Many Face'; Kelly and Barsade, 'Mood and Emotions'; Hatfield et al., 'Emotional Contagion' (1993) and *Emotional Contagion* (1994); Bartel and Saavedra, 'The Collective Construction'; Totterdell et al., 'Evidence of Mood'.

60 Barsade and Knight, pp. 23–24; the authors here cite as examples the research of the following: Dimberg et al., 'Unconscious Facial'; Hess and Fischer, 'Emotional Mimicry'; Lundqvist and Dimberg, 'Facial Expressions are Contagious'.

61 Lakoff and Johnson, p. 3.

62 Lakoff and Johnson, p. 3.

63 Lakoff and Johnson, p. 3.

# 5    Mood, Affect, Feeling, Emotion

Affects, feelings, emotions, moods: these exist as a murky and inter-contaminating pool of ideas. They are frequently interchanged and used to identify the same things but are, to be sure, different. Indeed, during the viva voce of my doctoral thesis, I noted this to the external examiners, who pressed me if such distinctions really matter. For the vast public, no; such distinctions mean nothing. However, if we follow the distinctions, a huge realm of inter-esting and meaningful understanding opens to us. They reveal knowledge of how we, as sensing and sensitive beings, feel our experiences. I will focus first on mood, mood-making functions and contagion of moods in more depth. To do so, I am going to shift from live performance to recorded media and explore ensemble or back-up dancing groups in music videos. Such groups, while present in live concerts as well, are an aesthetic collective ubiquitous through TV/film culture. I feel the inclusion of mediatised examples is important as music videos (or similar media) are hugely popular in mediatised culture and have dominated the music industry since the 1980s, when MTV (launched in 1981) and VH1 (launched in 1985) TV stations popularised the format through mass consumptive broadcast. In turn, music video came to influence music performance and user consumption in general. Music videos cannot be relegated to the realm of 'just entertainment' either. They achieve an artistry that ana-logises them to audio-visual poems or short stories.

In the early 2020s, it is now a format that both exists in and of itself, as a tool of music influence and one reciprocally influencing back onto live perfor-mance, with many concert performances enacting the video or aspects of it. Beyond TV, the internet and mobile technology have hyper-articulated music video with it becoming immediate, flexible and ubiquitous. Consumers now may experience full videos, samples, transposed elements as memes and engage with it legally or illegally with no real repercussions. They may even actively manipulate video themselves using editing software.

The notion of liveness operates in different ways in an intermedial world. Philip Auslander's *Liveness: Performance in a Mediatized Culture*[1] makes argu-ments that '[m]ediatized forms like film and video can be shown to have the same ontological characteristics as live performance, and live performance can be used in ways indistinguishable from the uses generally associated with

DOI: 10.4324/9781003205661-8

Mood, Affect, Feeling, Emotion    155

mediatized forms'.[2] The experience of mediatised arts like video offer key insights into what constitutes liveness at all. '[T]he best way of thinking about that relationship is to understand liveness as a historically contingent concept continually in a state of redefinition and to look at the meanings and uses of live performance in specific cultural contexts'.[3] Music videos offer a type of intimacy for the viewer that is not possible in live performance. They offer a 'relationship to cultural objects defined by proximity and intimacy'.[4] The camera and microphone offer a different type of entrance into aesthetic collectives.

In the music videos I look at aesthetic collectives, as back-up dancing groups, exist as characters within the event of the music video but also to produce and support the mood and atmosphere of the performance—as characters-as-roles and characterisers. Back-up dancers typically are not the main focus of attention. There is usually a leading act/performer on whom audiences focus. Instead, back-up dancing groups are often concomitant characters or elements of the background and spectacle. Without them, the lead performer(s) will undoubtedly continue to generate mood and atmosphere, but with them the performance is markedly more potent and the lead performer has a clear context established for them. I will focus on back-up dancers who are either the focus or are very strong presences in the performance. In using recorded videos, as opposed to a series of live concert events, their fixity and slight remove from live events demonstrates aesthetic collectives in non-live contexts and allows the viewer to exercise agency over the artwork's viewing. This feature allows me to break affect and effect of the aesthetic collectives down into specific, and pausable, detail. This also questions the mode of encounter and how we, as audience, experience the presence or aura of broadcast or recorded media—matters I address later.

## Mood-Making

The most important use and function of back-up dancers is as mood-makers, they facilitate atmospheric experiences. As characters, back-up dancers are generally on the edges of or even outside the narrative of the work. Almost like scenographic elements, the back-up dancers literally back-up the performance through mood-making, much more like the use of the khoroi. In Beecroft's installations or club dancing this was not the case. Those aesthetic collectives were definitively the centre of attention and artistic focus and there were no singular actors. Directors and artists often use back-up dancers to create or emphasise feelings and moods for their viewers. As shown so far, the climate of aesthetic spaces/performances was set and/or amplified by the aesthetic collectives operating in synchronicity with environmental and scenographic designs. They embodied and acted commensurately with the aesthetics of the event. While singular actors can set and/or amplify mood (and some quite powerfully), with collectives the combined focus of a group of common operating performers multiplies such effect and can broadcast that

156    *Precis*

mood from multiple loci and in multiple directions. Mood is the most definite and determined function: they produce moods and atmospheres in which their audiences become immersed. Immersion and atmospheres will be addressed in the final chapter in much more detail, but for the moment I introduce and hold the idea that aesthetic collectives immerse or contain the audience in their presence and the performance atmosphere.

Back-up groups help produce performance atmosphere. They are used to lend spectacle to the scene, to place focus on the lead performer(s) and, in many cases, to multiply the lead performer(s). They usually remain highly anonymous and even two-dimensional in their development. Physically they tend to be placed in diminutive locations relative to the lead performers (behind or to the sides), are usually unnamed, have a non-individuated role and are treated as a group with dispersed characterisation. The performers in these groups are often far more accomplished dancers than the lead performers they are supporting. Their anonymity or similarisation also works to ensure they do not detract from the lead(s) or that such heightened dance skill is not obvious. Again, focus is dispersed among the group, not on individuals, to prevent the redirection of focus away from the lead, making the back-up dancers more like background/scenery than people. They are present and affecting, but they should not have constant focus. However, there are instances in videos where they are the primary/mostly primary focus. These are not the majority of videos, though. This is because the lead singer(s) or music artists usually appear in their own videos, as 'the' artist. Such instances also require much more work as they are technically difficult to conceive, compose and execute due to the focus on the many moving parts of the collective.

Back-up dancing groups have entitativity. They are frequently closely clustered or used in lines radiating around and behind the lead performer(s). Their proximity makes them clearly grouped and distinct from the surroundings. In most instances the lead(s) is subsumed within the dancing collective, occupying a front and/or centred position. They are also carefully choreographed in shapes or designs, rarely in disorganised or amorphous patterns, although I will present one example using this shaping. Their similarity is varied. In some cases, they are transformed into identical versions of each other. In some they are thematically similarised but differ in their individual looks. In almost all cases they similarise in terms of their behaviour style, moving, acting and dancing with similar description and quality. They can also work as characters within the narrative, frequently shapeshifting between and filling several roles. Many of these features are identical with the use and purpose of khoroi. They are, at minimum, highly similar in their description and utilisation. One could further extend the comparison when the leading performer(s) integrates with them (again, usually front and centred), in which case they appear like the coryphaeus, the khoros leader and at times khoros' mouthpiece. I believe there is a rich site of comparison here, but I also think that to pursue that comparison lies slightly beyond the scope of this text.

Mood, Affect, Feeling, Emotion     157

I make these comparisons here to raise attention to the idea and to provide a contextual situating of back-up dancers within the purview here.

I advise the reader at this point to access the internet and watch the videos (links provided in the bibliography) to Janet Jackson's *Rhythm Nation*, Sia's *The Greatest* and Lady Gaga's *Bad Romance* and *Alejandro*. I have chosen these four examples from the myriad (literally hundreds of thousands) of possible examples for different reasons. A commonality between all four is that they are iconic videos that have created (or are currently creating) considerable discussion and/or discourse. *Rhythm Nation* is a pioneering example of music video dance and stands as one of the most influential dance-music videos ever created.[5] It is sampled, referenced and re-performed regularly and has been cited by music artists as an inspiration or influence in their own art. *The Greatest* I chose to include at first due to its homogenised aesthetic. From the grey colour wash and costuming to the uniform dancing actions. Additionally, the video posed a narrative problem to me as a viewer. The first few times I saw it I did not understand it. I attributed this feeling to its postmodern confusing mix of visual messages, de-concretised narrative and hyper-layered choreography. However, after repeat viewings and researching the video, I discovered a deeply affecting meaning derived as a response to a gun massacre. This immediately changed my response to it, subsequent viewings became emotional and I now recognise its potential as a commemorative anti-violence work. I chose both Lady Gaga videos for the impact and controversy they generated during their release. *Bad Romance*, like *Rhythm Nation*, has created a strong cultural response and has enmeshed itself within clubbing and partying culture. Indeed, when the song plays in clubs or at parties, I have noticed dancers enact choreography from the video almost every time. The video has had strong and deep penetration within cultural memory. *Alejandro*, on the other hand, has not. It is, as I outline in more detail below, a problem video. It appears more in keeping with arthouse video work and is meticulously and beautifully composed. However, its exhibition of sex, sexuality and the often-controversial effect they have when mixed with images of religion, gender, military and politics is in full force in the discourse that surrounds the video and its critique by cultural respondents. As such, I think its problematic nature is interesting and demonstrates how strongly the genre of music video is in arousing and piquing viewers.

*Rhythm Nation* was produced in September 1989 and was directed by Dominic Sena. The video is part of the longer film *Rhythm Nation 1814*; it concludes the film, finishing it as a statement piece. For this discussion I will mainly consider *Rhythm Nation* as a stand-alone video apart from its larger film. However, the whole film warrants viewing and has many of the same instances of the back-up dancing group as outlined in the following. The video takes place in an industrial plant in an undefined time, but the sense is that it is in some sort of post-apocalyptic, dystopian future. The environment is designed as a neo-noir: shot in black and white, use of haze, one-point lighting, long cast shadows, stark contrast, backlighting, multiple severe

158   *Precis*

camera angles and so on. All the cast are identically dressed in genderless, black, pseudo-military costumes. Even though there are dancers of all races and ethnic backgrounds, it is very difficult to identify one from the other. Jackson is herself differentiated from the others merely by the medals decorating her costume, her earrings and the fact that she sings and the others usually do not. Removed from the larger film there is no plot as such (within it, there is); instead, the video narrative is like a military demonstration wherein platoons demonstrate their proficiency in solidarity and uniformity while performing an exercise drill or routine. There is one non-collective cast member, a young black man, who cavorts around the industrial set as an outsider. At the beginning of the video he is shown crying before becoming aware of the collective. His interest in, flirtation with and spying on the collective echoes that of recruits before they join large organisations, like militaries, cults or fraternities of various natures. He is often shown through chain-link fences or behind piping and ducting. He is literally filmed to be on the outside looking in. His story is unresolved at the end of the video, and as such finishes the *Rhythm Nation 1814* film in slight ambiguity, perhaps suggesting that the choice to join the rhythm nation is entirely within the audience's own personal control.

The dancers and Jackson (positioned front and centre), looking much like an infantry, perform a choreographic routine of intense and exquisite technical proficiency. Indeed, this choreography and routine is one of the most recognisable and imitated in pop history. It is routinely reproduced or referenced in other media. A few examples include dance competition shows like *So You Think You Can Dance*, films like *Happy Feet 2,* and TV shows like *American Dad* and *Glee*. The technical demands in the choreography are impressively advanced, combining military marching, martial arts movements, angular robotic dancing, contemporary popping movements, street dance and waacking actions. The most complicated element is the extreme synchronicity required of all the dancers. They are in tight proximity, just at the borders of the personal space of each other, which adds to the difficulty in the action as there is a lot of arm movement. Each dancer must have exceptional proprioceptive and exteroceptive awareness in order not to hit another. Aside from an instance of break-away solo dance demonstration at minute 2:50 by five dancers, the choreography is all ensemble and uniform. The lyrics themselves are also a direct call to arms of the people of the world to unite, work together and effect change as a cohesive, not divisive, whole:

> Everybody sing it
> People of the world unite
> Are we looking for a better way of life
> We are a part of the rhythm nation
> People of the world unite
> Strength in numbers we can get it right

Mood, Affect, Feeling, Emotion    159

One time
We are a part of the rhythm nation[6]

These back-up dancers are solidly an aesthetic collective, and a rather severe one at that. One can even forget the lyrics emphasising collective identity, nature and unity; the visual demonstration in the video is strong enough to convey all these intended meanings.

*Rhythm Nation* serves as an example of when the back-up dancing group is the main character, and as such it is in the minority family of uses of them in music videos. This is not often done, but when it is, as here, it is usually for common reasons: to espouse feelings of cohesion, collectivity, power, control, uniformity and similarity.[7] The back-up dancers also produce the mood of the video in tandem with the scenographic elements. It is dark, dystopian and slightly aggressive. Yet, it is also hopeful and optimistic in the way that revolutionary propaganda can be: it seems to emphasise how the success and change after the battle outweighs the battle sacrifice itself. The carefully crafted and aesthetically specific environment creates a lot of mood in the video. However, the dancers animate and embody in themselves the mood of the environment. In inhabiting, intoning and bringing narrative to it a lived atmosphere emerges. They perform for the watching audience a story of what it is to exist in this fictional space. Without them, the video would simply be a series of landscape shots. With them, it becomes a living story and it can be related to by the audience.

The dancers embody a tapestry of affective experiences, which are transmitted to the viewer creating a response. Affective experiences are reactions to the external world for viewers. They register in intensity what is happening in the world surrounding them. For example, within the first minute of the actual dancing the group's movement and behaviour is rigid, angular and in fast tempo. Their expressions are severe and harsh. The choreography also has playfulness at times, fluctuating between being stiff or militant and being silly. For instance, at minute 1:14 they hustle step in an almost marching movement, but at 1:20 their side-shift movement is almost reminiscent of slap-stick comedy movement. Their behaviour simultaneously adopts the tone of the environment and responds to it. They register in their bodies the mood of the environment, but also advance it through their suggestive movement. The dancing group shows a series of affective reactions to the mood which the viewer then might experience and interpret. Consequently, the affective dimension of the video is a syntax of the space and its elements and the performers and their experience. The shafted lights, hazy air, industrial set, militant costumes, the style of the choreography, the facial expressions, the few vocalisations they make and so on all work together to transmit to the audience oppressive, dystopic, militarised affective elements.

These affective dimensions can more colloquially be understood as the video mood, feeling or emotional tone. I have previously explored these terms, but here define them more closely. Following my introductory notes,

160  *Precis*

affect, after Tomkins, is something fundamental and implicit in the body of the subject.[8] He theorised the affect system as a biological system of the body, alongside the pain, drive and cognitive systems. It offers immediate recognition of external stimuli and then quickly elicits responses that deem the stimuli positive or negative. The environment offers stimuli to the organism, which trigger responses that amplify the stimuli to the brain; this response is an affect. As the amplification increases brain activity shifts to focus on the stimuli and eventually to respond to it. Affects focus conscious awareness of encounters with the world. Affect, at its primal level, recognises external stimuli in terms of intensities and as intensity increases so too does focus/attention on the stimuli. It is also worth noting here how affects usually operate on the fringes of consciousness, only becoming truly in awareness when the affect is intensified to a strong enough degree. Operating on this edge of consciousness they are also wrapped-up in the proto-self.

People also communicate their affective states in the form of emotions and expressed feelings. I use *affect*, *emotion* and *feeling* here to define similar but different dimensions of experience, each pertaining to a variance in personal or public experience. To elaborate, I return to Anderson.[9] The affective dimension of *Rhythm Nation* includes the emotional and feeling-based aspects of how I receive and respond to the work.

> [I]n practice affect, feeling and emotion are indistinguishable. It is not that there are, first, separate layers that are then, secondarily, connected. Rather, affects and emotions are always-already entangled with one another in encounters—encounters that mix and render indistinguishable the personal and impersonal (but may involve processes whereby emotions come to be felt as personal).[10]

While watching *Rhythm Nation*, I am affected by it and its dark industrial vision and take-in the emotion or feeling of the work. This affective element of the work transmits to me. '[A]ffects are augmentations or diminutions of a body's "force of existing" that are expressed in feelings and qualified in emotions (and where emotions/affects become indistinguishable in experience)'.[11] The transmission of affect between the video and me, as viewer, happens through the performance of emotion to me. The dancing aesthetic collective did this. Jackson herself is a part of the collective, not simply a lead performer with a bolted-on back-up dancing group. They projected and performed this affective work for me, which is both performed and performative.

## Affective Dimensions

These affective dimensions can be developed through another example, that of Sia's *The Greatest*. Produced in 2016, this song is by Sia Furler, Greg Kurstin and Kendrick (Duckworth) Lamar and produced by Monkey Puzzle, RCA. Sia and Daniel Askill directed the video and Ryan Heffington choreographed

*Mood, Affect, Feeling, Emotion*   161

it. It features 49 dancers (Maddie Ziegler and an ensemble of 48 other young people) and is a tribute piece to the victims of the Orlando Pulse nightclub shooting in 2016. The video holds no true plot, and instead features only a suggestive narrative that loosely and abstractly dramatises socio-political struggles of gay culture culminating in such disturbing events as the Orlando shooting.

Maddie Ziegler's 'character' cries rainbow tears before the camera cuts to her inciting a ramshackle apartment complex of young, dirty, grey-clad and dystopian people to escape a cage and run into the building. Wildly, exuberantly, aggressively, defiantly they run about, dance and enjoy themselves, although usually with angry and determined facial expressions. The camera follows the group and Ziegler through corridors and rooms. Everywhere she goes she brings dance. At its end, they all arrive in a large open room made to look like a dancing club with a small stage and disco lights. The group dances and mimes a variety of actions before falling to the ground in front of a wall damaged by bullet-holes through which light pierces. The camera scans the bodies on the floor, Ziegler opens her eyes and looks into the camera before a cut returns to her rainbow-streamed face as at the beginning, crying. As an allegory on struggle, liberation and heart-breaking disappointment and loss, the video is a piece of abstract expressionist dance. The viewer is asked to interpret not only the pseudo-narrative but also the plethora of expressions, attitudes, incidental emotions and the rapidity with which they shift, change and present. As such it takes the viewer on a mimetic journey through a fractal world of expression and emotion.

The video also is highly like *Rhythm Nation* in the way it uses the dancers. The main focus point is the aesthetic collective, which includes Ziegler; different to Jackson, Ziegler differentiates from the collective a bit more. She not so much leads this group as compels it. They often automatically spring into action alongside Ziegler. She performs in the centre and at times front, although Heffington also choreographs Ziegler surrounded by the others, making her a positional and symbolic heart for the group. Again, without the dancers the video would just be a moody collage of environment shots, perhaps giving the impression of a space devoid of life, emptied of it or an endgame landscape. The mise-en-scène would still create an atmosphere, but it would not be the message (or set of messages) intended. With the dancers a host of possible narrative threads opens to the viewer and identification could be had with any of the members, individually or en masse. Moreover, the dancers offer specific emotional contexts for this piece through their actions, the quality of the movement, their speed and their expressions. In no order I read from it feelings of sadness, mournfulness, exuberance, free-spiritedness, love, triumph, defiance, strong-willed, power and terror amongst others. I read these feelings both from direct emotional expression of the performers and as intuited from the general mood of the video.

The emotional timbre is plastic and malleable, due mainly to the spectrum of emotional signals broadcast by the performers. Take for example the actions

162   *Precis*

of the dancing group in minutes 1:10–1:18. They simply stand, arms at the side, open their mouths and thrust their heads backwards several times. There is little expression to accompany this and it could mean anything. The action is not something that would be seen in almost any context, especially in its repetition, and feels more like an action in a ritual or warrior dance. For me, it conjures moments of shouting, garish smiling, biting and teeth and tongue display from the Maori haka dance. Later in the video there are several uses of the mouth and tongue/teeth that are similar (see minutes 2:19–2:28, 2:38–2:49, 3:22–3:28 and 3:36 to the end of the dancing). Much of the dance actions are like those in the haka, in fact: hitting and striking the body, wheeling of the arms, bent knee squatting postures and so on. This is not the only part of the video that simulates combat. In two instances (see minutes 1:50–2:09 and 2:17–2:27) the group uses boxing block poses while jumping or shifting weight left and right.

The dancing group clearly has made internal movement to solidify their purposeful existence. They are demonstrating scenes of struggle and battle through their dance. They have, to return to Barsade and Knight, affectively converged. Affective convergence leads them towards a more defined emotional culture. This aesthetic collective would not be successful if they could not achieve this. While the choreography and movement of the video is solid, the affective dimension of their performance is driving it. For me, as a viewer, they appear to be experiencing the same affective dimensions cohesively at the same time through their emotional culture. They appear similarised in affect, with an established emotional culture and in so doing to have strengthened the character, behaviour and objective of the group.

The video creates an affective response for me, the viewer. The group does this by creating a *mood*. This means that they embody, re/present and reflect the affective dimensions of the work in a globally pervasive way. A grimy, dusty, oppressive, abandoned condition pervades the video which the performers adopt in physical appearance and fight against in exuberant, aggressive and excited actions. Their action is both resonant with the environment and a re-action against it. On a representational level this is suggestive of the LGBTQ+ experience of fighting against intolerance and bigotry. A further link could be made between such struggling/fight experiences and colourful and exuberant gay rights demonstrations, parties, protests and pride events. The mood here both acknowledges the given conditions (the dirty, abandoned, run-down house of monochrome greys) and revolts against them.

*Mood*, following Anderson, is a collective condition, or 'some kind of collective affect [...] [that gives] an "enigmatic coherence" across life while also subtending life by persisting in the background [...] hinting towards how people are anchored in the world and to others'.[12] The notion of back-up dancers as something that operates as background and mood that 'subtend[s] life by persisting in the background' are clearly linked in their position relative to awareness. Both operate out of the foreground. The back-up dancers' performance formulates a mood, a collective affect. Practically, this happens

## Mood, Affect, Feeling, Emotion    163

through their movement and behaviour, both having specific energy and styles that relate to these moods. They are also expressing, mainly through their faces, various feelings or emotions. The group and video have a general mood, while each of the individuals exists within that mood differently (albeit very similarly) in their performance. The mood anchors the performers to each other and creates emotional coherence between their experiences and between them and me (as audience). In other words, this anchoring generates an affective experience for me that establishes coherence between my experience and the experience of the performers. The dancers work in a general mood within which several emotions also occur—they illustrate the interconnection of mood, affect and emotion. When experiencing the video, the emotion of the performers directs my attention, awareness and focus but is continually pervaded by the mood.

Moods, emotions and feelings differ in their focus, specificity of object and their duration. The mood of the video is the general affective tone that pervades, something I notice on a very low level of consciousness and which is not very specific. It is also something that everyone shares. The emotions in the video, however, are unique to each of the performers. Each person expresses emotions at different times, and while perhaps very similar to each other, they are unique. Moods and emotions are products of affect responses and operate in the external, broadcast and social environment. Drawing on Barsade and Gibson, moods '[g]enerally take the form of a globally positive (pleasant) or negative (unpleasant) feeling; tend to be diffuse—not focused on a specific case—and often are not realized by the perceiver of the mood...'.[13] Emotions, on the other hand, are '[f]ocused on a specific target or cause—generally realized by the perceiver of the emotion...'.[14] They are analogous with their cause or object(s) of origin. As such emotions operate in relatively binary and cause/effect fashions. The difference is that where emotions have an analogue object, moods do not or at least the connection is tenuous and often unrecognised.

In this video the mood is generally a tone pervading the whole encounter. *The Greatest* has a somewhat positive mood that feels rebellious or strong—that is of course except the opening and the very end when it feels generally poignant/sad. The emotion (of the performers) connects to the viewer (they look directly at us) and expresses something towards us. Their emotions are also very quick moving and transforming. They cycle through emotions very quickly. In fact, towards the end from minutes 3:34 to 4:42 there practically is an explosion of emotions. Collectively and individually, the dancers all express a kaleidoscope of emotions. The mood, differently, remains relatively constant throughout the video, only shifting between relatively positive (during the large middle part of the video) and negative (the opening and closing). Barsade and Gibson clarify that while an object(s) might cause moods, due to their more diffused nature, moods separate from that point of origin. We experience them as a pervading sense or a collective feeling.

164    *Precis*

The durations of moods and emotions also differ. Emotions are '...relatively intense and very short-lived [... whereas moods have] medium duration (from a few moments to as long as a few weeks or more)'.[15] *The Greatest* exaggerates this difference, with rapid-fire emotions contrasting the relatively stable, static mood. Barsade and Gibson further note that emotions can, after their phase of intensity, turn into moods. Moods are diffuse, do not specify on their causal object or perhaps any object, can be maximal or minimal in their intensity and last for longer periods of time. Also, while emotions are generally recognised by their perceiver, moods generally are not—they are something more elusive. The use of the terms focussed (for emotions) and diffused (for moods) are very good as comparatives. Emotions are like a sharp beam of aimed light; moods, a soft cast of generally directed light.

To return to the notion of character and characterisation, there is an obvious sharing of the experience they are having with each other. Their emotional culture is homogenic and they perform emotional states for us as viewers. In doing so, we might stand-in for them and experience their emotional culture as though having the experience ourselves. As stated above, these affects, and consequently emotions and moods, transmit between the participant individuals and us as audience. There is a contagion here. The dancers exist within, adopt and support a mood, which we the audience catch through our act of watching. By being within the broadcast presence of the dancing group we immerse in their mood and thus feel and are affected by it.

The catching/similarisation of emotional states in the aesthetic collective also supports the collective mood. Barsade and Gibson define *emotional contagion* as the 'processes that allow the sharing or transfer of emotions from one individual to other group members'.[16] It is the spreading of emotions through the group through a 'tendency to mimic the nonverbal behaviour of others, to "synchronize facial expressions, vocalizations, postures, and movements" with others, and in turn, to "converge emotionally"' (Hatfield, Cacioppo and Rapson, 1994).[17] So, as the aesthetic collective expresses their emotions, all of which are directed to be on similar paths, it creates a convergence of emotional range for the work, which is expressive of the same underlying affective dimension.

Applying Barsade,[18] the aesthetic collective of *The Greatest* has converged affectively and they display the behavioural norms and normative mechanisms of expression of collective affect.

> The second step of this primitive contagion process comes from the afferent feedback people receive from mimicking others' nonverbal behaviors and expressions—an automatic process. As myriad facial, postural, and vocal feedback studies have shown, once people engage in the mimicking behavior, they then experience the emotion itself (e.g. Duclos et al., 1989) through the physiological feedback from their muscular, visceral, and glandular responses (see Hatfield, Cacioppo and Rapson, 1994, for a review; Adelman and Zajonc, 1989; Laird and Bresler, 1992). One can

ultimately become aware of feeling this emotion, but the initial processes that lead to it are subconscious and automatic (Hatfield, Cacioppo and Rapson, 1994).[19]

This automatic self-construction of perceived emotion indicates that witnessing performed acts creates a multi-faceted experience for the viewer. On the one hand, I have a cerebral examination of the scene and thus an intellectually processed response. On the other hand, their emotion transmits to me and I may stand-in for them and feel that. The way an audience views and processes this collective perhaps simultaneously creates identification with the group. By contagion ('I am one of them—I *feel* what they feel') and by objective outsidership in intellectual processing ('they are a group; I am not one of them—but I *understand* what they feel') which allows experience from both within and without the aesthetic collective. Especially with recorded media like this, through a screen the viewer is definitely outside the physical aesthetic space of the aesthetic collective, but they still psychically project into it. This division does not stop emotional contagion.

> Cheshin et al. (2011) examined the emergence of shared group mood among group members working together virtually in a computer-based negotiation task and found that both text-based and behavior-based cues lead to emotional contagion (even in the absence of direct, in-person interactions).[20]

While the audience is not a physically present member of the back-up dancing group, the camera and microphone act as a proxy presence for the audience creating simulated membership through first, second and third person audio-visual entrance to the space of the collective.

## Mood Setting/Contagion

We can further examine mood setting and contagion with a set of videos by Lady Gaga. I have chosen *Bad Romance* and *Alejandro* as I read them as companion pieces, both working with similar motifs in content and visual construction. Both are from the 2009 album *The Fame Monster*. Both are strong, bass-driven club anthems with themes of love, sex, power and destruction. The lyrics of both proceed through open narratives. The aesthetic collectives perform character roles somewhat equal to Lady Gaga's character(s), but also serve as secondary characters. Unlike *Rhythm Nation* and *The Greatest* in which the aesthetic collectives are the focus point, here the aesthetic collectives are companion characters. Lady Gaga is a narrative character distinct and detached from the aesthetic collective, even though she does merge with them in each video on several occasions. The aesthetic collectives in each video weave in and out of the verses of the song but dominantly occupy, in the main, the chorus

166  *Precis*

parts. In that way they are typical of the more common use of back-up dancers in music video.

There is a direct comparison between these uses of aesthetic collectives and Greek khoros, which I think is in the nature of back-up dancers. They exist alongside the main action, sometimes participating, sometimes not. They connect directly with and ignore the audience. They support the main characters and at times perform with the main characters. The verse-chorus-verse-chorus pattern of song writing and video production also mirrors choral ode structure or even the entire play structure of a Greek tragedy in episode-ode-episode-ode pattern. *Bad Romance* even has the dancing chorus in extraordinary costumes complete with masks and elevated shoes—how khoroi would traditionally be costumed. Differently, *Alejandro* anonymises the male dancing chorus by casting very similar build, height and race men, identically dressing them, toning their skin with make-up/colour grading and putting them all in the same bowl-cut, exaggerated Kim Jong-Un/60s Beatles-like haircut/wig.[21] With this appearance the men could easily be out of a Beecroft installation. A direct comparison with Beecroft's collectives and how she similarised her members can be made regarding all the videos discussed thus far. In all cases the aesthetic collectives undergo cosmetic and costume transformation to become a visually cohesive, coordinated and identical group. In Gaga's videos, both are anonymised and used as characters and to characterise mood and spectacle in the videos.

While *Bad Romance* does follow an intelligible narrative plot, *Alejandro* does not and instead weaves together a pastiche of suggestive and fractal plot points. *Bad Romance* premiered first in November 2009. Lady Gaga wrote the song with Nadir Khayat and the video was directed by Francis Lawrence and produced by Red One and Lady Gaga (the Haus of Gaga). The video follows the story of the release of Lady Gaga from a coffin-pod container marked with a red crucifix and the word 'monster' along with six other women in similar coffin-pods. All seven are in skin-tight white latex leotard catsuits, thigh-high spike-heel and platformed boots and masks that cover, in Gaga, the face from the nose up and, in the others, the whole face except holes for eyes and mouth and extend above the head in crown-like spikes. This collective will accompany Gaga throughout the video in two further forms: during the second chorus they will appear alongside her numbering eight in white long-armed leotards, knee-high white spike-heel boots, and diamante forehead/skull caps; during the third and final chorus they appear along with Gaga, again numbering eight, in red leotards/bodysuits made of lace and lycra, black or red boots (again, with spike-heels), and red eye masks and on two or three of the members there are red tulle ruffs. In each chorus Lady Gaga dresses similarly, but differently, marking her the clear focus point. Each time she is positioned front and centre with the women fanned in two triangles to either side and slightly behind. The only variant to this is the beginning of the second chorus in which she begins in the centre, surrounded by the women. The second chorus is different to the other two as it is the only one that occurs in the

Mood, Affect, Feeling, Emotion 167

presence of the other characters in the video and as such within the verse/episode. The first and third choruses happen entirely in alternate, separated and unattended spaces, suggesting they operate more as cut-away moments of narration and commentary on the action of the plot. The actual plot of the video follows Lady Gaga's monster being forced into an underground black-market skin trade with a Russian gangster and, on the eve of his consummation of ownership of her, she burns him alive and, presumably, takes over his operation.

While the episodic characters do very little (including Gaga's character), the aesthetic collective (the only dancers in the video) do a lot. Their choreography, by Laurieann Gibson and Richard 'Richy' Jackson who also choreographed *Alejandro*, is very demonstrative, filled not just with dance steps, but with very specific gestures and limb movements. There is a lot of clawing, scratching, fist shaking, wrenching, twisting and heavily angular jerking of the whole body. Another very evocative gesture that the dancers use at the beginning and end of the video (see minutes 0:38–0:46 and 4:48–4:56) is a clapping action of the arms. This action on its own opens and closes the video, suggesting chomping jaws it implies that wrong love, or bad romance, is like a large set of teeth repetitively biting and slamming down on one. The clawing gestures, which can be seen throughout all the danced sections, similarly evoke feelings of frustration, anger and destruction and literally imply rending, ripping and lacerating. These feelings are further complicated by the costumes of the dancers, which are highly fetishistic and overtly sexual. The aesthetic collective has a visual tone that is Gothic and scary yet alluring and explicit—these women could be objects of pleasure or danger. Watching the video causes feelings of excitement and interest coupled with fear and caution. The mood set by this combination of feelings is strong and is accompanied by the pulse of the song. Having been to a number of clubs and in many dance situations this song always provokes dancing and duplication of the dance moves.

*Alejandro* too follows a verse-chorus-verse-chorus pattern of visual story-telling in which the aesthetic collective, this time composed of men, alternates with episodes of Lady Gaga doing a variety of things on her own or with members of the aesthetic collective and secondary characters. The aesthetic collective is again very much like a Greek khoros, playing characters (albeit very skeletally defined ones) and silent narrators. During the choruses of the song in which Lady Gaga dances with the aesthetic collective she is front and centre. The episode scenes are, however, not very clear in their plot, if one even really exists. The narrative here is more a montage of samples and homages to other artists and pieces of artistic work, such as Madonna (in particular in look and action to the videos for *Like a Prayer*, and *Justify My Love*), the film *Cabaret*, Eva Perón and *Evita* and a variety of military and erotica references. Its referential nature creates a confusion in the video, reducing its narrative to a series of visual statements and absent meanings; the meaning of the video has a particular postmodern dismissal of rational and linear thought,

168    *Precis*

leaving meaning up for interpretation in the viewer. Although Lady Gaga and director Steven Klein claim not to reference other artists intentionally (particularly Madonna) but only to have been influenced by them, the video is a bricolage that does allow such reference and linkage even if not intended.

While reviews in *Rolling Stone* magazine, *CBS News, New York, The Sunday Times* and *Billboard* were mixed (some were glowingly positive, some were lukewarm, some negative), and generally placed the video as lesser than *Bad Romance*, I would argue it is a superior piece of work. I suspect that poorer reactions are to the lack of clear plot, expecting/needing meaning be explicated within the video. The obvious comparisons to the above artists and artworks also frustrated reviewers slightly. Indeed, Camille Paglia's article 'Lady Gaga and the Death of Sex' acerbically attacks her and this video. Paglia argues that Gaga is both too manufactured, synthetic and superficial to be sexy and that she is simply a thief of others' work:

> In fact, Gaga isn't sexy at all—she's like a gangly marionette or plasticised android. How could a figure so calculated and artificial, so clinical and strangely antiseptic, so stripped of genuine eroticism have become the icon of her generation? Can it be that Gaga represents the exhausted end of the sexual revolution? In Gaga's manic miming of persona after persona, over-conceptualised and claustrophobic, we may have reached the limit of an era [...] Bob Fosse's dazzlingly aggressive choreography in that blockbuster film [*Cabaret*] was adopted by Madonna for her videos and stage shows—all of which have been doggedly imitated by Lady Gaga. Gaga has borrowed so heavily from Madonna (as in her latest Alejandro video) that it must be asked, at what point does homage become theft? [...] she is a ruthless recycler of other people's work. She is the diva of déjà vu.[22]

Paglia's comments reflect a number of critiques of her work, suggesting that she, and in particular this video, is simply too referential and a skilled plagiariser. Much of the critical discussion of *Alejandro* is pervaded by an obsession with sampling and referencing. If such judgements are put aside, this video can be read as more narratively complex and technically better executed than *Bad Romance* and many of her other videos. As to meaning, also a negative critique in critical and popular discussion, Lady Gaga has stated that the video is not so much a story, as a commemoration to her relationship with gay culture:

> The video is about the 'purity of my friendships with my gay friends', Gaga had explained [...] 'And how I've been unable to find that with a straight man in my life. It's a celebration and an admiration of gay love—it confesses my envy of the courage and bravery they require to be together. In the video I'm pining for the love of my gay friends—but they just don't want me'.[23]

Mood, Affect, Feeling, Emotion    169

I am going to walk through the video sequence by sequence. The aesthetic collective portrays a series of military men who dance for, with or around Lady Gaga's character, nominally some sort of deceased political military dictator's wife/partner, and her internal visions of herself. They dress in three ways: in black combat boots and black brief underwear; black combat boots and high-waisted black trunk underwear; in full p/leather military outfits. Their appearances in the video are a bit more elaborate than in *Bad Romance* and I will focus mainly on their dancing appearances, as opposed to their more incidental appearances as characters (in flashbacks, the present or flashforwards). They appear first as backlit silhouettes performing a military demonstration, stomping, marching and squat marching to introduce the video (0:29–1:00). This was similar in action, but more extreme, to the warrior-like dancing in *The Greatest* and, compared to Greek khoros, very much like khoros warrior dance, a pyrrhikhe.[24] This dance happens almost as a prologue to the video, immediately setting the tone with a mood of anonymity, aggression, masculinity and domination.

The second appearance of the aesthetic collective occurs at minute 2:19–3:40 when they dance alone for Gaga's character (the set suggests in the courtyard below a balconied residence). Until minute 3:16 the dancing is in an organised shape with the men staggered in diagonal lines and the camera cuts between their dancing and Gaga singing. Their choreography here mixes standing routines and floor routines with the men flipping, wheeling and punching. It still has a military and athletic feeling to it and it is well co-ordinated. A mood is conveyed in emotional projection through their bodies and stern faces (at times you can even see, but not hear, them shouting). At minute 3:16–3:41, the dancing changes, though, and they dance in an inward facing circle and then break into three couples and a group of four. The choreography here utilises sparring and fight moves as choreography. There is neck grabbing, half barrel rolls and moves that look simultaneously like fighting and tango. There is a lot of homoerotic aggression and violence to this section (it ends with a member of the three couples being violently thrust face-first into the ground). Like *Bad Romance*, the men generate a mood of sexual desire tinted with danger and overt sado–masochism; this chorus is designed to arouse the audience and disturb them.

Gaga is introduced as a performer with the aesthetic collective in both the third episode and chorus. In the episode she and three of the men (who in addition to the costume outlined above also wear high heel shoes) enact scenes of underwear-clothed-sex and S&M rope play on three single sized, steel-frame, military issue beds; the men explicitly writhe with ropes. At minute 4:10, five of the aesthetic collective are re-introduced (and they will serve as the second chorus dancers) along with Lady Gaga dancing (front and centre) with them. From here until and through the actual chorus (at minute 4:31–4:58), the action cuts between the episode scenes, the chorus dancing and scenes of a Joan of Arc-like Gaga on a bed with a crucifix. The dancing is now more overtly sexual and combines both stereotypically male and female

170   *Precis*

sexual behaviour (hands sliding over breasts and crotch, actions of male masturbation, writhing). The energy levels in each subsequent choral dance noticeably increase and the dancing becomes more intense and expressive. This happens alongside a more direct sexual motif. The increase in energy interjaculates the video mood more assertively into the audience's viewing. I found this section to be the most effective in the video. The visual tone alone is powerful and very stylish, but the attitudes of the dancers and the innate eroticism throughout are also very infectious and affecting.

Barsade might echo my assertion here. She states that '[a] high-energy display of positive or negative emotion may also transfer emotion more powerfully because it communicates the emotional message more clearly and accurately than a low-energy display'.[25] None of the previous dancing in the video could be categorised as low-energy, but energy increases as timecode moves forward. While Barsade's research is developed alongside research on depression[26] and extroversion,[27] when used here illustrates how low-energy states do not transmit as well or as accurately as extroverted behaviour. Furthermore, Barsade makes a physiological point:

> Last, physiological studies of emotion show that energy intensifies emotional experiences. High arousal has been found to lead to an increase in autonomic nervous system responses (e.g. heart rate acceleration, sin conductance, facial activity) and has been shown in longitudinal blood pressure studies to be an important indicator of affective involvement (Jacob et al., 1999). These effects, along with the psychological effects of energy on emotional experiences, leads to [a hypotext]: [...] The same emotional valence (pleasant or unpleasant) expressed with high energy will lead to more contagion than if expressed with low energy.[28]

As the energy level in *Alejandro* increases the viewer is carried along as well with each verse-chorus-repeat evolving the energy. For instance, in the second verse the synth bass line is the predominant music, pushing the lower pulse of the song more. This has the effect of pulsing or even forcing the mood at the audience. This second episode-chorus is interesting as well as the camera work literally pulses at the viewer, using extremely fast cuts (some are only parts of seconds) between the three action scenes. The first episode and chorus have consistently longer lingering shots, more tracking moves and more fluid and liquid-like dolly movement of the camera. Comparatively, the second episode and chorus become faster, more aggressive and the camera both moves faster and has faster editing cuts. Interestingly, the shots of the aesthetic collective dancing with Lady Gaga have fairly long-held shots in the first half of the chorus; in the second half, the cuts in the scene on the beds and of the chorus dance become very rapid, at times almost strobing. This increase in speed and energy will develop yet further in the third episode-chorus and in the fourth, outro. In a subtle way, the visuals, the camera control and the editing style are developing through the video, pulsing and thrusting at the

Mood, Affect, Feeling, Emotion    171

viewer, heightening the mood and mimicking the actions, rhythms or patterns of sex.

The video now moves into an extended bridge in which Lady Gaga is the primary focus, but the aesthetic collective is still cavorting with her. In minutes 4:59–5:36, they rise from the floor around her and then encircle her and throw her up in the air while the video intercuts with images of her swallowing a rosary and singing. During this section, the expressions on the men's faces (and Lady Gaga's face) convey further feelings of effort, tension, elation and serenity. The video then returns to a strobe-editing effect, both with fading in the video and cutting between different takes. The collective, now dressed in full military dress, marches around Lady Gaga who sings and dances in homage to a scene from a Sally Bowles performance in *Cabaret*. This bridge is preparing the viewer for climax. The use of the aesthetic collective here is a sense is recapitulating what has happened before launching the viewer into another bridge-chorus dance with them (see minutes 6:16–6:36). This one, with very high energy and fairly athletic choreography moves from standing to ground work very quickly. The choreography is in fact a combination of parts of the material that has already been presented. From that point on the video works towards its literal and figurative climax in the fourth chorus by using a vamp or loop from the chorus and adding instrumentation bit by bit. The visuals are a complex montage of characters, riot and battle imagery, flashbacks from all of the video presented, and other bits and pieces. The cuts are fast, relatively even and alternate in visual appearance (some in black and white, some colour, some new material, some already seen etc.). The fourth chorus, and climax, to the piece occurs at minute 7:34 and lasts to the end of the video. It is a development of the same third chorus dance and then an acted scene between Gaga and the aesthetic collective in which they surround her. She removes her clothing (except underwear) and they writhe together in actions that mimic an orgy.

An enormous amount happens in this video. It is fast moving and the visual tone is skilfully crafted and designed (Steven Klein is a photographer by trade so perhaps this comes as no surprise). The aesthetic collective is fully entitative and displays an incredible level of cohesion. The mood in the video emerges from a strong combination of the design of the visuals, the song music (and in particularly the driving electronic bass and pulse) and the attitude and behaviour of the performers.

As a viewer, the collective in this video feels very cohesive and joined. Apparent difference has been eliminated between the performers. They look and act similarly while also holding the same character/ising roles. '[E]xternal observers judge[] groups in which there [i]s greater diversity in emotion among the group members as sharing less of a common fate and holding less shared responsibility for group outcomes'.[29] This group, though, is highly convergent in their emotion and they imply a great sense of common fate. '[T]he degree of affective diversity among people is an indicator that people use when judging the "groupiness" of a group'.[30] Likewise, the collective in *The Greatest* also

## 172   Precis

converge in their emotion and common fate, indeed they even terminate in a literal common end fate. That affective state or emotional culture then transmits to the audience. The collectives in these videos move their shared affective state and mood of the aesthetic collective to me, the audience. Returning to Fuchs' notion of standing-in for the character, I can stand-in for these collectives and experience the moods, and by extension the affective dimension of the work, and feel a sense of insidership with the performance. I would argue this is supported by the voyeurism of the camera-as-eye/microphone-as-ear, which literally moves within and about the aesthetic collectives.

Taken together, the back-up dancers in all these videos demonstrate potential uses of aesthetic collectives. They can be used in capacities as characters within the narrative of the video: as characters, as narrators, as chorus/khoros, as dancers, as background, as primary focus points, as scenery for the main performer(s). They also produce mood; they work in tandem with the mise-en-scène and design to produce an affective dimension which the viewer experiences. There are correlations between the emotions performed and the transmission of that emotion to the audience. A return to elements of entitativity shows that the more similarised in action the group the clearer the emotional message is and thus the easier its transmission to the audience: clarity and cohesiveness in communication is linked to the same in messages. Next, the precipitation of mood links with the actions the dancers perform. On the one hand, there is the control over facial expression, the image suggested by the action, gesture, posture and general body language. As dancing examples, choreography further contributes to the conduction of mood. The repetition of actions and the nature of the dance create tones and feelings for the audience. Their energy levels also correlate to contagion. This relates to several different aspects, such as the force of expression, the speed or rhythm of their movements, the intensity of their embodiment, the relative exaggeration of their emotions and so on. The greater the energy, the stronger the contagion.

Having started this chapter and the last discussing the uses, functions and purposes of the cases of aesthetic collectives under study it ends with the observation that one clear and common purpose is the creation and transmission of mood, emotion, feelings and affect between performers and audiences. Another is that collectives work in tandem with environmental aspects to achieve this transmission. Like in clubbing crowds, the emergence of affect, feeling, emotion and mood was reliant on the environmental design, especially the music. Without the music, the experience would cease to exist; but this is not a unilateral relationship. Without the dancing crowd the club would fail as well. Beecroft's installations could exist perhaps anywhere, but the specific locations she chose and the organisation of the participants and their prägnanz determined the reception of them by the audience. She framed the installations with the space and the duration of the performance. The environment relied on the members and the members on the environment for those installations to succeed. The khoroi examples similarly relied on the performance contexts in which they appeared and the design/scenography of

Mood, Affect, Feeling, Emotion   173

those spaces to affect the audience fully. Each instance illustrates how intertwined aesthetic collectives and their environments are to establish an emotional culture for them, the performance experience and effective communication with audiences.

## Notes

1 Philip Auslander, *Liveness: Performance in a Mediatized Culture*, 2nd ed. (London and New York: Routledge, Taylor & Francis Group, 2008).
2 Auslander, p. 184.
3 Auslander, p. 184.
4 Auslander, p. 184.
5 For an assessment of this claim, please see Joseph Vogel, 'The Nation …'. In this article, he compares Jackson's *Rhythm Nation* to other key musical albums of the 1980s, before and beyond.
6 Janet Jackson, *Rhythm Nation*, A&M Records (1989), online video clip www.youtube.com published on 16 June 2009 [accessed 15 July 2017].
7 See comment 5 in Appendix C for other examples.
8 See Silvan S. Tomkins, *Affect, Imagery, Consciousness: The Complete Edition* (New York: Springer Publishing Company, 2008).
9 See Ben Anderson, *Encountering Affect: Capacities, Apparatuses, Condition* (London: Routledge Taylor and Francis, 2016).
10 Anderson, p. 84.
11 Anderson, p. 85.
12 Anderson, p. 107.
13 Sigal G. Barsade and Donald E. Gibson, 'Why Does Affect Matter in Organizations?', *Perspectives*, 21:1 (2007), 38.
14 Barsade and Gibson, p. 38.
15 Barsade and Gibson, p. 38.
16 Barsade and Gibson, p. 38.
17 Barsade and Gibson, p. 38; see also E. Hatfield, J. Cacioppo and Richard Rapson, 'Emotional Contagion', *Current Directions in Psychological Science*, 2 (1993), 96–99.
18 Sigal Barsade, 'The Ripple Effect: Emotional Contagion and its Influence on Group Behavior', *Administrative Science Quarterly*, 47:4 (2002), 644–675.
19 Barsade, p. 648. See also Pamela K. Adelmann and R. B. Zajonc, 'Facial Efference and the Experience of Emotion', *Annual Review of Psychology*, 40 (1989), 249–280; Sandra Declos and others, 'Emotion-Specific Effects of Facial Expressions and Postures on Emotional Experience', *Journal of Personality and Social Psychology*, 57:1 (1989), 100–108; James D. Laird and Charles Bresler, 'The Process of Emotional Experience: A Self-Perception Theory', *Review of Personality and Social Psychology*, 13 (1992), 213–234.
20 Sigal G. Barsade and Andrew P. Knight, 'Group Affect', *Annual Review of Organizational Psychology and Organizational Behaviour*, 2 (2015), 31; see also Arik Cheshin, Anat Rafaeli and Nathan Bos, 'Anger and Happiness in Virtual Teams: Emotional Influences of Text and Behavior in Others' Affect in the Absence of Non-Verbal Cues', *Organizational Behavior and Human Decision Processes*, 116 (2011), 2–16.
21 See Comment 6 in Appendix C.
22 Camille Paglia, 'Lady Gaga and the Death of Sex', *The Sunday Times* (12 September 2010), https://www.thetimes.co.uk/article/lady-gaga-and-the-death-of-sex-lnzbcd70zj3 [accessed 10 August 2017].
23 Caitlin Moran, 'Come Party with Lady Gaga', *The Times* (22 May 2010), https://www.thetimes.co.uk/article/come-party-with-lady-gaga-pb2ln3zrmp3 [accessed 10 August 2017].

174   *Precis*

24  See comment 7 in Appendix C.
25  Barsade, 'The Ripple Effect', p. 650.
26  K. M. Prkachin et al., 'Nonverbal Communication Deficits and Response to Performance Feedback in Depression', *Journal of Abnormal Psychology*, 86 (1977), 224–234; A. C. Gerson and D. Perlman, 'Loneliness and Expressive Communication', *Journal of Abnormal Psychology*, 88 (1979), 258–261.
27  R. P. Buck, *The Communication of Emotion* (New York: Guilford Press, 1984).
28  Barsade, 'The Ripple Effect', p. 650.
29  Barsade and Knight, 'Group Affect', p. 25.
30  Barsade and Knight, 'Group Affect', p. 25.

# 6  Encountering Atmospheres

The final points about aesthetic collectives follow in more detail the types of encounter and immersion in the cases discussed and how both roles—participant and audience—interact with the performance. I have already noted the encounter itself positioning participants and audiences within the entitative presence of these aesthetic collectives. I have been confederating notions of *presence*, *effect* and *aura*. Whilst all slightly different, I use these terms to represent the same core thing experienced with these collectives. I will address these as a *field*, something that extends out into surrounding space and matter, and experiencing these fields as *atmospheric* encounters. A fundamental aspect of these encounters is that participants and audiences were always within, surrounded by or projecting into the field of aesthetic collectives. This 'being-in' is immersion. The roles of audience and participant define the type(s) of immersion and the structure the experiences take. Participants are always physically 'in' and 'a part' of the collectives. With audience roles, though, this becomes less the case as their physical location at times is removed from the physical domain of the collectives but contained nonetheless within the aura of the aesthetic collective as a work of art.

I use Walter Benjamin's term *aura* here to imply how as original works of art these examples created an affective, aesthetic field about them through their presence. Aura, from mythology, is a goddess of the breeze. Like a breeze, an aura surrounds, moves about and affects all where it occurs. Benjamin asserts that works of art hold around them a field of influence, an aura, that engulfs its audience in their aesthetic commands—meaning within an aura, performances exert aesthetic effects on those present. Audiences for aesthetic collectives, while not always physically contained within them, are still immersed and contained in their aesthetic field. In that space we affected and were affected by the other things, subjects and objects co-present. For Benjamin, *aura* is the unique aesthetic presence of performances as works of art. *Aura* derives from their '*presence* in time and space, [their] *unique existence* at the place where [they] happen[ed] to be [...] The[ir] *presence* [...] [was] the prerequisite to the concept of authenticity [all emphasis added]'.[1] As I have emphasised, aura is tied to presence and unique existence, and Benjamin himself relates aura and presence.[2]

While there is potential for a wider extension of Benjamin's theoretical principles of aura here, I am only taking and addressing the notion of aura, as

DOI: 10.4324/9781003205661-9

176    *Precis*

with presence, as a field property of artworks. The aura is a field in which the relationship, exchange and impact between participants and audience become crucial dimensions of the work. For my purposes, this field addresses the inhabited environment of aesthetic collectives. There is the sense of their fields occupying and extending through space. In my analysis, I find aesthetic collectives to have a common core of properties demonstrative of these notions. They all seem to extend perceptually beyond their physical containment (that being the bodies of the individuals and the collective domain). Extension beyond the material of bodies creates a dimensionality that includes the space between members and surrounding them. Fields, by definition, are distributed forces through spaces. Indeed, the fields of aesthetic collectivesare filled with an aesthetic force or effect and create aesthetic experiences and feelings. Engaging or encountering them is an encounter of or interaction with(in) that field, constituting and creating the conditions for intersubjective exchanges.

At the outset, I clarify my use of the term *immersion,* much as I did in the introduction, as a descriptive term. At times, my various examples did use/ have immersive tactics/production styles and performance methods à la immersive theatre (e.g. using headphones to draw distanced audiences in, strategically placed projections to bring the visuals closer/at greater scale, moving audiences through performance spaces, direct participation and so on). Those tactics do bare on how performances might engender sensations of immersion. However, I am focussing on the issue of being or feeling inside/outside of these fields specifically. I will first touch on immersive qualities in review of the experiences discussed. I then will unpack this further in regard to a discussion of immersivity in performance framed in a more detailed way through critical discourse on what immersion might/can mean.

## The Encounter

An encounter is a meeting, a coming together with/against, where one thing is faced with another. An encounter sets the scene for an experience and the experience modifies or affects the encounter. Encountering the clubbing crowds, the audience came together with the aesthetic collective and could become contained in its field or concatenate/fused with it. In the Beecroft and khoroi examples, the audiences were not physically contained in the collectives. They were delineated from them and organised into a distinct audience body but contained in another way, within the field of those aesthetic collectives. With back-up dancing groups the viewer could both objectively view the dancing groups and experience them from within through the lens of the camera and the microphone. Whatever the case, the fields of the aesthetic collectives engulfed and transfixed their audiences.

Going a bit deeper into what constitutes their fields, I follow Böhme's[3] concept of how things radiate their presence outwardly into the surrounding world. He posits that things (all types of things, including material objects and living people) radiate part of their living essence about; he refers to this as the *ecstasy* of the thing. *VB46* had extension from the individual women's presence into space as well as the combined collective presence for them as a totality, for example. These presences were not simply a sense of them being there, but also *how* they existed in that space together. How they exist, this ecstasy, is an affective dimension. How they are *affected* and how they *affect*. How their presence is coloured and tinted by affect, their mood or emotional tone. In all the cases, I examined the presence, these ecstasies, of the participants and the audiences felt like tangible fields affecting and tuning the surrounding space. In other words, their fields felt like overlapping, radiating and enmeshed ecstasies of everything there.

These radiations were directed through the focus of so many present people; mainly, the audience focussed towards the performance and the performers at the audience but also in more nuanced directions. Each audience member was first present with the rest of the audience. This co-presence encompassed them. They were physically in the audience and each was situated within the audience field. Following Böhme's argument, as a subject in that space they were in the audience-collective's field, their ecstasy. Equally, the performing collective was caught in the audience field. In this sense, the fields to the khoros and the audience overlapped and interpenetrated each other. In other words, being *in* both, both groups were immersed in these fields. These spaces were "'tinctured'" through the presence of things, of persons and environmental constellations, that is through their ecstasies. They [we]re themselves spheres of the presences of something, their reality in space'.[4]

Delineating the participant-performer experience of immersion in each other's presences more I return to Beecroft's installations. As a confluence of individual presences they were affecting and being affected by each other. Because so little was directed to happen in those installations, the very presence of the participants, as individuals and as collective, became an objectified element of the work. Their presences/radiating ecstasies were affected in a number of ways. First by Beecroft's own directorial hand. The members had to focus on the explicit instructions Beecroft gave them. In turn, their individual agency, as discussed earlier, reduced and denuded to become the form Beecroft designed. Their individual presences transformed into a version designed to Beecroft's idea for that aesthetic collective: a homogenous blueprint. Second, they were affected by their co-presence, as discussed in chapter two, of which they were both strongly aware but instructed to remain apart from (by restricting communication and indicating they should have feelings of individual responsibility for the work). Third, they were affected by objectification felt from the imposing audience presence. Such objectification further contained and segregated them from the audience. So, each individual participant affected and was affected by aesthetic choices, cohabitation and the environment. For the performers, a plural presence emerged creating a sense of similarity and autonomy. They were all made to be the same and a multiplication of that collective homogenous presence—as a totalising and radiating field. Audience members were then engulfed within that expansive collective

178   *Precis*

field, experiencing the specific ecstasy of the-collective-as-thing. In the encounter of those cases, the perceiver and perceived were immersed in each other's fields, bathed in the ecstasy of the other.

For performers, immersion was always physical (being in the collective) and always within the collective field. Since their field had affective dimensions, the type of entrance or immersion conditioned the affective experience. For example, being a participant/audience in the clubbing crowds had very powerful and immediate affective effects on me, in part as that is an experiential role, one in which I personally make entrance to the aesthetic collective. Comparatively, the experience of the khoroi, where I was not a participant, was more objectified and less personal. I was removed from them physically and their field had to be diffused across the whole audience. The music videos were even more objectified as I was fully removed from the event (in their space and time of happening). However, since their viewing format is personal, occurs in a chosen environment and offers control over the video timecode they had a more intimate experience and I could feel very much 'in' them.

Returning to audiences, how they enter into or are immersed in the fields of aesthetic collectives is an important aspect that conditions the experience. This experiential inside/outside is not just a physiospatial positioning, it is also psycho-perceptual. I see three broad forms of immersion: physical immersion within the collective; being physically outside the collective but within its field; being physically outside the collective but projecting/being absorbing into its field. Clubbing cases, for example, are physically immersive where the audience is within the collective domain and in their field. This is physical immersion of one body within another body, which entails presence within the field. Attendants entered and became part of the dancing crowds. Differently, some aesthetic collectives still immerse audiences in their field but are experienced from an external physical perspective. For example, in watching the khoroi the audience projected themselves into the aesthetic collective on-stage while being in the different physical space of the audience, outside the collective domain. This was immersion of our thoughts and minds through sensory projection into these collectives while remaining physically separate to them. Beecroft installations and music videos, where audiences could choose their physical perspective relative to the aesthetic collectives or stand-in through the entering eye of the camera, show an in-betweenness. These had elements of both physical immersion and removal.

These experiential positionings, first, illustrate how the encounter of aesthetic collectives is multi-modal and, second, demonstrate a variety in types of immersion. Before going further with the nature of immersion it is relevant to clarify the modal geometry of encounters *as bodies* here—that is, how participants and audience bodies are situated and relate to each other in terms of intersubjective paths. To me there are also three general options for how audiences situate in relation to aesthetic collectives: the audience and aesthetic collective are distinct and non-intersecting bodies; the audience and aesthetic

## Encountering Atmospheres    179

collective bodies intersect yet are distinct; the audience and aesthetic collective are one group, intersecting and also the same. Some encounters use more than one of these options.

In the first option, aesthetic collectives are distinct from audiences. This was the case with the khoroi, music video and the Beecroft cases. These aesthetic collectives were designed to be objectively separate and differentiated from the audience, particularly in space. As an audience member for the khoroi and music videos, I was very much a separate and outside audience member looking in/at the performances. In this relationship, the audience tends to observe and watch the aesthetic collective. This has the effect of keeping the aesthetic collective at a certain intersubjective, third-person remove: the audience is allowed to objectify the aesthetic collective as an aesthetic object.

In the second option, aesthetic collectives and audiences intersect or can have intersection as bodies. Depending on viewing choice, the clubbing cases and Beecroft's installations could be encountered in this way. Audiences had the agency to enter the dancing crowds or installed collectives and view from within, like walking amongst them, giving them third and second person perspective. In the Beecroft examples, there was no instruction to the audience stating they should *not* move through the installation. However, as reported in chapter two this never happened. There was an assumption to stay separate (I believe encounters in galleries tend to imply distance). Audiences in this option can engage with and cavort amongst collectives. This creates a blurring of distinctions for the audience between aesthetic-object and self-as-aesthetic-object.

In the third option, aesthetic collectives and audiences are the same or there is no distinction between them. This was the case with the clubbing crowds; although a caveat here might be that as a dancer I could stand back and watch the dancing as though an audience, which is why they also have the second option just mentioned. In fact, I did this very often during my dancing to gain a more objective perspective. In this relationship, the audience is the aesthetic collective and thus experiences the aesthetic event from the first-person perspective, from 'within', in addition to third- and second-person perspectives. Thus, they simultaneously can be aesthetic object and audience.

Whatever option, encountering these aesthetic collectives is always being immersed in their fields. To limn, at *Oresteia* I was both objectively watching the khoroi and felt enclosed/surrounded by them. Their field expanded beyond the stage to encompass us. Moreover, upon reflection I can say that I felt like I was encountering them both as myself, an attendee, but also as a member of the *body* of the audience. I both watched and focussed on certain, individual khoros members, but also watched and focussed on the group. My encounter had multiple levels of attention or relationship from me to them, including my own individuated perspective and a collectivised perspective of *we-the-audience*. The attention or relationship returned from them was similarly multi-layered. At times, a member of the khoros or several of them directly viewed me. This happened when their gaze and attention fixed on me. A particularly exciting

180   *Precis*

experience of this happened when I was singled-out and performed to during one ode. Several of them made eye contact with me at the same time. At other times, they vaguely directed their attention in my general area encompassing me and the immediately surrounding audience. At yet other times, they directed their attention elsewhere in the audience, not in my general area. It still felt like I was being attended to vicariously through those other audience members, though. It was as if any address to the audience was an address to *us* and thus to *me*. This intersubjective experience holds a unique plurality of directions and connections. In this example, intersubjectivity is not simply bilateral between the aesthetic object and me as viewer. In different ways this was the case with all the different aesthetic collectives. The encounters of them had multiple, simultaneous intersubjective experiences—plural intersubjectivity.

The plural intersubjectivity in my encounter of the khoros of *Oresteia* occurred between singular khoros members and me/we (the audience) as well as the totality of the khoros and me/we. Compared to my dyadic relationship with the actors playing the episodic characters, my encounter of the khoros was polyadic. Experiences with the singular performers offered an intersubjectivity that existed as a one-to-one or many-to-one relationship. I felt like an individual (one) or one-of-many-in-an-audience-body (many) encountering an individual (one). I also took the plurality of the audience for granted, again feeling the *we* of the audience as *me*, my experience nestling together both individual and collective perspectives. The collective perspective as an audience body often surreptitiously rested deeper in my awareness. I did not pay attention to my status as part of the collective audience body. This sense of audience totality pervaded my experience on a less conscious level of awareness.

My awareness would amplify and I would shift my conscious attention to it, though. My spectatorship in audiences constantly is ruptured by ambient stimuli. Usually at the fringes of my awareness, at times it becomes fully conscious, though. For example, when there is an audience disturbance (coughing, sudden movement, someone leaving the auditorium) or when we were addressed directly as an audience. Suddenly, I become very conscious of our presence as an audience and the activity occurring within our space. At The Globe, this was often the case. The khoroi addressed us often and the sunlight/flood lighting illuminated and exposed us. This also happens in clubbing experiences where our activity includes both dancing for ourselves and for each other. Clubbing experiences have patterns of self-awareness interlacing heightened and relaxed states. In any club, communication with people around me draws attention, at least for us, to our dancing behaviour. In watching music videos there is a kind of super-imposition of experiences. While my attention directs at the screen, I also am immersed in all the sensory information of the space in which I watch them. So, attention to my position as an audience or as being part of the *we* of the audience came into and out of awareness, shifting positions. These observations indicate audience members

Encountering Atmospheres 181

can and do experience these encounters alternately as individuals and as a plural audience, in a [one-or-many]-to-one relationship.

For the performer this is also the case, but since they have an imperative to perform to *all* audience members, not just one, the situation elaborates. From the position of a performing member to an aesthetic collective, there is principally a need to operate in a one-to-many relationship. The role requires members to perform to all audience members. This creates an experience of the audience as a sort of flowing series of encounters as attention shifts from one to another. From their perspective they encounter the audience as a whole body, as smaller groups and as individuals as their focus moves across and through the audience. As attention moves from audience member to audience member, a series of one-to-one or one-by-one encounters may occur. Background attention to the audience as a whole, however, still permeates this kind of dyadic experience as subliminal awareness. Based on my own experience in performing within khoroi and other types of aesthetic collectives, the audience is always encountered at the fundamental level as a collective totality, as *the* audience. From the perspective of the singular performer, the experience of the performance can be felt as one-to-one and as one-to-many. Layered yet further onto this, though, the encounter of the audience also includes the performer's own sense of totality as the aesthetic collective. A sense of *we-as-the-collective* conditions their sense of one/me, just like my own sense of me/we as the audience. Different to my audience experience as a *we*, though, this is a core principle of their role and performance and this awareness/role compliance is required and necessary.

To emphasise this point turn again to Beecroft, where the sense of totality is more directed, cultivated and individual agency reduced. Returning to *VB46*, like much of her other work, an erasure of individuality within plurality occurs. As I described them earlier, they appear as a collective of clone-like members, an undifferentiated mass. Her collectives can be encountered like a singular entity. The exaggerated similarity of the members depreciates the members as individuals and heightens, even forces, the encounter of them as a totality. Just as the audience may be treated as a many-as-one, the aesthetic collective here is perceived as the totality of members and treated more as a body, a singular entity. This encounter as many-as-one intensifies the experience. Indeed, I believe this is part of Beecroft's artistic rationale: to demonstrate the deindividuation of many into a singular entity. In her own words:

NW:   The performances are scripted, they are created in response to a set of
      formal conditions and enacted according to a set of instructions. But
      what happens is that they can sustain that script for only a limited
      period before breaking down—literally, in the sense that fatigue sets in
      and structurally in that the rigid formations begin to decompose. In a
      structural way, are they battlefields between order and disorder, will
      and its relaxation?

182    *Precis*

*VB:*    Yes. And I set this up against my interest as it really aggravates me to witness this loss of precision and this meltdown every time. In fact only those who witness the performances know this as a fundamental aspect of the work. The people who own the photographs are supporting my work but they miss its manifestation in its full form.[5]

The experience of many-as-one and its breakdown is central. This is a witnessing of deindividuation, collective decay and the balancing/battlefield between plural and singular states. Moreover, directly addressing why she uses or focusses on collectives and not individuals, she has stated in interview that the group is more powerful than the individual:

[Interviewer] How do you perceive the women you represent? Why collective and not individual?

[VB] The women are often there as a physical equivalent of what I am going through. She is not alone because she is speaking for a group, for more than one person and because a group is stronger and more convincing than an individual. The women have similar aspects but there are also differences between them. They are organized in a hierarchical formation in which there are privileges and unbalance, symmetries and color-schemes.[6]

The structure of her encounters for audiences is also individualised and a somewhat more private experience. Since her work sits somewhere between the disciplines of installation art and live art, the audiences themselves are less formalised as observing collectives (than say theatre audiences). They enter and exit the space as they please, can choose their viewing perspective and distance, control the duration of the experience and can comment on it while in attendance (like before a painting). Here, attendants encounter the work more as they would a piece of fine art in galleries and museums. Placement, direction of attention and perspective are within the individual audience members' control. Differently, in the khoroi instances the audience was collectivised by their mostly static, arranged physical placement, direction of attention, the more determined duration of viewing and the more restricted sense of attention (people generally did not talk at those events).

Compared to khoroi, Beecroft's audiences have more agency over their experience and a lessened, though not deleted, many-as-one feeling. Clubbing crowds, by further comparison, have even more agency in their placements, direction of attention and perspectives as they are the agents of the aesthetic collective. Viewing the music videos discussed in chapter five creates yet an even greater sense of agency. Unless viewed in environments where another person controls the video, the viewing of video is generally from an individual perspective with control of the time-code, play-rate and volume of the work. In that position, one controls the video almost entirely. The work is experienced

Encountering Atmospheres 183

almost fully from the perspective of one-to-many. However, music video also initiates an experience that positions the viewer as part of a larger, dispersed and anonymous audience. When Lady Gaga's *Alejandro* is watched on YouTube, for instance, you are one of 463,522,999 viewers (as of 7 September 2021). This greater, intermedial audience poses further multiplications of audience numbers.

To sum up these relational experiences and perspectives, the encounters for the audience and for the aesthetic collectives included dyadic forms (one-to-one, [many-as-one]-to-one, one-by-one) but also more elaborate plural options (such as the one-to-many, the many-to-many, or even the [many-as-one]-to-many, many-to-[many-as-one] and [many-as-one]-to-[many-as-one]). All of these, of course, depend on choices in watching and performing and the interpretation of the encounter by both audiences and performers. These relational options can all be experienced simultaneously, as well, which happened to me during several of the encounters surveyed. Particularly in clubbing cases and theatre performances, the experiences were noticeably multi-layered and I simultaneously felt several of these relationships to the rest of the audience and to the aesthetic collectives.

Stepping out of the perspectives of both the audience and the performer for a moment, we can also consider these events from a further external point of view. That is, from the perspective of an observer of both groups (as I had in conducting this research). For example, in the case of the Metropolis clubbing event I had the opportunity to stand on the first- and second-floor balconies and observe the dancing collectives on the floors below. While there was still active dancing surrounding me on my own floor, I could observe the lower aesthetic collective with a bird's eye view. What I saw was both a crowd of people watching the dancing crowd as well as the dancing crowd performing for each other *and* for the watching crowd. I noticed this at the other club events as well. I attended *Bakkhai* twice to utilise and test this perspective. At my second viewing, I took a backrow seat and paid closer attention to the audience than to the performance. Again, I noticed how the audience was behaving and the reciprocal nature of their experience and the experience of the performers. From this third observational point of view, it was clear that the experience of encountering aesthetic collectives, regardless of interpretation, was and is a situation of many encountering many. It is masses encountering masses. There are many bodies encountering many bodies and having corporeally multi-modal experiences.

I think it is more often the case that performances do not physically immerse audience members in aesthetic collectives. The clubbing experiences stand as an obvious exception and were naturally physically immersive. While immersive theatre/performance writ large (where the audience is physically placed within the work) has recently gained a lot of attention and popularity I believe it still is less frequent than physically separated audience work. The Beecroft installations, Greek khoroi and music video examples were not particularly physically immersive. For example, in three of the khoroi examples (*Medea*, *Bakkhai*, *Chorus*) the audience could not be a participant and was physically outside the aesthetic collectives, occupying a delineated

184   *Precis*

audience space. Moreover, those performances actively kept the audiences in positions with limited agency—they could not meaningfully influence the performance or interact with it short of interrupting/disrupting it or stopping it. So, if the audience had no definite agency and were physically outside the aesthetic collectives how might they have been immersed? Again, the issue of style of production method or immersive practice (as in immersive theatre practice) are not the core issue here. Rather, I move to this question: how are feelings of immersion created and broadly generate experiences that immerse audiences and participants in the affective-atmospheric fields of the aesthetic collectives?

## Immersion

I turn to the writing of Catherine Bouko and Gareth White on immersive performance as noted to address issues of immersion more fully. Bouko considers how immersion is not necessarily determined by physical dimensions nor by agentic ones.[7] Moreover, she argues 'immersion is not a characteristic but rather an effect which a work may produce on the participant'.[8] Her use of the term *participant* is specifically denoting a participating audience member. She goes on to discuss that the rupture or penetration of critical distances is often confused with immersion, that one's body must actually be within the container of the work in order to be immersed in it. Such placement of the spectator clearly creates a feeling of immersion as one literally perceives the work from within it. Echoing these assertions, White observes how in immersive experiences the audience is in search of some depth in the work, some interior to the artwork where its truest meaning might be found. He notes how audiences will readily confuse the metaphor of depth and interiority with the spatio-physical. '[W]e move within the artwork, intimately close to it, but still distinct from it. To be immersed is to be surrounded, enveloped and potentially annihilated, but it also is to be separate from that which immerses'.[9] His comments are accompanied by a language metaphor he creates, *The Artworks are Containers*, that he uses to deconstruct into a variety of conceptual premises that might be inferred.[10] I have already used this same container metaphor throughout this text. White asserts that if they are containers then artworks have insides that hold something and that something, which the audience pursues as a meaning centre, is something into which we can go.

Bouko states that as an audience member we conceive this idea of meaning in physical terms.

> [T]he assimilation of the immersant's body acts as a more significant lever for immersion and interactivity than the narrative dimension [...] the immersant's sensory appeal constitutes an experience which places his body at the heart of the dramaturgy. The immersant's body experiences first-hand the fluctuation between what is real and what is imaginary.[11]

*Encountering Atmospheres* 185

White offers a counterpoint to this physical immersion, however, by clarifying that the experience, and indeed meaning, of works of art is actually within the audience themselves.

> In a very real sense, then, the spectator is not inside the work, in the way that the body is inside the dome [here referring to the experience of James Turrell's *Bindu Shards*], but the work is inside the spectator. We might see in this an image of spectator or audience response to all artworks: the works are nothing without the 'eye of the beholder' (and we might substitute here ear, body, sensibility).[12]

So, while physical entrance to the artwork can create an immersivity, it is not in and of itself the means of immersion; physical immersion is merely a tactic of immersion, not a definitive of it.

I have shown immersivity in a variety of ways as a physical ordination tactic, and they fall along a spectrum. The clubbing cases are very much at one end of the spectrum, identified as complete physical immersion. Moving away from that pole the Beecroft examples would follow, where one can manipulate proximity to the aesthetic collective and *could* even enter it. Next, less physically immersive, are the khoroi of *Oresteia*, as they occasionally moved within the audience space (in the groundlings' area of The Globe) but mainly performed on the separated stage. Next would be *Chorus* where the audience was in opposing banks with the performance vaguely in the round and with the performers entering and exiting through lanes bifurcating each bank; lastly *Bakkhai* and then *Medea* were respectively the least physically immersive, with the audience clearly separated in a front-on arrangement limiting their sight of other audience members. These last two had little to no overlap of performance/audience spaces (*Bakkhai* had a few entrances and exits of characters from the audience space, but not the khoros; *Medea* had none). At the farthest end are music videos, where such physical immersion is not even possible.

Situating the bodies of audience members within the performance indeed does allow unique access. A more sensorially immediate immersion, it allows direct, perhaps interactive, engagement with the narrative dimension as well. To return to the proxemics of Edward T. Hall, physically immersed audiences experience aesthetic collectives within personal and intimate spaces, instead of the social or public spaces. The experience of being in that space subsequently can create personal and intimate feelings. Physical immersion of the sphere of the audience within that of aesthetic collectives allows Diderot's fourth wall to enclose the audience within it. The audience is within the performance reality, not just looking in at it.

The same order of cases from strongest to weakest occurs in agency as well: the audience had greatest agency and authorship in the clubbing experiences and least in the *Bakkhai* and *Medea*. It is expected in clubbing experiences that one pursue the experiences individually; in *Oresteia*, the audience was engaged on and off throughout the performance to help generate energy, to become

186    *Precis*

scenery or phantom characters and to move in and out of performers' paths. This involvement and ability to assist, become dramatis personae/features of the world, and to choose to participate in the fantasy reality of the performance transformed these performance contexts from passive to more active experiences. Even though the audience in *Oresteia* had predetermined paths and outcomes (these roles were 'cast' over us and required no action on our part) we still felt as though we were involved and participating or, as Bouko would argue, interacting with the performance.

Comparing models of interactivity drawn from Marie-Laure Ryan, David Saltz, Dominic M. McIver Lopes and Steve Dixon, Bouko defines *interaction* and outlines how it is connected, often conflated with, but distinct from immersion.[13] She comments how 'the notion of interactivity covers a multitude of definitions and is often linked to other concepts (sharing, participation, exchange, sense, immersion etc.), which leads to the specificity of each diminishing'.[14] Central are involvement, agency, control and choice-making on the part of the audience member. One of the ultimate determinants of real interactivity with all three is the effect the audience member has on the work of art. Put another way, the strongest and purest form of interactivity is the measure of how much the audience member has adopted or assumed authorship of the artwork. To change the work of art by interacting with it blurs the line between the role of audience and the role of artistic agent or performing participant.

The *Bakkhai* and *Medea* performances actively suppressed and discouraged audience agency to the point that any action was felt as disturbance and which might be met with aggression and anger. This is perhaps a consequence of these two examples not being designed as immersive experiences in terms of style, but rather to absorb their audiences, which required more silent and directed attention from a passive audience. One instance in the first of my two viewings of *Bakkhai* illustrated this through a disruption of the performance by an audience member. A man sitting in the second row far house right began to cough early in the performance, perhaps one minute into the opening. Ben Whishaw, playing Dionysos, was centre stage delivering the opening monologue of the play and the man coughed. It is perhaps noteworthy that for some audience there was interest in this performance only to see Ben Whishaw.[15] There was a heightened sense of importance to his celebrity presence that was perceptible in some of the audience, particularly the younger audience members. I sat at the very back of the theatre and from that vantage point I could see how everyone's heads were directed. No one responded to the coughing at first, keeping their heads directed at the actor. The coughing continued for another ten seconds at which point I noticed the disturbance of the cough moving through the crowd. At first, people were just shaking their heads to the coughing.

After 20 seconds of this one audience member in the third-row centre swung her head quickly to the side to see who was coughing; the man sitting next to

*Encountering Atmospheres* 187

her did the same. Suddenly about a third of the crowd did the same. This did not happen to the people sitting immediately around the man, however. They seemed to know exactly who was coughing and kept their gaze firmly fixed on the stage action (I could see the faces of these people as the audience banks curved at the edges). The looks came from elsewhere in the theatre. There was an intense moment of piercing gaze in his direction trying to identify the offending cough. People held this gaze for about one or two seconds, then they returned their gaze to the stage. As soon as they had returned their gaze, though, many more who did not look at first turned their gaze towards him, watched for one or two seconds, then similarly returned to the stage. The coughing continued and though most did not gaze at the man again, I could notice how different audience members throughout the theatre were upset: they shook their heads, inhaled deeply with raised shoulders then huffed their exhalation, moved their gaze distractedly around the stage. Occasionally, one or two people would fully direct not just their gaze, but their entire shoulder carriage to look at the man. I had the impression that people were now not just trying to identify the interruption, but to shame him with (passive) aggressive body language. After about two minutes of continuous coughing (which felt much longer and was very uncomfortable), the man stood and exited the theatre through the back, hunched over with his jacket over his mouth and face, coughing into his chest. He appeared ashamed and distressed. There was then a silence and a full stillness in the audience; focus was intently directed at the stage. It was as if no one wanted to move lest they next distract from the event—even a slight movement would attract attention. This continued until the audience grew slightly fidgety in their seats during the first of the choral odes when many people relaxed and began to shift to find comfortable positions. I did not see the man again until 20 minutes later during the second choral ode, forced to sit that time with the stewards at the back.

While not changing the nature of the performance itself (although Ben Whishaw did smile an acknowledging smile once the man left the theatre), this man's inadvertent agency disturbed the performance and changed the reception of it for the rest of the audience. In a sense his interference blurred the line of audience member and artist by directing the experience for the others. A similar experience (although not as intense) occurred at The Globe (and this happens during every performance that I attend there) when a helicopter or plane flew overhead (a hospital is nearby). These moments strain concentration for the audience. I have noticed actors on that stage have even become accustomed to attempting to incorporate this as an environmental feature of their performances (e.g. a sign from the gods, a disturbance in nature and so on).

Elias Canetti discusses this phenomenon of crowd behaviour in *Crowds and Power*.[16] He outlines how crowds operate within rigid unspoken, but fully understood, behavioural codes. He discusses how in such crowds *stagnation* occurs, which he defines as the compression of the crowd on itself.

188 *Precis*

[I]t is impossible for it move really freely. Its state has something passive in it; it waits [...] The more people flow into that formation, the stronger the pressure becomes; feet have nowhere to move, arms are pinned down and only heads remain free, to see and to hear, every impulse is passed directly body to body. Each individual knows that there must be a number of people there, but because they are so closely jammed together, they are felt to be one.[17]

This was precisely the feeling in the *Bakkhai* audience. We were so close together and so formally positioned in rows of seats that movement, while possible, was minimal, constrained and would garner notice from others, mostly from neighbouring attendants. Such proximity and behavioural expectation means even small actions affect those around us. Writing directly about experiences at the theatre or at a music concert Canetti notes even more intense behaviour:

Late-comers are received with slight hostility. There they all sit, like a well-drilled herd, still and infinitely patient. But everyone is very well aware of his own separate existence. He has paid for his seat and he notices who sits next to him. Till the play starts, he leisurely contemplates the rows of assembled heads [...] But their spontaneous reactions to it [the performance] are limited. Even their applause has its prescribed times; in general people clap only when they are supposed to [...] Stagnation in the theatre has become so much a rite that individuals feel only a gentle external pressure [...] But one should not underestimate the extent of their real and shared expectation, nor forget that it persists during the whole of the performance. People rarely leave a theatre before the end of the play; even when disappointed they sit it through, which means that, for that period anyway, they stay together [...] [This is even more striking] in *concerts*. Here everything depends on the audience being completely undisturbed; any movement is frowned on, any sound taboo [...] no rhythmical effect of any sort on the listeners must be perceptible [...] all outward reactions are prohibited. People sit there motionless, as though they managed to hear *nothing*. It is obvious that a long and artificial training in stagnation has been necessary here [all emphasis in the original].[18]

Interruptions from outside a performance (such as the coughing man) draw the audience attention away from what they want; that interruption prevents feeling immersed in the performance (the object of desire) and the reaction toward that interruption is not kind. In Silvan Tomkins' analysis, the prevention of interest with a goal of enjoyment is the definition of the affect shame/humiliation—the audience in this example felt such an obstacle to their interest and because it was sustained the audience then began to experience distress, then anger. As a result, they began to direct shame and humiliation at the offending man. In performances

*Encountering Atmospheres* 189

like *Medea, Bakkhai, Chorus* or the Beecroft installations, restricting the audience into a determined space transforms them into a crowd, a collective all its own. Not physically immersed in the performance space, audience agency reduces.

So, why is this considered immersion and not simply engagement with or direction of concentration at the performance? To address this, a comparison with the encounter of another art form, literature, will prove useful. 'Dramatic immersion distinguishes itself from literary immersion by the tangibility of the world into which the individual is plunged, as opposed to the world of literature into which [a] reader is absorbed'.[19] *Bakkhai* and *Medea* felt more like pieces of art that absorbed me, rather than immersed me, so perhaps they stray closer to absorption than immersion?

> For Ryan (2001: 14), [the world of literature] produces an imaginary relationship with a literary world, which leads the addressee to metaphorically plunge into the tale. Richard Gerrig (in Ryan 1999: 116) links literary immersion with the concept of "transportation", through which a reader of fiction distances himself from his immediate physical environment in order to "lose" himself in the story.[20]

Indeed the performances of *Bakkhai* and *Medea* had this sense about them, and I experienced 'losing' myself in their stories. Their worlds, however, were tangible (in the sets, actors, soundscapes) and my relationship with those performances was not imagined, it was embodied before me. Consequently, transportation to an imaginary place was both not necessary and necessary. I experienced what was literally before me, but also I had to imagine and construct parts of the narrative or background of characters that were off-stage or out of time. The literal action before me was where my sensory focus was located, though. While absorbed in the stories, I was immersed in the constructed, performed worlds.

Direct address of an audience by performers also augments immersion. In extant Greek tragedies khoroi directly address and are aware of the audience. In Beecroft installations the performers can look right at the audience. To return to a study of character, they can operate internally with the performance and externally with the audience. At least in the khoroi I saw, they would address the audience directly, make eye contact, assume our watching perspective at times, refer back to us; in short, they would be us, be characters in the drama and be able to shift between the two with ease. Operating like a bridge between both realities they pulled me as an audience member into the drama in a way that the other performers did not.

The argument developing here is that there are multiple tactics of immersion in these performances. There is the physical immersion of the audience in the space of the performance, but also there is also projected entrance. Gareth White contemplates this kind of entrance and absorption and the depth that they imply. He notes:

190    *Precis*

[W]e talk of "immersing ourselves" in other experiences—new situations, cultures, environments—as well as in more conventional art works like books and films, when we want to commit to them wholeheartedly and without distraction. The implication of the term "immersive theatre" is that it has a special capacity to create this kind of deep involvement.[21]

Notably, performance allows an experience to occur and as an audience one has the faculty to allow that experience to expand or contract in quality and value. In White's discussion, immersivity follows a material analogy in which the audience member as subject is plunged, submerge, immersed, or put into a position where the performance flows, like a body of water, around them. In fact, he offers three metaphors to help clarify immersivity which I will reproduce here:

*The Experience Is a Body of Water Metaphor*
Experience Is a Body of Water
Experience Flows around Us
Experience Can Be Shallow or Deep
Experience Can Be Dangerous...
*The Art Is Immersive Metaphor*
Art Is Immersive
Art Experiences Are Shallow or Deep
Successful Art Experiences Are Deep...
*The Immersive Performance Metaphor*
Performance Can Flow around Us
Participation Can Sweep Us Away
Participation Makes Waves in the Performance[22]

The progression of metaphors used here conceptualise immersivity like being a body in fluidal space. I shift from fluid, though, to the actual conductive substance betwixt and between us in performance: air, its modalities and atmospheric nature.[23] For White, the immersive is further detailed as being contained within the performance, not just exterior to it looking inward; again, '[t]o be immersed is to be surrounded, enveloped and potentially annihilated, but it also is to be separate from that which immerses'.[24] The argument being that to be truly immersed in a work of art is first to be within its containing apparatus and then to be ever closer to its centre, its heart, and thus the truth of the work. We can assume 'lesser' immersivity suggests being exterior to the work, yet being able to see within it, followed by containment and perceiving the work from inside, followed yet by interactive complicity in the work where one collaborates with the artwork to facilitate its being. White proposes that audiences are looking for the essence of truth in the work of art in these found depths. Frustratingly, immersivity does not in and of itself allow more access to such a metaphysical thing. The suggestion of further interiority and hidden depth which can be accessed is actually an illusion of art, perhaps

*Encountering Atmospheres*  191

*the* illusion; the interiority, depth and real truth is again within the audience themselves.

> Ontologically speaking, immersive [performance] can only achieve what other forms of performance can achieve: a relation in which the event of a work of art occurs between its material being and the person who encounters it. If it has claims to make—as well as its persuasive claims for having found new and excitable audiences—they must be to do with its potential to stimulate these relations, rather than with creating realms of experience not available in other kinds of work.[25]

Recall Bouko's framing, immersivity is a tactic or strategy of performance, more a shaping of the way we experience the performance; a 'game of coming and going [becoming interior with or exterior to the performance] which constructs and deconstructs physical and mental immersion…'[26]

One further way immersion in collectives' fields happens is in the commitment to the conventions of the event and our roles. There are usually relatively clear expectations and rules for the roles of audience and performers. The Almeida theatre events, for instance, required clear and relatively traditional theatrical conventions. We sat in assigned seats, we faced towards the performing space, we kept silent, we applauded at intervals and the end, we neither socialise nor interact during the performance. As an audience we participated in the construction of the aesthetic event by agreeing, silently, to abide by understood, though unwritten, rules and conventions of spectatorship in that space. We engaged in the aesthetic realities of *Bakkhai* and *Medea*, suspending our disbelief and inhibitions, and abided (complied?) by rules and regulations. This applied equally to the performers. The performers took their roles and conducted a performance in agreement with the design for that experience.

These dependencies and relations existed so the events and happenings could occur and be successful. They formalise the event and condition it so that a theatrical experience could unfold. On a basic level, events and encounters of aesthetic collectives set up spheres of space and time.[27] Immersed in those spheres, all present agreed to become a part of it and while in it regard the performing collectives as objects of art/aesthetics. Returning to Barsade and Knight these spheres present as micro-cultures and emotional cultures: social experiences where the emotional nature is self-contained, codified and whose existence lasts the duration of the event. Rules and regulations shift and change from event to event. Some are more lasting and persist in performance culture (as outlined above); some are purposefully subverted in contemporary performance. All are agreed and adopted appropriate to the aesthetics and drama of the event—a type of social contract—and such agreement and adoption sustained collective immersion in the experiences. Audiences agree and behave in a myriad of fashions as assumed for events: to be silent and still,

192    *Precis*

to be walking and engaging, to be responding, dancing and participating and so on. This grants attention and seriousness to the event. In doing so, we (the audience) also at times become passive recipients. From such identity work in our roles, performances can be believable spheres of experience, a space and time in which the cultures of the performances come to life. However, we can also break that. Again, I would cite the instance of the coughing man at *Bakkhai*. Broadly true of all performance, not just immersive ones, disturbances or breaking the conventions of the theatre can shatter the aesthetics of the event, rupturing into the spheres of others.

## Foam Structures—Atmospheres

Co-presence conditions encounters quite heavily and the immersion and experience of one is impinged on by the immersion and experience of the others. As I indicated in the introduction, these cases are, after Sloterdijk, *foam* structures.

> [M]ultichamber organization[s] that [were] referred to with the notion of co-isolated associations: each chamber or cell [individual] [made] up its own microspherical world; it [wa]s separated from other chambers, but since adjacent cells [others] share[d] the same wall or boundary, they [we]re characterized by cofragility, as the dissolution of one cell will affect its neighbouring cells.[28]

My dancing in the clubs affected others around me and I was affected by them. In theatre audiences, the disturbances from each other affected each of us. Equally, for the participants in khoroi, Beecrofts or back-up dancing groups, if one member behaved in ways not collectively shared or agreed, it could lead to the dissolution of the experience for the others. Audiences and participants affected and were affected by their neighbours. The geometry of foam structures with plural intersubjectivity 'contain[ed] […] a high degree of internal tension, or tensegrity, between the […] co-isolated spaces [individuals] that their shared existential risk can be expressed in [this] co-fragility formula'.[29] As a participant in an aesthetic collective, one is always immersed within the plural inter-subjective condition created by the collective field. As an audience, immersion within that field situated us all as co-present. Either participant or audience immersed in this plural intersubjective field creates an affecting/affected relationship between the individual and everyone else.

I would like to observe one further element of immersion with aesthetic collectives. In discussing ontological metaphors, Lakoff and Johnson explain a general principle of metaphor: that we understand experiences through entity and substance metaphors. My experiences and encounters of these aesthetic collectives are addressed and framed in language demonstrative of these metaphors:

*Encountering Atmospheres* 193

Our experience of physical objects and substances provides a further basis for understanding [...] Understanding our experiences in terms of objects and substances allows us to pick out parts of our experience and treat them as discrete entities or substances of a uniform kind. Once we can identify our experiences as entities or substances, we can refer to them, categorize them, group them, and quantify them—and, by this means, reason about them. When things are not clearly discrete or bounded, we still categorize them as such [...] Such ways of viewing physical phenomena are needed to satisfy certain purposes that we have [...] Human purposes typically require us to impose artificial boundaries that make physical phenomena discrete just as we are: entities bounded by a surface. [O]ur experiences with physical objects (especially our own bodies) provide the basis for an extraordinarily wide variety of ontological metaphors, that is, ways of viewing events, activities, emotions, ideas, etc., as entities and substances.[30]

In the precis to part two, I observed how I applied a container metaphor to the examples of aesthetic collectives. I outlined there how the encounter of clubbing crowds, for example, automatically generates understanding of them as contained, like our own bodies, and containing. At that point, I outlined how I perceived those aesthetic collectives and thought of them as bounded and contained entities. Earlier in this chapter, I detailed how we, as audiences, experience aesthetic collectives from inside or outside their physical containment; but from whatever perspectival position, we are always within a field (of presence, aura or effect). This field and immersion or projection in it produce an intersubjective experience laden with and conditioned by affective dimensions. Aesthetic collectives and their field, and through my experience of the examples, create atmospheric experiences. They, 'atmospheres[,] circumscribe or fill the space we inhabit, and they may define moments for individuals as well as for human collectives [...] [they are] the premises that lay the ground for the sensuous and emotional feel of a place'.[31] To refer to categorise, group and quantify such experiences of this atmospheric collective field, we must conceptualise and reify them into not only an entity, which I have established, but also some sort of encountered thing/substance.

Encountering aesthetic collectives brings into consideration the intersubjective space itself, where and in what that experience happens. First, have the collective domain, a volume of space that surrounds and interpenetrates the collective and demarcates 'their' space from 'other' space. This space also appears to 'hold' an entitative energy. Considered as containers, aesthetic collectives hold within them events, encounters, activities, actions; but we also consider the totality like or in terms of human subjects. The examples given illuminate that whatever the distance or spatial remove of the audiences, the collectives created about them a field that engulfed and immersed the audiences. Like White's analogy to a body of water in which the audience swims, these examples created fields in which audiences were plunged, immersed and experienced emanations beyond the space of the collective domain. The

194  *Precis*

encounters were a "going into" these fields. They are things that we can be inside or outside of, but always within their field of presence. These fields pervade, overlap and imbricate with our own. With that, affective dimensions tint and tone the experience of their pervading, overlapping and imbricated presence. Encountering and being within the fields of aesthetic collectives carries with it affectively charged experiences.

While a fine analogy, considering immersion as like going into a body of liquid, does not fully correlate to these cases or aesthetic collectives generally. As above, performance takes place in air-filled spaces, in literal atmospheres, and immersion in the medium of air more accurately defines them. The performances were within an envelope of gaseous air that we all shared. Compared with liquids, gases or vapours behave less definitely, less observably and allow more action to occur through them (e.g. sounds, visuals, telegraphed or broadcast elements all usually move more effectively through the medium of air). While there are similarities with liquid bodies, the language that describes encounters with aesthetic collectives aligns more with the vernacular of gases. For example, liquids require distinct edges to hold them and behave with substantial and observable activity. In describing the edges and boundaries of the club dancing crowds, they were 'hazy', 'indistinct', 'blurry', 'cloudy' or 'fuzzy'. These terms are much less distinct or tangible than the physical boundaries of bodies of water, whose edges are more defined. In terms of tangibility we, audiences, encountered these fields as something non-material and occurring in and through space filled and permeated with air, not with liquid. Immersion in their fields was immersion in a charged, gaseous space—in an atmosphere.

*Atmospheres* have multiple enfolded meanings, though, and are themselves hazily delineated and indistinctly understood. Generally, we recognise and can easily point to something that happens in our own experiences as 'an atmosphere'. For example, if asked what the atmosphere of a performance is, an attendant would likely respond with some mood-linked description—that they are perhaps tense, depressing, gloomy, joyful, energetic, frenetic, gothic, romantic and so on. Discussing, analysing or detailing those descriptions, however, is less straightforward as they are largely constructed out of dynamic human psychological elements, but also material things (sets, lights, sound etc.). This quasi-nature makes them evade clear definitions.

To delineate them better, we can structure and conceptualise them in terms of more defined, immediately describable and conversable concepts. There are two immediate conceptual meanings to *atmosphere*. The first is meteorological and relates to the weather. The second is a human characteristic, something conditioning the intersubjective engagement in a space, i.e. the mood, energy or tone of a space. When we speak of atmospheres as weather we conceptualise the enclosed, demarcated space of the air, with matter and energy filling it. We think of wind, clouds, fog, rain, snow, sleet, sunlight, tornadoes, hurricanes, lightning and so on. These are the living things of the Earth, moving and with perceivable intensities. Weather also works well as a metaphor for the second meaning, of human characterising, helping structure how we understand something as evanescent and intangible as 'human atmospheres'. Thinking of these mood, energy and toned atmospheres as parallel with planetary weather 'allow[s] us [...] to use one highly structured and clearly delineated concept to structure another'.[32] This metaphor ontologically and structurally grounds understanding of these human atmospheres in the more understandable experience of planetary weather. Aesthetic collectives occupy space and through their fields contain around them their members and the present audiences and put things (air, matter, energy, moods, emotions) into living action with perceivable intensities. Their performance and the environmental elements create a space of shared moods, a transmission of affect between participants, audience and space. The memberships and audiences engaged in intersubjective realities through those moods. Atmosphere is both content and medium of transmission. When deconstructed conceptually in this way, the examples of aesthetic collectives show themselves to be containing, mood-making, atmospheric entities.

Through a theory of atmospheres, to which there is now a quickly emerging literature, I can reconsider aesthetic collectives and how it is like to be *in their field* (of presence/aura/effect) and what kind of experience that is. Their field—what it is, how it works, what effects it may cause—is a conditioning of experiences. The discipline of performance studies does not address this concept, certainly not regarding plural entities such as these. A major contribution to the literature sits here, with this analysis of atmospheric properties of collectively inhabited and viewed space. I am going to pierce the idea of conditioning to expand on this—how conditions in the cases both founded the atmospheres and how the atmospheres conditioned the encounters. Lastly, I will address weather-making and weathering as notions of how these experiences felt or might be felt.

## Conditioning

Atmosphere is the master conditioning of experience. If we use the examples analysed throughout this text, some fundamental conditions were the choices in aesthetic and production. The environments, their designs, the collectives, their component individuals and the audiences all conditioned each other to formulate experiences. Conditioning is how experience is manipulated or modified: the properties, circumstances and modalities of the encounter or indeed anything else that comes to determine or influence experiences and its interpretation. This broadly organises into three categories: environment, participants and audience. These three structure, fashion and frame sensory-perceptual encounters and the affective dimensions to experiences. In other words, the interplay of environment, participants and audience precipitates atmospheric experiences. Nor are affective experiences unilaterally dictated. All three elements are fully complicit in the structuring and generation of the affective dimensions, conditioning the encounters in different but complimentary ways.

196   *Precis*

First, environmental conditioning. Lights and sound tuned the club environments to create dancing and partying environments. Beecroft's work was site-specifically situated and used the spaces that she chose. In the khoroi, everything took place in theatres, where the entire experience was designed to situate and condition the experience of spectators as audience. Lastly, in the music videos, the viewers have control over their viewing environment, but they have to shut-out/mute that environment and direct/absorb their focus into a screen. Through the mediation of technology, audio–visual displays psychologically pulled the viewer into the work while also maintaining the body's openness to stimuli from the viewing environment—a superimposition of one atmosphere onto or into another. In all cases, the encounter immersed all present in aesthetic designs and in spatially determined ways. The term *scenography* covers this, but here I broaden its definition to include the full aesthetic space, inclusive of audience/spectator areas, and not just the design of the performance spaces. Aesthetically suffused spaces immersed and conditioned me, the audience, and the aesthetic collectives, participant-performers.

Participant-performers crucially had to work in tandem and in congress with the environment to achieve a harmony between the aesthetic elements. Narrowing only to their perspective, the environments conditioned them individually and their experience of collective entitativity. A fundamental reason for this is that the environmental airspace is a part of the collective domain, a part of the entitative totality. This is a key difference between singular (individual) and plural (collective) entities. For example, *VB45* I understand as a bounded collective of women. With a perceivable perimeter the women occupy a space, and in so doing they differentiate their collective space. They territorialise that space in inhabiting it, and audiences respected that and remained outside of it. The totality is the space, the occupying discrete bodies *and* the air/matter between them. In the performance photographs, the regularity and uniformity of this space matches the regularity and uniformity of the bodies. Indeed, as noted in chapter two, the sculpting and geometric use of negative space is as much a part of the performance as the positive, the bodies.

With a singular person this kind of space does not exist. If I focus on only one member in *VB45* and temporarily detach her from the collective, there is space that surrounds her body and her body singly occupies one undisrupted volume of space. I read her only as her material body and a spheroid negative space surrounding her—her personal space. That space anchors perception of her and her sense of self. Refocusing on the collective body differently involves negative spaces between the members. There is also no centre or core here. With the individual there is a framing and focus given to her by her space and we see the face, usually, as their 'centre' of being (perhaps as it is their centre of perceptual activity). Disruption of bodies in the collective by space diffuses focus across them. There is literally a geometric centre to the group roughly equidistant from the edges, but there is no central core to the entity, no 'home' for its essence or centre of perceptual activity. Moreover, their

*Encountering Atmospheres* 197

spatiality transformed and evolved in terms of volume and topography, how much space they occupied and its shape. The lone individual participant cannot do this on the same scale or in the same way, nor can she simultaneously inhabit multiple spaces or interrupted spaces like this—ones that have holes or expanses of emptiness. All collectives are composed in this way, with spaces in between and surrounding members that shape-shift continuously.

These spaces between the women are crucial. At the outset, the equidistant, gridding of them allowed the audience to view them in rank and file, like an army. As the performance progressed, this perfect structure shifted and changed with the bodies of the members, but also in the way the spaces between them appeared. That negative space shifted and formed itself in relation to their transformation. Moreover, the hall in which they were installed conditioned the viewing of them. I can only speak to the visual elements from photographs such as light, volume and their displayed emotional tone. The quality of light in the room weighs down on the women. There is darkness above them and light upon them. The floor beneath is also reflecting some of the light. They are somewhat backlit as well, so they cast forward angled shadows. There is also the scale of the space; the hall is enormous. The women occupy a large amount of space collectively. Individually, they have a volume of space around them that is at least eight times their own body volume (or one additional body space in all lateral directions). Lastly, the air appears clear with nothing diffused or hanging in it (such as fog, mist or haze). In turn the women also appear pristine. All these visual cues contribute to feelings of being sanitised, clean and ordered. I can imagine that being in that space would also have a very aired, sterile sensation.

The space in the collective totalities also conducts the breaking and refracting of our viewing focus and attention in many directions simultaneously. Focus and attention are diffused across collective bodies. I observed in chapter one how dancing crowds have a sense of density in their geometric centre; not the same thing. The members at the edges were just as 'in' the essence of the crowd as those at centre and I viewed them just as much (even more as they were easier to see, whereas the dense centre was hidden). As foam structures, I can draw a more literal comparative. Foams are amalgams of bubbles that enclose gaseous space; space (empty of everything but air) composes *most* of what a foam is. If the examples throughout this text are reviewed, you will notice how much space divides them. Most of the time, the aesthetic collectives had a lot of space between the members. Clubbing crowds prove to be the most elastic in this regard, often contracting the negative space into the more personal and intimate (e.g. Debbie and Oslo had very little space dividing members, while Metropolis and Morrisons had significantly more). As foam structures, a layered experience presents to audiences. The space, its charge with their presence and the environmental components of that space conditioned my perception and reading of them. Furthermore, grasping them as totalities required constant perceptual scanning. Their decentred nature agitates focussing at any one point. Only by scanning and compositing the

198    *Precis*

individuals and their space can I perceive and experience the whole. My perceptual focus was decentred or dissevered. In fact, I found and find it difficult to maintain focus on one member throughout a duration of time—I *want* to look at the rest.

The dynamism of this interpenetrating space is also vital. Its constant changes keep the collective lively, but it is also filled with other interpersonal activity. Returning to *VB45,* environmental space was always dynamic and in-flux as the suspension in which their experience lived-out and was broadcast. Any movement or shift in the individual members changed the space and that in turn impacted on other participants or semiotically signalled something to the audience. Again, micro-dramas emerge out the impact of the environment shifting and changing in this way. Furthermore, the participants' non-verbal communication moved through that space. Visually, both participants and audiences could see or sense the body language and expression of the members. Consequently, movement, communication and the energy with which members performed made the space an unfolding condition experienced over and through time. Perception of these aesthetic collectives includes this intra-member space and the activity that occurs through it as a part of the collective. I can make three immediate points about how this space conditions them and in turn conditions their encounter by audiences.

First, the conditioning of space in between and around members by environmental and aesthetic designs conditions the totalities. That is, the environments are part of them. They hybridise the participant members and the environmental ambiance—*the ambient* being that which goes around and surrounds. Ambiance in this sense somewhat follows Jean-Paul Thibaud's observation of it as being something considered 'to emphasize more the situated, the built and the social dimensions of sensory experience while atmosphere is more affective, aerial and politically oriented'.[33] His analysis goes on to confederate the terms, but for my purposes I carry on with *ambiance* referring more to the environmental features. For instance, when we examine the clubbing crowds it is not just the dancers that we observe and 'see' as part of the crowd. It is also the scenography of the space (lights and haze notably) and the space between the members (also filled with haze catching the beams of light).

Second, spaces between and around members are physically dynamic. Their composition frequently shifts in volume, shape and order in direct relation to the members' action. As members move and change, these spaces move and change. As such these spaces became spaces of tension: between balance and imbalance, harmony and discord, expansion and contraction and so on. Take, for example, the Oslo clubbing experience. I observed and noted that during the dancing any opening of vacant space, say when a dancer left the floor, was immediately filled and rebalanced. Such an action, of the sudden emptying of an area, changed the space. It created a vacuum that required filling. It imbalanced the space between dancers and that created a tension or energy in the surrounding members; dancers quickly appropriated the space to establish balance and gain more personal space, to improve their comfort levels. It was a move towards balance and comfort. Oppositely, *VB45* began as a regular and perfect composition, but as time progressed both the women and the space between them decomposed into messier and more chaotic forms until the end signalled a prescribed return to the initial image. Its chaotic and irregular spatial transformation was bookended and framed by these opening and closing images of perfection.

Third, the space in between members is neither vacant nor empty. The spaces are indeed vacant of bodies, but also filled with other things—sometimes material but more often something psychological. The air filling these spaces becomes a suspension in which psychological stimuli move, are broadcast and received. In the main this is the communication and signals between members or with audiences. Information—ideas, thoughts, affect—moves through that air. In clubbing crowds this was evident through various communication conducts: glance, gaze, expression, physically tele-graphed emotions, mimicry across spaces, performative character dancing, filling the space with body smells and pheromones. Even the manipulation of spatial relationships and kinaesthetic response between members was a type of communication. Moving away, moving closer, avoiding, engaging, inserting others between and so on all sent information about the experiences being had.

These signs and communication are apparent to other participants and audiences. In external positions in clubbing crowds, I could observe and sense the progression of engagements through the space. At times, this was much like a narrative, especially when I observed people engaging in romantic or aggressive activities. People courting or fighting played out almost like scripted dramas. Differently, but also following the same principle of transmitting signals, the music videos had dancing groups that broadcast directly to the viewer. They directly shared and engulfed us in their emotional culture—through the space between them and the camera and then through time and virtual space to us as viewers. Nowhere is this clearer than in the examples of *The Greatest* and *Bad Romance*, where they look into the camera and direct themselves at the viewer. The nature of the information moving about and the mode of transmission through these spaces are conditions for the experience. They interpersonally condition the experience.

## Climate and Human Weather

These spaces and their conditioning allude to and are intermeshed with the second interpretation of atmosphere, that of climate. As above, atmosphere is a term of climate, referring to the weather-like environment and the gaseous spheres surrounding the planet and smaller environments that sustain life. As something so pervasive and constant, it is a taken-for-granted feature of the environment. For instance, The Globe theatre is open air and operates through the summer. Temperature in the summer is something that routinely

200   *Precis*

disrupts performances there as it can make the environment uncomfortable or oppressive. Audience members often faint or find the performance difficult to stand through (as groundlings). Despite knowledge that hot temperatures, direct sunlight and standing for hours can oppressively push the body into such a state of fatigue and stress, audiences often do not pay attention to or notice these conditions until they become very uncomfortable. Similarly, the climate in the club often becomes very hot, humid, loud and personal space minimises. You do not recognise how uncomfortable it can be until it distresses you. While not necessarily about the climate of her chosen spaces, Beecroft's installations even foreground the impact of time in a climate/position in space with her revelations of fatigue and strain on her participants. The impact of climate on individuals was slow and surreptitious, something noticed over the large course of time in the installations. Sometimes we notice climate instantly. At Debbie, for instance, I did notice the aforementioned discomfort of the environment as soon as I entered—I was hit by a wall of hot, wet air—but I regulated to that and my body established a sense of comfort. This maintained until I was dancing, at which point my body heat and sweating made my clothing wet and uncomfortable and the presence of so many bodies against mine made me feel claustrophobic.

Climate is generally unrecognised, though. Sloterdijk discusses how 'ordinary inhabitants have a user relationship to their environment, that they instinctively and exclusively consume it as a silent condition of their existence'.[34] While we sense climates, we do not often attend to them. As climate, *atmosphere* is also the constant, surreptitious presence of the air conditioning the environment. Moreover, in performances the air holds other things that in turn climatise or further condition our experience. This includes, for instance, vapours and hazes, caught or refracted light, smells, air pressure or mobility, static electricity, human gaseous products like pheromones, breathe, body odour, flatulence and so on. In any of the performances noted, when the climates became uncomfortable or shifted suddenly, we became aware of them and adjusted ourselves or used technologies to adjust the environmental climate. As an example of a very welcomed technology, in Metropolis there was air conditioning and fanned circulation in some of the spaces. This kept that environment more tolerable and more enjoyable, unlike at Debbie. Returning to The Globe, while it did not happen at my viewing of *Oresteia,* rain often disrupts or changes the viewing experience. Audiences then introduce different types of clothing (rain jackets) or technologies to stay dry (umbrellas) or simply *weather* it. *Oresteia* did, on the other hand, fill the air with haze and smoke. The atmosphere then had a different visual experience and tactile response. The air felt heavy, oily, sticky and thick. The haze also caught the lights, creating architectural impressions and smoky appearances. This conditioned the experience to feel these ways as well.

Climate has several concentric levels. There is the climate of a geographic area which relates to barometric pressure, precipitation, temperature, humidity, cloud cover, wind and the like. These directly impact on our sensory system,

Encountering Atmospheres 201

conditioning our presence in performance spaces with surrounding and physically impressing sensations and stimuli. We do not have agency over this kind of climate—although the catastrophe of global warming and pollution show that we have a collective agency in weather and effects of nature. That aside, we have no immediate or individual control over this kind of climate, it is a feature of nature. There is also architectural climate, the environment as established within built architectural spaces. Such structures shield or manipulate interior space(s) to be more controlled environments: dry, moderate in temperature, aired, and lighted (theatrically in most of the cases). This climate is a human intervention in space. The environments of the performances reviewed were manipulated with materials and technologies to make them more inhabitable and comfortable. There is personal intervention on the smaller climate scale. This is the climate of co-occupied spaces. In my examples, this was our immediate surroundings (and this extends to chambers, rooms, beds, cubicles, cells and seating areas). In these spaces, which are more intimate as we share personal and even intimate space, a more individual manipulation of environment occurs. We adjust the climate features to the comfort level of ourselves and nearest occupants. On an even smaller scale, we manipulate our own spaces of individual inhabitation. This is on the close personal and intimate levels through our choices in clothing, special garments or individual materials/technologies that are immediately near or against the skin. Again, we do not pay attention to, think about or consider these climate aspects of atmosphere, until they shift, become uncomfortable or are uninhabitable.

At least one other performance that I have attended at The Globe rain became so heavy that I eventually had to leave. It completely overpowered the experience. I was uncomfortable, cold and the sound of the rain striking the audience, roof and ground was as loud as the performers. Moreover, audience members were variously distressed by this. Some were agitated but fine; some herded together in more sheltered areas; some reacted with excitement; some immediately left the theatre; some did all these things in sequence. The distress in that audience was causing constant interruptions to the rest of the audience. Those who had them, used rain jackets and umbrellas—umbrellas being very visually and spatially disruptive to those standing around. To return to an earlier point, the climate affected them and they were affecting the rest of us. I could not focus or concentrate on anything else. In drizzling rain, I could have managed. With that heavy rain, I was not able to weather it.

The use of haze mentioned in *Oresteia* similarly conditioned my experience of that performance, characterising it with feelings of heaviness, thickness, oiliness and stickiness. This intentional design of the space via set, lights, haze, smells (burning incense), vibration in the air/materials, verticality of levels, temperature, sound volume and direction and so on were aesthetic outcomes of climate control. These climate-atmospheres came to condition our perceptual and sensorial processes. Far from existing in a vacuum, the perception and sensations in these cases existed within and through these atmospheric airspaces and were

## 202 *Precis*

by extension conditioned by it; the production teams/artists conditioned the environments.

Climate can be a way of conceptualising how participants and audiences also condition their atmospheric spaces—how they *made weather. Human weather* labels the ways in which we (participants and audiences) change the climate around us, individually and collectively. Different to changing the pressure, temperature, precipitation, cloud cover, wind and the like, we create and change the affective weather in encounters. What I have discussed previously as affective dimensions or moods are these human weathers, conditioning the space surrounding us through our fields of presence. We emanated into space an affective energy, or to return to Böhme, ecstasies, that shifted the tone and timbre of the experiences. Human weather is the affective dimensions and mood in atmosphere.

Taking *Bakkhai*, a mood pervaded the space that we, the audience and the performers shared. There was anticipation from the audience, a sense of expectation, excitement; from the performers there came a feeling of tension. Their moods being scripted, directed and rehearsed. Together we experienced the performance commonly through those moods, which shifted and moved. The khoros was one of the strongest producers of this atmosphere. They worked to create moods of calmness, aloof distance, heightened anxiety and religiosity. Throughout the episodes of the play, they also characterised the experience as still scenery posed around the perimeter of the stage, watching the actors engage with each other. This, while absent of action, worked as well to create a mood of observance and directed focus. These moods were a large part of the human weather constituting the atmosphere at that performance. As an audience, we too emanated our own focussed engagement into the performance space. Our silent and directed attention energised the environment.

This affective charge was is the atmosphere of the performance.

> [These a]tmosphere[s] were the common reality of the perceiver and the perceived. [They were] the reality of the perceived [the khoros] as the sphere of its presence and the reality of the perceiver [the audience], insofar as in sensing the atmosphere [w]e [were] bodily present in a certain way.[35]

Taking this in pieces, the atmosphere of *Bakkhai* was the felt reality of our shared space—the audience and the performers, the perceivers and the perceived. Dramatic reality imbricated the actual reality of the theatre space and together they constituted our theatrical experience—our reality. Working in concert, our co-presence and our responses to those realities created human weather. Ideally in performance, the constructed, performative reality overtakes and superimposes on the actual reality of the performance arena. Not dissimilar to the first interpretation of atmosphere, there is a conditioning of the environment here, but now it is also the intersubjective, affective conditioning of the encounter.

*Encountering Atmospheres*   203

Everyone produced the human weather of that *Bakkhai* experience, even if subtly done. The coughing man disturbed and ruptured the experience for others, which in turn shifted the human weather of the auditorium drastically. Affective feelings of guilt, shame, distress and displeasure very quickly moved and spread over the audience like a constant stinking wind. Upon his exit from the theatre the weather shifted drastically again towards stillness and silence toned with caution—no one wanted to be seen as a disturber of that new peace. I cite this example again as an instance in which the affective weather of the audience contagiously overpowered the performance. Something as small as a cough, when persistently done, completely ruptured the dramatic reality and superimposed unwanted affective feelings and moods on the audience.

Performance encounters become closed systems of experience—self-contained space in which we all affect and are affected by each other in a continuous feedback loop. The human weather of the audience affecting the collectives, in turn collectives produce different weather back (or, as in clubbing crowds, this occurs internally). While this might sound like a call and response relationship, I do not mean to imply it is so dyadic or polar. Weather production here is again operating with field properties and is simultaneously occurring in all directions and at all levels. Again, as foam structures, the total structure is formed and deformed by each adjacent or superimposed presence—co-tensile and co-fragile.

Due to their aeriform, intangibility and pervasive elemental nature, atmospheres like these are naturally immersive. We exist in them at all times.

> [We we]re immersed in atmospheres, and the manifest sp[oke to us] from atmospheres. Immersion in the conductive element ma[d]e them originally *there* and open for environments. Space as atmosphere [wa]s nothing but vibration or *pure conductivity* [all emphases in the original].[36]

Here I use Sloterdijk's words on the omnipresence of the atmospheric to illustrate how in cases of aesthetic collectives, atmosphere is the conductive suspension in which all communication and interactivity happens. It is the site of intersubjective exchange, indeed in my examples it was our intersubjective exchange.

Constantly shifting, changing and evolving, atmospheres are never stable or static. I return to the *Oresteia* performance where this kind of exchange amplified and was very noticeable, mainly because of the nature of lighting in Shakespeare's Globe. With our (the audience's) faces completely visible to the performers (there is even, full flood lighting of the entire space) our reactions and responses (human weather) were clear and evident to everyone. Perhaps because of this exposure by light, audience members were far more expressive and reactive, both with the performers and with each other (as compared with audiences in standard darkened auditoria). The atmosphere, as read in audience behaviour, evolved as a cooperative activity.

204  *Precis*

> [They] vibrate[d] [...] with the timbre of a mood or a defining *climate* [emphasis added]. But moods [...] are initially never the affair of individuals in the seeming privacy of their existential ecstasy; they form as *shared* [emphasis added] atmospheres—emotionally tinted totalities of involvement [*Bewandtnis*]—between several actors who tint the space of closeness and make room for one another in it.[37]

This activity and transformation was usually so subtle as not to be noticed. At times, it shifted radically and very quickly to produce large dramatic effect: the entrance of bodies on an altar in *Oresteia* (which I will address below); a large lighting change and shift in music type in the clubs; a thematic, refrain or narrative change in the music videos; the participants of a Beecroft taking a step or sitting/laying on the ground. Like climatological weather, our human weather shifted and changed.

> [T]heir *fields* of closeness [made us] [...] *weather makers*, casting sun and rain spells at every moment. [Our] faces [...] the headlines of the inner states; [our] gestures and moods radiate[d] both storms and brighten[ed] up into the shared [all emphasis added].[38]

The mood of *Oresteia* in text is serious, ominous, violent, dark, vengeful and gloomy, but in performance indulges in those moods to allow enjoyment and even humour. The mood contagion and human weather of the audience mirrored it. Frequently, members would turn to each other and convey re-actions to what was happening on stage. At the end of *Agamemnon*, an altar heaped with fake body parts of Agamemnon and Cassandra was wheeled onstage to show Clytemnestra's murderous work, herself doused in fake blood. The props were obviously fake, but moderately real, and the image called to mind slasher-porn horror films. This was a sudden and dramatic change in the weather of the performance, an introduction of gratuitous gore. The audience groaned, and many people turned to show humorous disgust, some laughing, at the sight.

   The fakeness of the props allowed humour here, but in a different theatrical environment this scene probably would have been met with greater silence and deeper solemnity. I can directly compare and contrast it with a late scene from *Bakkhai* in which Agave (played by a man) ran onstage holding a staff with the head of her son, Pentheus (previously played by the same man), his blood covering her body. The theatre of *Bakkhai* was dark, very dramatically lighted, and had the audience in seats aimed at the stage. These props were just as realistic/fake as those in *Oresteia* and the scenes of both had equally campy qualities in their execution (in *Bakkhai* this was literal with gender cross-dressing). However, in the audience of *Bakkhai* we did not react as at *Oresteia*. We sat, silently, and stared at the unfolding scene. While a few audience members I saw in both productions of *Bakkhai* did turn to each other and did convey emotion through facial expression, they were very much in the

Encountering Atmospheres 205

minority. Most people did not move at all. In *Bakkhai*, the weather within the audience was tense, contemplative and discomforted by the sight onstage. Mood vibrated through the still, forward facing audience, resonating within the individual bodies of the audience members as well as in our collective body.

As audiences we experienced both the weather of these khoroi onstage and of our audience responses. As weather-makers, we were *creators* of or *contributors* to the atmospheres. As active agents, we *made* weather. This does not imply that we were purely active agents. We also experienced the weather of each other as receptive subjects as well—we *weathered* it and were *weathered* by it. Thus, as weather-makers, we operated simultaneously as active and passive agents of the weather created. Within that reciprocating loop the weather was being iteratively exchanged, transmitted and circulated.

Ben Anderson's Encountering *Affect: Capacities, Apparatuses, Conditions,*[39] has helped me conceptualise the substrate of this weather, affect, as something existing along a continuum of definitions 'as developed through Gilles Deleuze's (with Felix Guattari) encounter with Baruch Spinoza, and subsequent experiments by Brian Massumi and others in contemporary cultural theory'.[40] His examination leads to referring to affect as a dual capacity in which one is both *affecting and is affected*, phraseology I have used throughout. The atmospheric weather production that occurred in these cases was an affecting/affected condition wherein our affect transmitted and exchanged, propelling the experiences. It was conditioning our experiences.

> On the one hand, [it] refers to [our] capacity to be affected through some form of affection. On the other hand, affect describes the capacity [our] bod[ies had] to affect something outside of itself. "Being affected-affecting" are therefore two sides of the same dynamic shift [...] It is [a] relational version of affect as a "force of existing" (Deleuze 1978).[41]

The term 'force' here connects Tomkins' perspective of affect as 'intensity' readings. The fields of aesthetic collectives are this force of existing, operating with intensities that are felt upon our bodies and in our minds.

Moreover, affect does not just happen apropos of nothing. In performance they are stimulated. Performances, in a sense, stimulate new affective experiences or extend/remind audiences of the affective dimensions tinting/toning the experience. Using aesthetic collectives, we can cast or shift mood and atmosphere in directions. Khoroi often had to shift moods and atmospheres along their affective spectrum, entering and exiting the dialogue to introduce variations on the general mood of the performance; or as silent and still reminders of the pervading mood. Back-up dancing collectives are there nearly entirely to magnify or amplify the affective tone of music videos through their collective bodies. They are there to 'back-up' the performance, give it the affective background to impact the viewer. 'Feelings express[ed our] affected body's existing capacity to affect and be affected, or what Massumi

## 206 *Precis*

(2002a: 15) describes as perpetual bodily changes "in which powers to affect and be affected are addressable by a next event and how readily addressable they are".[42] Aesthetic collectives create pervasive affective backgrounds and interventions in the affective fabric of the performance to shift/change the atmosphere, moving the performance along.

Although affects can biologically be linked to chemical reactions in the body, I sidestep the pinpointing of it as a specific thing in the subject/their body. I take affect as a combinatory field in which subjects and the environment coexist. I use the word *combinatory* to specify how this field of coexistence has, as a principle, assimilatory properties. Two (or more) things combine to produce something new. Again, as Böhme illustrates with his notion of ecstasies, the subject and environment are not fully bounded or contained. Instead, they radiate out of themselves and into space and into each other; they permeate the surrounded space with their field (of presence/aura), their ecstasy. Aesthetic collectives bask in their own field of radiance. The participants are immersed in that field that affects them and through which they affect each other. They then collectively affect outwardly into the audience. They establish their fields around and within themselves, a contained weather environment—generating and establishing atmospheres.

As I conclude, I return to the awareness of atmospheres that I had in these closely read cases and the surprising importance atmospheres played in my experiences. As indicated, my role within the atmospheres functioned in a complex balance of active and passive states. I passively existed within the atmospheres and was affected by them. I also actively transmitted, 'made', that atmosphere. In Sloterdijk's terms, I injected my own experience, my own weather, into the atmosphere. To return to an earlier point from Sloterdijk, this state of affairs is taken for granted: as 'ordinary inhabitants [we had] a user relationship to [our] environment, that [we] instinctively and exclusively consume[d] as a silent condition of [our] existence'.[43] I was not purposefully attending to or at times even noticing these atmospheric states or effects, it was usually a background phenomenon, one that surreptitiously defined the experiences I was having.

> The one thing that can never be kept quiet because [...] it makes the manifest shared *character* palpable is the atmosphere, the encompassing tinting of the space that *impregnate[d* the] inhabitants. Thus for most people, the weather of their own relationships remains more important, and far realer, than all great politics and 'high' culture [...] the tinted endosphere is the first product of densely dwelling communities, and its mood is their first message to themselves. To seal, round it, regenerate and brighten it is the first human-creating project [all emphasis mine].[44]

Character in the cases was brought out through atmosphere. Per Fuchs, it was the characterising of the total spaces, human elements and spectacles. As with my discussion in chapter four, the idea that these atmospheres entered the

Encountering Atmospheres 207

body and virally began to generate life within us supports the notion of contagion and affect movement as viral, along paths. Atmospheres moved around us, into us, out of us and became part of us. Sloterdijk goes so far as to state that these actions of crafting and managing atmospheres constitutes the first major project of humanity and of being in community; the work of community and being together is the atmospheric.

> Humans are not only sensitive to the weather in groups, however; in all that they do in the shared field, they themselves act as microspherically climate-active creatures through the division of the immediate surroundings. The world of closeness arises from the sum of our actions towards one another and our suffering through one another.[45]

If atmospheres, and weather-making, are assumed and constant features of our interaction, Sloterdijk's assertion is not wrong. There were two very clear entities involved: the human 'makers' and the environmental enclosures from, in, with and on which they 'make' weather: co-present, co-tensile, co-fragile.

## Notes

1 Walter Benjamin, 'The Work of Art in the Age of Mechanical Reproduction', in *Illuminations*, trans. by Harry Zohn, ed. by Hannah Arendt (New York: Schocken Books, 1969), p. 3.
2 For a discussion of authenticity in Benjamin's sense see comment 8 in Appendix C.
3 See Böhme, 'Atmosphere as the Fundamental Concept of a New Aesthetics', trans. by David Roberts, *Text Eleven*, 36 (1993), 113–126; Böhme, *The Aesthetics of Atmospheres*, ed. by Jean-Paul Thibaud (Abingdon, Oxon: Routledge, 2017). These arguments equally extend to the similar notions of ecstasies, atmosphere and affect already presented in Brennan, Anderson, Barsade, Barsade and Knight and, as will be presented shortly, Sloterdijk.
4 Böhme, 'Atmosphere as the Fundamental...', pp. 121–122.
5 Neville Wakefield, 'Vanessa Beecroft: South Sudan', *Flash Art* (November-December 2006).
6 Elena Cué, 'Interview with Vanessa Beecroft', *Alejandra De Argos* (2017), http://www.alejandradeargos.com/index.php/en/all-articles/21-guests-with-art/41536-vanessa-beecroft-interview [accessed 24 July 2018].
7 Benjamin, p. 3; Catherine Bouko, 'Interactivity and Immersion in a Media-based Performance', *Participations: Journal of Audience and Reception Studies*, 11:1 (May 2014), 254–269. Bouko is here drawing on a vast body of related research on interactivity and immersion in performance. I will follow her assertions, but for further discussion and background context see also Frances Dyson, *Sounding New Media: Immersion and Embodiment in the Arts and Culture* (Ewing: UC Press, 2009); Helen Freshwater, *Theater & Audience* (Basingstoke and New York: Palgrave Macmillan, 2009); Steve Benford and Gabriella Giannachi, *Performing Mixed Reality* (Cambridge MA: The MIT Press, 2011); Josephine Machon, *Immersive Theatres: Intimacy and Immediacy in Contemporary Performance* (Basingstoke and New York: Palgrave Macmillan, 2013); Nathaniel Stern, *Interactive Art and Embodiment: The Implicit Body as Performance* (Canterbury: Glyphi Limited, 2013).
8 Bouko, p. 260.
9 Gareth White, 'On Immersive Theatre', *Theatre Research International*, 37:3 (2012), 228.

208   *Precis*

10  Similarly applying George Lakoff and Mark Johnson, *Metaphors We Live By* (Chicago and London: University of Chicago Press, 2003).
11  Bouko, p. 263.
12  White, p. 228.
13  Ryan puts forth the interactivity literary model which examines interactivity as literary and figurative which she further categorises into weak and strong interactive forms. Saltz and McIver Lopes consider a minimal level of interactivity as an issue of control over experience (terms Bouko advises against conflating). Dixon further explores interactivity through four stages of engagement (names navigation, participation, conversation and collaboration). For further information see also Steve Dixon, *Digital Performance* (Cambridge: The MIT Press, 2007); Dominic M. McIver Lopes, 'The Ontology of Interactive Art', *Journal of Aesthetic Education*, 35:4 (2001), 65–81; Marie-Laure Ryan, 'Immersion vs. Interactivity: Virtual Reality and Literary Theory', *Substance*, 28:2 (1999), 110–137; Marie-Laure Ryan, *Narrative as Virtual Reality: Immersion and Interactivity in Literature and Electronic Music* (Baltimore: The John Hopkins University Press, 2001); Marie-Laure Ryan, 'Beyond myth and Metaphor: Narrative in Digital Media', *Poetics Today*, 23:4 (2002), 581–609; Aaron Smuts, 'What is Interactivity?', *Journal of Aesthetic Education*, 43:4 (2009), 53–73.
14  Bouko, p. 255.
15  Wishaw has established a strong base of fans through his cinema status. His return to the theatre created a celebrity urge to see the performance.
16  Elias Canetti, *Crowds and Power*, trans. by Carol Stewart (New York: Farrar, Straus and Giroux, 1960).
17  Canetti, p. 34.
18  Canetti, pp. 36–37.
19  Bouko, p. 260.
20  Bouko, p. 260.
21  White, p. 225.
22  White, p. 227.
23  While there probably are performances that take place in liquids, liquid conducted performance is certainly in a very small minority, and, as shall be shown shortly, even then one would probably be contained within an air-packaged suit or vessel of some sort.
24  White, p. 228.
25  White, p. 233.
26  Bouko, p. 260.
27  Following Sloterdijk, the term *sphere* does not necessarily imply the perfect geometric form, but rather an enclosure, albeit one that is roughly spherical in shape and form as it extends in all directions more or less equally. Spheres also are not necessarily spatial in nature but are also figurative, metaphoric and analogous.
28  Christian Borch, 'Organizational Atmospheres: Foam, Affect and Architecture', *Organization,* 17:2 (2009), 226.
29  Peter Sloterdijk, *Foams: Spheres Volume 3: Plural Spherology*, trans. by Wieland Hoban (California, USA: Semiotext(e), 2016), p. 48.
30  Lakoff and Johnson, p. 25.
31  Mikkel Bille, Peter Bjerregaard and Tim Flohr Sørensen, 'Staging Atmospheres: Materiality, Culture, and the Texture of the In-between', *Emotion, Space and Society*, 15 (2015), 31.
32  Lakoff and Johnson, p. 61.
33  Jean-Paul Thibaud, 'The Backstage of Urban Ambiance: When Atmospheres Pervade Everyday Experience', *Emotion, Space and Society*, 15 (2015), 40.
34  Peter Sloterdijk, *Terror from the Air,*trans. by Amy Patton and Steve Corcoran (Los Angeles, CA: Semiotext(e), Foreign Agents Series, 2009), p. 28.

Encountering Atmospheres  209

35 Böhme, p. 122.
36 Peter Sloterdijk, *Spheres: Vol 2*, p. 136.
37 Sloterdijk, *Globes: Spheres Volume 2: Macrospherology*, trans. by Wieland Hoban (South Pasadena, CA, USA: Semiotext(e), 2014), p. 138.
38 Sloterdijk, *Globes: Spheres Volume 2*, pp. 139–140.
39 Ben Anderson, *Encountering Affect: Capacities, Apparatuses, Condition* (London: Routledge Taylor and Francis, 2016).
40 Anderson, p. 78; see also Gilles Deleuze and Félix Guattari, *A Thousand Plateaus*, trans. by Brian Massumi (Minneapolis: University of Minnesota Press, 1987); Gilles Deleuze and Félix Guattari, *What is Philosophy?*, trans. by Hugh Tomlinson and Graham Burchill (London: Verso, 1994); Brian Massumi, *Parables for the Virtual: Movement, Affect, Sensation* (Durham, NC: Duke University Press, 2002).
41 Anderson, pp. 78–79; see also Gilles Deleuze, 'Lecture of 24.01.1978', (trans. unknown), https://www.webdeleuze.com/textes/14 [accessed 26 July 2019].
42 Anderson, p. 80; see again Massumi.
43 Sloterdijk, *Terror from the Air*, p. 28.
44 Sloterdijk, *Globes: Spheres Volume 2*, pp. 140–141.
45 Sloterdijk, *Globes: Spheres Volume 2*, p. 139.

# Conclusion

Aesthetic collectives. Like the climate, unacknowledged or unaddressed until it shifts/changes/becomes uncomfortable, these performance bodies have been woefully under-examined as a phenomena. When I started this research, I was mainly amazed by how overlooked as a rich site of human activity they were. I have always been thrilled, excited, scared or confused by these kinds of cultural, collective bodies. When I see audiences watching them, I am equally intrigued by what makes them so compelling: masses watching masses. There is something happening there that is truly interesting and uniquely human. My review is limited to clubbing crowds, installation performance art, Greek theatre khoroi, back-up dancing groups in music videos. As noted at the start, the list of potential examples, however, is far more extensive. The appearance of aesthetic collectives pervades cultures, demographics and geography. Seemingly simple, 'they are just groups', my progression here has illustrated a complex depth and fundamentality, delving into human emotions, communicative processing, agency, individuality, deindividuation, conformity and so on.

Conceptualised like entities, human entities or at least aspects of them, facilitated better understanding of them. They have also proved to evade definition, either of concrete or psychological matter and ipso facto any strong categorisation. A plurality of subjects composed the memberships, but I cannot tether the perceived entity of the totalities to any one individual subject. Moreover, the totalities are neither objects nor have subjectivity as traditionally understood. Instead, I have shown how they operate in terms of a perceived ontological categorisation, often vacillating between ontological constructs. I have outlined and detailed what kind of entity they *can be considered* through measures of entitativity and this has shown them to have more than one ontological state—often simultaneously or shifting depending on perceptual interpretation. Never with true subjectivity, at least not in the way we address and hold people as individuated subjects. Rather, they exist *like entities*, they hold properties *like entities*, we understand them *like entities*. I am left pondering their ontologically polysemy.

To explore that, I applied a theory of entitativity. In the process I broke examples down into different conceptualising processes that we use and employ. Progressing through four entitative elements in my analysis, drawn from

DOI: 10.4324/9781003205661-10

Conclusion    211

Donald T. Campbell, I grounded understanding in a complex matrix of metaphor. As a thing, aesthetic collectives are 'not a concept that has a clearly delineated structure; whatever structure it has it gets only via metaphors'.[1] I developed understanding of them through a bricolage of metaphoric thinking. Via metaphor I compared aspects of them with other, more readily understood, things. Through the reconstructive assembly of these disparate pieces of defining information they became more fully understandable.

The first element, proximity, established how we conceptualise these aesthetic collectives in spatialised terms and understand them as a body. Participants nearer to each other coalesce as a body, or to observing audiences participants nearer to each other appear to be unified as a body. The spacing of participants also showed proximal limits: when too far apart participants do not feel part of a collective body nor are they perceived as part of that body by audiences; when too close together the comfort of the participant is decreased or threatened and they revert to focussing on themself and their personal space. To an audience this also appears as a break in cohesion and connection with the collective body. Proximity, I later returned to in chapter six illustrating how that the space between participants was as much a part of the collective body as the participants themselves. The shifting state and features of that space as well as its material composition (anything in the air or the communication signals moving through it) became conditioning factors of aesthetic collectives. Moreover, this space I came to define as a field in which the entitative totalities exuded their presence and immersed their participants and audiences.

My application of the second element of entitativity, prägnanz, revealed further how discrete individuals became perceived as a collective body through both a bounding/enclosing and increases in physical order. Prägnanz shows collective bodies to be conceptualised as contained in some way, and for the participants to be *inside* while the audiences are *outside*. Being *in* or being *out* was a motif throughout. In chapter six, it came to structure encounters, immersion and absorption in performance. Broadening the crux of these arguments I identified a surrounding and emanating field feature. Within that field, which I detailed as their presence or aura, a sense of immersion occurs. As a descriptive property, immersivity notes being or feeling inside/outside or contained/not in the field of the collectives. Being physically within/out of the bounded space of the collectives was not itself determinant of this kind of immersion. Moreover, one's role (as participant or audience) in the encounters alters the perspectival experience. The more interaction performances offer the greater the becoming an agentic part of it/the collective and thus the sense of immersion or being 'in'.

In examining the third element of entitativity, similarity, I worked through the transformation of participants' physical self as well as their agentic capacity. Similarising participants does two things. One, it creates an increased sense of visual cohesion and togetherness, emphasising the inside and outside principles noted above in terms of belongingness and outsidership. Two, it highlights the deindividuating effect on the participant-as-member and the types of loss in

## 212   Conclusion

agency that occur for them. Recurring themes of individual agency and what happens when that agency is sacrificed, lost or exchanged for collective agency permeated the rest of the text. By-products (compliance, unity, cohesion, obedience, anonymity and a sense of safety within the group) arose through the similarisation of the participants. I illustrated how those by-products also have an outward projection to audiences, exhibiting images of collectivity and strong bonds in the group. In chapters four and five, I would extend this notion, emphasising how such strength creates greater shared emotional cultures for these collectives and stronger group character. The strength of that emotional culture and group character is something further contributing to the effectiveness of aesthetic aims.

The last entitative element, common fate, I detailed as creating bonds and cohesion through time. Perception of the participants in the collectives showed them having the same objective or goal, making them similar in terms of motivations and movements towards those objectives or goals. In other words, collectives become more entitative because members draw together for the same reasons, behaving in the same ways, in pursuit of those reasons. Like with similarity, this is a similarity of purpose that transcends, or can feel like it transcends, the present moment. Objectives, goals and purposive action are also connected to motivations, drives and a sense of biographic continuity. This is a feature of personification, relating aesthetic collectives, human motivations and drives. In chapter four, I expanded on this as a character role or characterising role. With character role, aesthetic collectives generate or adopt character features in their manifestation, appearing more like a reflection of a human being or archetype; with characterisation they characterise or generate/produce characteristics for the experience.

This entitative analysis and the unpicking of its metaphoric conceptual structuring foregrounded how important awareness of the experience of their encounter is. Entitative analysis established that aesthetic collectives contain themselves, creating insides and outsides, and that the experience of their encounter, either for audiences or participants, is characterised by immersion in their presence. That could be within the body of the collective or in their emanated field. In either situation (or both), one is within their field. This field is characterised by a sense of co-presence: with others, with environment/matter and with the affective. Entitative analysis led aesthetic collectives as atmospheric encounters and experiences. They are the confluence of participants, environment and aesthetics that audiences encounter. Dancing collectives (clubbing crowds or back-up dancers) became physicalisations of the music and/or its thematic content; installed collectives (Beecroft) came into harmony with and were strongly framed by the space in which they were installed; Greek khoroi reflected and embodied the theatrical drama in which they found themselves, conveying commentary on the narrative and meaning of the performance from both within and without the drama in which the other actors are trapped.

*Conclusion* 213

Aesthetic collectives are not any one element, but all elements complicitly creating their effects. Their atmospheric nature frames and constitutes their experience. 'Atmospheres are indeterminate. They are resources that must be attuned to by bodies [...] exceed[ing] clear and distinct figuration because they both exist and do not exist'.[2] As something that cannot be fully or properly determined, and as they both exist and do not exist they move past normal ontological figuration.

> On the one hand, atmospheres require completion by the subjects that "apprehend" them [...] On the other hand, atmospheres "emanate" from the ensemble of elements that make up the aesthetic object. They belong to the aesthetic object. Atmospheres are, on this account, always in the process of emerging and transforming. They are always being taken up and reworked in the events of lived experience.[3]

The participants in collectives are the material focus, but they are not the full experience. They work among and with other elements that determine the sensory-perceptual experience. They are totalities that include as a part of themselves the environmental space, the air filling it and the affective interface that occurs through it. The environmental space between and around the aesthetic collectives and the audience is overlooked but highly conditioning of the experience, indeed is the interface in which encounters and experiences happen. Crucially, the space includes the material of the air that occupies it. How much space, how much air, their formation and dynamics participate directly, and strongly, with the other elements constructing, determining and conditioning the experience.

Aesthetic collectives are confluences of elements that create affective life, a combination of elements that work together towards specified or implied goals. They construct encounters in which affective purposes are fulfilled. They work towards the crafting, participating in and conducing of affective life within each of their contexts. This 'creates an intensive space-time. A space-time that exceeds lived or conceived space, even as [they] "emanate" from the material and representational elements that compose the art work[s]'.[4] Their space-time *exceeds* lived or conceived space, superimposing or interpolating other feelings, thoughts or experiences on/out of 'normal' reality and normal affective life. Encountering them creates a felt and affected response, which in turn induces intelligent apprehension.

> The[ir] atmosphere[s] [...] disclose the space-time of [...] "expressed world[s]"—[they do] not represent objective space-time or lived space-time. [They] create a space of intensity that overflows a represented world organised into subjects and objects, or subjects and other subjects. Instead, it is through [their] atmosphere[s] that a thing, person or site [... take] on a specific presence.[5]

214  *Conclusion*

This dual analysis, of conceptualisation through entitativity and through atmospheric theory, is not something previously done. These kinds of plural experiences reside outside of normal ontological discussion, which tends to focus on dyadic experience. I propose that plural intersubjectivity moves beyond this.

Beyond normal ontology further means that they fit neither subject nor object categories, but do fit as a type of *thing*.

> [Things are] the concrete yet ambiguous within the everyday [… They] function […] to overcome the loss of other words or as a place holder for some future specifying operation […] to index a certain limit or liminality, to hover over the threshold between the nameable and the unnameable, the figurable and unfigurable, the identifiable and the unidentifiable.[6]

Things, here defined through Bill Brown's theory of things, are the present, but indeterminate. Tonino Griffero in *Quasi-Things: The Paradigm of Atmospheres*[7] offers a clear outline of the properties of things, which I will quote at length:

> Things are roughly taken to be tangible and well-determined entities with a regular shape that, being three dimensional, cannot be exhausted by their representations. They are harmonious in their parts, which are not too distant or different both materially (cohesion) and qualitatively (homogeneity). They can be singled out and therefore, unlike substances, they can be measured based on their genus and species (individuation). They have a continued existence (persistence) and peculiar spatial-temporal properties. Such things, perhaps transcendentally possible only if the analysis is temporally detached from the syntext, probably gather the projection of the ideal in-itself that a constantly threatened being like a human feels to be lacking.[8]

Griffero augments Brown's definition with additional features that help identification of things. Addressing gases, particularly the air, Griffero classes them as something not quite thing-like. 'It might not be strictly a thing, but the air we breathe is still a very concrete experience, both climatic and affective'.[9] The air, as a thing that does not fully fit thing definition, he classes in a subset of things: *quasi-things*.

The quasi-thing, which Griffero goes to extraordinary, deeply involved lengths to detail, ruptures from other things. First, quasi-things are 'beings that do not respect borders (primarily between the external and internal world)…'[10] While I have a bit of trouble with the use of the word 'beings' here, I will avoid critique and instead focus on how Griffero outlines quasi-things as something between the worlds of inner and outer conception—thought and matter. This means that quasi-things might be of the external world and be matter, of the

Conclusion 215

internal world and be thought, or even something between those two, in an interstitial place of existence.

> [I]t is easy to discover instead that these quasi-things [...] brightly colonize a vast territory in between the (so-called) qualia and things in the proper sense. However, as I have said, we must resist the recurring temptation to remove them, whether by forcedly turning them into things (for example, by reifying distal vagueness at all costs) or by tracing them back to perceptions so chaotic and decontoured that they are as anomalous (if not pathological) as experimentally produced ones.[11]

So, quasi-things exist and have some material substance to it (some-thing that is/does something) but are completed through the apprehension of the mind and its sensorium.

Aesthetic collectives enclose and incorporate space and air within them, are atmospheric phenomena and by this logic, are quasi-things. There are elements of material in them (air, pheromones, dust, people, objects), but they are also imbued and animated by affect. The participants and audiences were also both *in* the atmosphere and *a part of them*. These atmospheres were *conditions* in which subjects, objects things and quasi-things came into relationship with each other and experienced each other. They were 'both an effect of a gathering of elements and a mediating force that actively change[d] the gathering it emanate[d] from'.[12] A force of collective presence in aesthetic collectives structures and creates these atmospheric conditions. Their atmospheric nature allowed me to affect the encounter and be affected by it.

*I return to my encounter at the Tower of London watching* Storm the Wall *and the 202 dancers twisting, revolving, spinning, shifting, turning and moving about the stage as one massive, simultaneous and synchronously performing group. As I watch I pay attention to how my mind is processing what I am experiencing. My cognitive thinking, my perception and my aesthetic tastes are all stimulated at the same time. Fluctuations between them are happening; there is a sort of hypnotism in effect. The dancers' behaviour captures me on an affective level. I feel the mood in this space with these other watching people. Our co-presence (we as audiences and them as participants) establishes a tension between us all and this environment. The dark and threatening sky above is suggesting a meteorological storm (climate-weather!) at any moment. The oppressive backdrop of the tower itself. Our fixed attention aimed at the stage. By-passers further back are stopping and watching from a great distance. The drumming music. At times these are fully sensory experiences, allowing all of this to wash over me and invoke feelings for me.*

*At times, I engage with these stimuli in a cognitive capacity. My strongest experience of this is during a late dance when a corps of 12 or so dancers mimetically dance/act a series of execution methods. I am moved by the implicit terror of enforced death and my own political and humane response to this, but I am also entertained by the humour of puzzling out some of the semiotic suggestions of the dancing and the patterns of movement they are performing. I cognitively assemble the thread of suggested narrative into some form*

216    *Conclusion*

*of statement or comment on execution and its historical place here at the tower. We all feel the throbbing, beating music, literally as it vibrates through our bodies—I am aware of the fixed attention at this point on the dancing collective. I am also aware of its strong effect on us as audience as many people begin to film or photograph this part. (A sure sign that something is considered valuable or at least memorable.)*

*I return to my first question about these collective bodies on-stage, 'what are "they"'? Obviously, they are the individual people, the young dancers. But this conglomerate they create in their dance—what is it and how does it capture both them and us? This question, like my initial questions about groups in performance, spawned this research. I was initially concerned with how collective bodies have presence* as a collective. *What I conclude is that the encounter of things like these aesthetic collectives is an atmospheric experience in which the capacity to affect/be affected is live, active, present. Aesthetic collectives charge the air between us and around us with affective dynamics. They create a collective atmosphere of being together, communally sharing and experiencing their/our presence. What distinguishes aesthetic collective phenomena is that those affective feelings are generated by and fixated on our being together and they make us think about this relationship between the self and the social. Unique to these collective or mass experiences is the feeling of being-with and thoughts of co-existence. Jean Luc Nancy points out that there is a co-existence implicit in existence itself. 'That which exists, whatever this might be, coexists because it exists. The co-implication of existing [l'exister] is the sharing of the world'.[13] There is no existence in a world without an existing 'with'. In the case of human beings, it is* with *others: 'there exists something ("me") and another thing (this other "me" that represents the possible) to which I relate myself in order for me to ask myself if there exists something of the sort that I think of as possible. This something coexists at least as much as "me"'.[14] Nancy's notion that there is no existence before existing with, before co-existence, perfectly encapsulates the premise of the atmospheric—that co-existence is shared and transmitted. In performance, the substrates of this co-existence in atmosphere (presence, aura, shared affect) is the primary encountered thing. Aesthetic collectives anchor this atmosphere in their bounded space and field. Through the art of performance, aesthetic collectives allow us the direct encounter and experience of witnessing and being with other human beings on an expansive or even cosmic scale. Allowing us to rupture our boundedness and to permeate/be permeated by the feeling of our great social being-with; co-present, co-tensile, co-fragile—the feeling and knowledge of us in all our discreteness; together yet isolated.*

## Notes

1 George Lakoff and Mark Johnson, *Metaphors We Live By* (Chicago and London: University of Chicago Press, 2003), p. 110. In this quotation, Lakoff and Johnson are discussing *love* as a concept; the extension to my needs here is appropriate given the similar degree of a lack of structure with aesthetic collectives.

2 Ben Anderson, *Encountering Affect: Capacities, Apparatuses, Condition* (London: Routledge Taylor and Francis, 2016), p. 145.

3 Anderson, p. 145.

4 Anderson, p. 143.

5 Anderson, p. 144.

6 Bill Brown, 'Thing Theory', *Critical Inquiry*, 28:1 (2001), 4–5.

7 Tonino Griffero, *Quasi-Things: The Paradigm of Atmospheres*, trans. by Sarah De Sanctis (New York: SUNY Press, 2017).
8 Griffero, p. 4.
9 Griffero, p. 8.
10 Griffero, pp. 4–5.
11 Griffero, p. 5.
12 Anderson, p. 156.
13 Jean-Luc Nancy, *Being Singular Plural* (Stanford, CA: Stanford University Press, 2000), p. 29.
14 Nancy, p. 29.

# Bibliography

Adelmann, Pamela K. and R. B. Zajonc, 'Facial Efference and the Experience of Emotion', *Annual Review of Psychology*, 40 (1989), 249–280.

Aeschylus, *Oresteia*, adapted by Rory Mullarky, dir. by Adele Thomas (London: Shakespeare's Globe, 2015).

Anderson, Ben, *Encountering Affect: Capacities, Apparatuses, Condition* (London: Routledge Taylor and Francis, 2016).

Andrews, Hazel, '"Tits Out for the Boys and No Back Chat": Gendered Space on Holiday', *Space and Culture*, 12:2 (2008), 166–182.

Ashforth, Blake E. and Ronal A. Humphrey, 'Emotion in the Workplace: A Reappraisal', *Human Relations*, 48:2 (1995), 97–125.

Auslander, Philip, *Liveness: Performance in a Mediatized Culture*, 2nd ed. (London and New York: Routledge, Taylor & Francis Group, 2008).

Austin, J. L., *How to Do Things with Words*, 2nd ed., ed by J. O. Urmson and Marina Sbisà (Cambridge, Massachusetts: Harvard University Press, 1975).

Barsade, Sigal, 'The Ripple Effect: Emotional Contagion and its Influence on Group Behavior', *Administrative Science Quarterly*, 47:4 (2002), 644–675.

Barsade, Sigal G. and Andrew P. Knight, 'Group Affect', *Annual Review of Organizational Psychology and Organizational Behaviour*, 2 (2015), 21–46.

Barsade, Sigal G. and Donald E. Gibson, 'Why Does Affect Matter in Organizations?', *Perspectives*, 21:1 (2007), 36–59.

Barsade, Sigal G. and Olivia A. O'Neill, 'What's Love Got to do with It? A Longitudinal Study of the Culture of Companionate Love and Employee and Client Outcomes in the Long-Term Care Setting', *Administrative Science Quarterly*, 59:4 (2014), 551–598.

Bartel, Caroline A. and Richard Saavedra, 'The Collective Construction of Work Group Moods', *Administrative Science Quarterly*, 45 (2000), 197–231.

Beecroft, Vanessa, from the Deitch archive notes on *VB16* (1996), http://www.deitch.com/archive/vb16-piano-americano-beige [accessed 6 May 2016].

Beecroft, Vanessa, as quoted in Goddard, Peter, 'Artist Exposed in Film', *The Star* (2007), https://www.thestar.com/news/2007/02/21/artist_exposed_in_film.html [accessed 29 September 2018].

Beecroft, Vanessa, 'Vanessa Beecroft' in interview with David Shapiro, *Museo Magazine* (2008), http://www.museomagazine.com/VANESSA-BEECROFT [accessed 6 May 2016].

## Bibliography 219

Beecroft, Vanessa, *Vanessa Beecroft: Performances*, ed by Marcella Beccaria (New York: Rizzoli International Publications, 2003).

Beecroft, Vanessa, 'The Very Best of Vanessa Beecroft', *The New York Time* (2016), http://www.nytimes.com/slideshow/2016/05/19/t-magazine/the-very-best-of-vanessa-beecroft/s/19tmag-beecroft-slide-7RKB.html [accessed 6 May 2016].

Benford, Steve and Gabriella Giannachi, *Performing Mixed Reality* (Cambridge MA: The MIT Press, 2011).

Benjamin, Walter, 'The Work of Art in the Age of Mechanical Reproduction', in *Illuminations*, trans. by Harry Zohn, ed. by Hannah Arendt (New York: Schocken Books, 1969).

Bennett, Susan, *Theatre Audiences: A Theory of Production and Reception*, 2nd ed. (London and New York: Routledge, 2003).

Bergl, Skylar, Skylar Bergi Instagram account. www.instagram.com/skylarbergl [accessed 15 May 2016].

Bille, Mikkel, Peter Bjerregaard and Tim Flohr Sørensen, 'Staging atmospheres: Materiality, Culture, and the Texture of the In-between', *Emotion, Space and Society*, 15 (2015), 31–38.

Bion, W. R., *Experiences in Groups* (New York: Tavistock Publications Limited, 1961).

Blake, Robert R. and Jane Srygley Mouton, 'Conformity, Resistance, and Conversion', in *Conformity and Deviation*, ed. by Irwin A. Berg and Bernard M. Bass (New York: Harper & Brothers, 1961).

Böhme, Gernot, *The Aesthetics of Atmospheres*, ed. by Jean-Paul Thibaud (Abingdon, Oxon: Routledge, 2017).

Böhme, Gernot, 'Atmosphere as the Fundamental Concept of a New Aesthetics', trans. by David Roberts, *Text Eleven*, 36 (1993), 113–126.

Borch, Christian, 'Organizational Atmospheres: Foam, Affect and Architecture', *Organization*, 17:2 (2009), 223–241.

Bouko, Catherine, 'Interactivity and Immersion in a Media-based Performance', *Participations: Journal of Audience and Reception Studies*, 11:1 (May 2014), 254–269.

Brennan, Theresa, *The Transmission of Affect* (Ithaca and London: Cornell University Press, 2004).

Brown, Bill, 'Thing Theory', *Critical Inquiry*, 28:1 (2001), 1–22.

Buck, R. P., *The Communication of Emotion* (New York: Guilford Press, 1984).

Butler, Judith, *Gender Trouble: Feminism and the Subversion of Identity* (New York: Routledge, 1990).

Calleja, Gordon, *In-Game: From Immersion to Incorporation* (London and Cambridge: MIT Press, 2011).

Campbell, Donald T., 'Common Fate, Similarity, and Other Indices of the Status of Aggregates of Persons as Social Entities', *Behavioral Science*, 3:1 (1958), 14–25.

Canetti, Elias, *Crowds and Power*, trans by Carol Stewart (New York: Farrar, Straus and Giroux, 1960).

Cavendish, Dominic, '*Medea*, Almeida Theatre, review: "Fiercely intelligent and at times ferocious"' *The Telegraph*, 1 October 2015, https://www.telegraph.co.uk/theatre/what-to-see/medea-almeida-theatre-review/ [accessed on 16 August 2018].

Cheshin, Arik, Anat Rafaeli and Nathan Bos, 'Anger and Happiness in Virtual Teams: Emotional Influences of Text and Behavior in Others' Affect in the Absence of Non-Verbal Cues', *Organizational Behavior and Human Decision Processes*, 116 (2011), 2–16.

## 220 Bibliography

Clapp, Susannah, 'As You Like It Review—Out with Merriment, in with Humour', *The Guardian The Observer* (2015), https://www.theguardian.com/stage/2015/nov/08/as-you-like-it-polly-findlay-review-national-theatre [accessed 22 August 2018].

Cué, Elena, 'Interview with Vanessa Beecroft', *Alejandra De Argos* (2017), http://www.alejandradeargos.com/index.php/en/all-articles/21-guests-with-art/41536-vanessa-beecroft-interview [accessed 24 July 2018].

Damasio, Antonio, *The Feeling of What Happens: Body, Emotion and the Making of Consciousness* (London: Vintage Books, 2000).

Declos, Sandra, James D. Laird, Eric Schneider, Melissa Sexter, Lis Stern and Oliver Van Lighten, 'Emotion-Specific Effects of Facial Expressions and Postures on Emotional Experience', *Journal of Personality and Social Psychology*, 57:1 (1989), 100–108.

Deleuze, Gilles, 'Ethology: Spinoza and Us', in *Incorporations*, ed. by Jonathan Crary and Sanford Kwinter (New York: Zone Books, 1992).

Deleuze, Gilles, 'Lecture of 24.01.1978', (trans. unknown), https://www.webdeleuze.com/textes/14 [accessed 26 July 2019].

Deleuze, Gilles, *Spinoza: Practical Philosophy*, trans. by Robert Hurley (San Francisco: City Lights Books, 1998).

Deleuze, Gilles and Félix Guattari, *A Thousand Plateaus*, trans. by Brian Massumi (Minneapolis: University of Minnesota Press, 1987).

Deleuze, Gilles and Félix Guattari, *What is Philosophy?*, trans. by Hugh Tomlinson and Graham Burchill (London: Verso, 1994).

Derrida, Jacques, *Of Grammatology*, trans. Gayatri Chakravorty Spivak (Baltimore & London: Johns Hopkins University Press, 1976).

Derrida, Jacques, *Writing and Difference*, trans. Alan Bass (London & New York: Routledge, 1978).

Dimberg, Ulf, Monika Thunberg, and Kurt Elmehed, 'Unconscious Facial Reactions to Emotional Facial Expressions', *Psychology Science*, 11:1 (2000), 86–89.

Dixon, Steve, *Digital Performance* (Cambridge: The MIT Press, 2007).

Dyson, Frances, *Sounding New Media: Immersion and Embodiment in the Arts and Culture* (Ewing: UC Press, 2009).

Elfenbein, H. A., 'The Many Faces of Emotional Contagion: An Affective Process Theory of Affective Link', *Organisational Psychology Review*, 4 (2014), 326–362.

Ellamil, Melissa, Joshua Berson, Jen Wong, Louis Buckley and Daniel S. Margulies, 'One in the Dance: Musical Correlates of Group Synchrony in a Real-World Club Environment', *PLOS One* (2016), https://journals.plos.org/plosone/article?id=10.1371/journal.pone.0164783 [accessed 12 April 2019].

Euripides, *Bacchae: After The Bacchae of Euripides*, trans. by Colin Teevan (London and New York: Oberon Books Ltd, 2001).

Euripides, *The Bacchae in The Complete Greek Tragedies: Euripides V*, trans. by William Arrowsmith, ed. by David Greene and Richmond Lattimore (Chicago and London: The University of Chicago Press, 1968).

Euripides, *Bakkhai: A New Version by Anne Carson* , trans. by Anne Carson (London: Oberon Books Ltd., 2015).

Euripides, *Bakkhai: A New Version by Anne Carson*, trans. and adapted by Anne Carson, dir. by James Macdonald (London: Almeida Theatre, 2015).

Euripides, *Hekabe*, in *Grief Lessons, Four Plays by Euripides*, trans by Anne Carson (New York: New York Review Books, 2006).

## Bibliography   221

Euripides, *Medea*, a new version by Rachel Cusk, dir. by Rupert Goold (London: Almeida Theatre, 2015).

Euripides, 'The Trojan Women', in *The Complete Greek Tragedies, Euripides III*, trans. by Richard Lattimore (Chicago: The University of Chicago Press, 1958).

Fischer-Lichte, Erika, 'The Art of Spectatorship', *Journal of Contemporary Drama in English*, 4:1 (2016), 164–179.

Foster, Susan Leigh, *Choreographing Empathy: Kinesthesia in Performance* (London and New York: Routledge, Taylor & Francis Group, 2011).

Freeman, Nate, 'The Most-Viewed Work of Performance Art in History: Vanessa Beecroft on Ditching the Art World for Kanye West', *Artnews* (17 February 2016), http://www.artnews.com/2016/02/17/the-most-viewed-work-of-performance-art-in-history-vanessa-beecroft-on-ditching-the-art-world-for-kanye-west/ [accessed 29 September 2018].

Freshwater, Helen, *Theatre & Audience* (Basingstoke and New York: Palgrave Macmillan, 2009).

Fuchs, Elinor, *The Death of Character: Perspectives on Theater after Modernism* (Bloomington and Indianapolis: Indiana University Press, 1996).

Gerson, A. C. and D. Perlman, 'Loneliness and Expressive Communication', *Journal of Abnormal Psychology*, 88 (1979), 258–261.

Goddard, Peter, 'Artist Exposed in Film', *Toronto Star* (2007), https://www.thestar.com/news/2007/02/21/artist_exposed_in_film.html [accessed 07 November 2021].

Griffero, Tonino, *Quasi-Things: The Paradigm of Atmospheres*, trans. by Sarah De Sanctis (New York: SUNY Press, 2017).

Hainley, Bruce, 'Vanessa Beecroft; Gagosian Gallery' *Artforum* (Summer, 2001), https://www.artforum.com/print/reviews/200106/vanessa-beecroft-48549 [accessed 12 August 2018].

Hall, Edward T., *The Hidden Dimension* (New York: Anchor Books published by arrangement with Doubleday, a division of Random House, Inc, 1990).

Hamilton, D. L. and S. J. Sherman, 'Perceiving Persons and Groups', *Psychological Review*, 103:2 (1996), 336–355. 10.1037/0033-295X.103.2.336

Hatfield, E., J. Cacioppo and R. L. Rapson, *Emotional Contagion* (Cambridge: Cambridge University Press, 1994).

Hatfield, E., J. Cacioppo and R. L. Rapson, 'Emotional Contagion', *Current Directions in Psychological Science*, 2 (1993), 96–99.

Heidegger, Martin, *Being and Time*, trans. by Joan Stambaugh (Albany: State University of New York Press, 2010).

Heidegger, Martin, *History of the Concept of Time: Prolegomena*, trans. By Theodore Kisiel, in *The Phenomenology Reader*, ed. by Dermot Moran and Timothy Mooney (London and New York: Routledge, Taylor and Francis Group, 2002).

Hill, Logan, '"Art Star" Vanessa Beecroft: Slammed at Sundance', *Vulture* (January 2008), http://www.vulture.com/2008/01/vanessa_beecroft_slammed_at_su.html [accessed 25 February 2018].

Hess, Ursula and Agneta Fischer, 'Emotional Mimicry: Why and When We Mimic Emotions', *Social and Personality Psychology Compass*, 8:2 (2014), 45–57.

Husserl, Edmund, *Ideas Pertaining to a Pure Phenomenology and to a Phenomenological Philosophy, First Book*, trans. by F. Kersten (The Hague: Nijhoff, 1983).

Idhe, Don, *Listening and Voice: Phenomenologies of Sound*, 2nd ed. (Albany, New York: State University of New York Press, 2007).

Jackson, Janet, *Rhythm Nation*, A&M Records (1989), online video clip www.youtube.com

222    *Bibliography*

published on 16 June 2009, https://www.youtube.com/watch?v=OAwaNWGLM0c [accessed 15 July 2017].

Johnstone, Nick, 'Dare to Bare', *The Observer* section of *The Guardian* (2005), https://www.theguardian.com/artanddesign/2005/mar/13/art [accessed 29 September 2018].

Jovchelovitch, Sandra, *Knowledge in Context: Representations, Community and Culture* (London: Routledge, 2007).

Kaldor Public Art Projects, http://kaldorartprojects.org.au/projects/project-12-vanessa-beecroft [accessed 8 May 2016].

Kashima, Yoshihisa, 'Communication and Essentialism: Grounding the Shared Reality of a Social Category', *Social Cognition*, 28:3 (2010), 306–328.

Kashima, Yoshihisa, 'Culture, Communication, and Entitativity: A social Psychological Investigation of Social Reality', in *The Psychology of Group Perception: Perceived Variability, Entitativity, and Essentialism*, ed. by Vincent Yzerbyt, Charles M. Judd and Olivier Corneille (New York and Hove: Psychology Press, 2004).

Kashima, Yoshihisa, Emiko Kashima, Chi-Yue Chiu, Thomas Farsides, Michele Gelfand, Ying-Yi Hong, Uichol Kim, Fritz Strack, Lioba Werth, Masaki Yuki and Vincent Yzerbyt, 'Culture, Essentialism, and Agency: Are Individuals Universally Believed to be More Real Entities than Groups?', *European Journal of Social Psychology*, 35 (2005), 147–169.

Kellein, Thomas, 'The Secret of Female Intimacy' originally printed in *Vanessa Beecroft: Photographs, Films, Drawings* (Berlin: Hatje Cantz, 2008), www.vanessabeecroft.com [accessed 8 May 2016].

Kelly, J. R. and S. G. Barsade, 'Mood and Emotions in Small Groups and Work Teams', *Organisational Behaviour and Human Decision Processes*, 86 (2001), 99–130.

Lady Gaga, Bad Romance, Red One and Lady Gaga (2009), online video clip www.youtube.com published on 24 November 2009, https://www.youtube.com/watch?v=qrO4YZeyl0I [accessed 15 July 2017].

Lady Gaga, *Alejandro*, Red One and Lady Gaga (2009), online video clip www.youtube.com published on 8 June 2010, https://www.youtube.com/watch?v=niqrrmev4mA [accessed 15 July 2017].

Laird, James D. and Charles Bresler, 'The Process of Emotional Experience: A Self-Perception Theory', *Review of Personality and Social Psychology*, 13 (1992), 213–234.

Lakoff, George and Mark Johnson, *Metaphors We Live By* (Chicago and London: University of Chicago Press, 2003).

Le Bon, Gustave, *The Crowd: A Study of the Popular Mind* (New York: Cosimo Classics, 2006).

Lehmann, Hans-Thies, *Postdramatic Theatre*, trans. by Karen Jürs-Munby (London: Routledge, 2000).

Lickel, B., D. L. Hamilton, G. Wieczorkowska, A. Lewis, S. J. Sherman, & A. N.Uhles, 'Varieties of Groups and the Perception of Group Entitativity', *Journal of Personality and Social Psychology*, 78:2 (2000), 223–246. 10.1037/0022-3514.78.2.223

Liu, J. H. and D. Mills, 'How the Past Weighs on the Present: Social Representations of History and Their Role in Identity Politics', *British Journal of Social Psychology*, 44:4 (2005), 537–556.

Lundqvist, Lars Olov and Ulf Dimberg, 'Facial Expressions Are Contagious', *Journal of Psychophysiology*, 9:3 (1995), 203–211.

Machon, Josephine, *Immersive Theatres: Intimacy and Immediacy in Contemporary Performance* (Basingstoke and New York: Palgrave Macmillan, 2013).

## Bibliography  223

Massumi, Brian, *Parables for the Virtual: Movement, Affect, Sensation* (Durham, NC: Duke University Press, 2002).

Mayo, Elton, *The Human Problems of an Industrial Civilization*, 8 vols (New York: The Macmillan Company, 1933).

McDougall, William, *The Group Mind: A Sketch of the Principles of Collective Psychology* (New York: G. P. Putnam's Sons, 1920).

McIver Lopes, Dominic M., 'The Ontology of Interactive Art', *Journal of Aesthetic Education*, 35:4 (2001), 65–81.

Milgram, Stanley, *Obedience to Authority: An Experimental View* (London: Harper Perennial, 2009).

Moran, Caitlin, 'Come Party with Lady Gaga', *The Times* (22 May 2010), https://www.thetimes.co.uk/article/come-party-with-lady-gaga-pb2ln3zrmp3 [accessed 10 August 2017].

Moscovici, Serge and Miles Hewstone, 'Social Representations and Social Explanations: From the "Naïve" to the "Amateur" Scientist', in Hewstone, Miles (Ed), *Attribution Theory: Social and Functional Extensions* (Oxford: Blackwell, 1983).

Nancy, Jean-Luc, *Being Singular Plural* (Stanford, CA: Stanford University Press, 2000).

Noland, Carrie, *Agency and Embodiment: Performing Gestures/Producing Culture* (Cambridge Massachusetts: Harvard University Press, 2009).

Noland, Carrie, 'The Human Situation on Stage: Merce Cunningham, Theodor Adorno, and the Category of Expression', *Dance Research Journal*, 42:1 (2010), 47–60.

Paglia, Camille, 'Lady Gaga and the Death of Sex', *The Sunday Times* (12 September 2010), https://www.thetimes.co.uk/article/lady-gaga-and-the-death-of-sex-lnzbcd70zj3 [accessed 10 August 2017].

Prkachin, K. M., K. D. Craig, D. Papageorgis and G. Reith, 'Nonverbal Communication Deficits and Response to Performance Feedback in Depression', *Journal of Abnormal Psychology*, 86 (1977), 224–234.

Rayner, Alice, *Ghosts; Death's Double and the Phenomena of Theatre* (Minneapolis, MN: University of Minnesota Press, 2006).

Reynolds, Dee, 'Kinesthetic Empathy and the Dance's Body: From Emotion to Affect' in *Kinesthetic Empathy in Creative and Cultural Practices*, ed. by Dee Reynolds and Matthew Reason (Bristol: Intellect Ltd, 2012), pp. 123–136.

Rokeach, Milton, 'Authority, Authoritarianism, and Conformity', in *Conformity and Deviation*, ed. by Irwin A. Berg and Bernard M. Bass (New York: Harper & Brothers, 1961).

Ryan, Marie-Laure, 'Beyond Myth and Metaphor: Narrative in Digital Media', *Poetics Today*, 23:4 (2002), 581–609.

Ryan, Marie-Laure, 'Immersion vs. Interactivity: Virtual Reality and Literary Theory', *Substance*, 28:2 (1999), 110–137.

Ryan, Marie-Laure, *Narrative as Virtual Reality: Immersion and Interactivity in Literature and Electronic Music* (Baltimore: The John Hopkins University Press, 2001).

Sallis, John, *Crossings: Nietzsche and the Space of Tragedy* (Chicago: The University of Chicago Press, 1991), pp. 89–90.

Saltz, David, 'The Art of Interaction: Interactivity, Performativity, and Computers', *Journal of Aesthetics and Art Criticism*, 55:2 (1997), 117–127.

Schechner, Richard, *Between Theater and Anthropology* (Philadelphia: University of Pennsylvania Press, 1985).

## 224   Bibliography

Schechner, Richard, *Performance Studies: An Introduction*, 2nd ed. (New York: Routledge, 2006).

Searle, John, 'How Performatives Work', *Linguistics and Philosophy*, 12:5 (1989), 535–558.

Seigworth, Gregory J. and Melissa Gregg, 'An Inventory of Shimmers', in *The Affect Theory Reader*, ed. by Gregory J. Seigworth and Melissa Gregg (Durham and London: Duke University Press, 2010).

Shakespeare, William, *As You Like It*, dir. by Polly Pindlay (London: The National Theatre, 2015).

Shearing, David, 'Intimacy, Immersion and the Desire to Touch: The Voyeur Within', in *Theatre as Voyeurism: The Pleasures of Watching*, ed. by George Rodosthenous (London: Palgrave Macmillan, 2015).

Sia, *The Greatest*, Kurstin (2016), online video clip www.toutube.com published on 5 September 2016, https://www.youtube.com/watch?v=GKSRyLdjsPA [accessed 15 July 2017].

Sloterdijk, Peter, *Globes: Spheres Volume 2: Macrospherology*, trans by Wieland Hoban (South Pasadena, CA, USA: Semiotext(e), 2014).

Sloterdijk, Peter, *Foams: Spheres Volume 3: Plural Spherology*, trans. by Wieland Hoban (California, USA: Semiotext(e), 2016).

Sloterdijk, Peter, *Terror from the Air*, trans. by Amy Patton and Steve Corcoran (Los Angeles, CA: Semiotext(e), Foreign Agents Series, 2009).

Smith, Roberta, 'Critic's Notebook; Standing and Staring, Yet Aiming for Empowerment', *The New York Times* (6 May 1998), http://www.nytimes.com/1998/05/06/arts/critic-s-notebook-standing-and-staring-yet-aiming-for-empowerment.html [accessed 19 November 2016].

Smuts, Aaron, 'What Is Interactivity?', *Journal of Aesthetic Education*, 43:4 (2009), 53–73.

Stanislavski, Constantin, *An Actor Prepares*, trans. by Elizabeth Reynolds Hapgood (New York: Routledge, 1989).

Steinmetz, Julia, Heather Cassils and Clover Leary, 'Behind Enemy Lines: Toxic Titties Infiltrate Vanessa Beecroft', *Signs*, 31:3 (2006), 753–783.

Stern, Nathaniel, *Interactive Art and Embodiment: The Implicit Body as Performance* (Canterbury: Glyphi Limited, 2013).

Tanghe, Jacqueline, Barbara Wisse and Henk Van Der Flier, 'The Formation of Group Affect and Team Effectiveness: the Moderating Role of Identification', *British Journal of Management*, 21:2 (2010), 340–358.

Thibaud, Jean-Paul, 'The Backstage of Urban Ambiance: When Atmospheres Pervade Everyday Experience', *Emotion, Space and Society*, 15 (2015), 39–46.

Thorpe, Chris, *Chorus*, dir. by Elayce Ismail (London: Gate Theatre, 2016).

Thurnell-Read, Thomas, 'What Happens on Tour: The Premarital Stag Tour, Homosocial Bonding, and Male Friendship', *Men and Masculinities*, 15:3 (2012), 249–270.

Tomkins, Silvan S., *Affect, Imagery, Consciousness: The Complete Edition* (New York: Springer Publishing Company, 2008).

Totterdell, P., S. Kellett, K. Teuchmann and R. B. Briner, 'Evidence of Mood Linkage in Work Groups', *Journal of Personal Social Psychology*, 74 (1998), 504–515.

Turner, Victor, *The Ritual Process: Structure and Anti-Structure* (London: Routledge & Kegan Paul, 1969).

Vogel, Joseph, 'The Nation That Janet Jackson Built', *The Atlantic* (2014), https://www.theatlantic.com/entertainment/archive/2014/09/the-world-changing-aspirations-of-rhythm-nation-1814/380144/ [accessed 14 October 2018].

## Bibliography

Wagner, Wolfgang and Nicky Hayes, *Everyday Discourse and Common Sense: The Theory of Social Representations* (New York: Palgrave-Macmillan, 2005).

Wagner, Wolfgang, Peter Holtz and Yoshihisa Kashima, 'Construction and Deconstruction of Essence in Representing Social Groups: Identity Projects, Stereotyping, and Racism', *Journal for the Theory of Social Behaviour*, 39:3 (2009), 363–383.

Wakefield, Neville, 'Vanessa Beecroft: South Sudan', *Flash Art* (November-December 2006), https://flash---art.com/article/vanessa-beecroft-2/ [accessed 07 November 2021].

Westcott, James, 'Black Tie vs. Black Face', *The Drama Review*, 49:1 (2005), 114–118.

White, Gareth, 'On Immersive Theatre', *Theatre Research International*, 37:3 (2012), 221–235.

Wilson, Peter, *The Athenian Institution of the Khoregia* (Cambridge: Cambridge University Press, 2000).

Worth It featuring Kid Ink, Fifth Harmony, online video clip, www.youtube.com, published 28 March 2015, https://www.youtube.com/watch?v=YBHQbu5rbdQ [accessed 20 July 2018].

# Appendix A

**IMAGE 1:**

Morrison's Budapest:

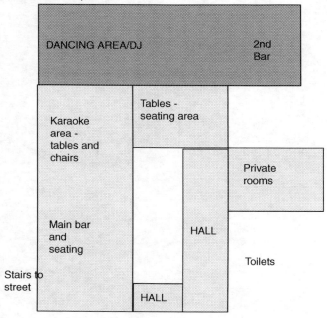

## IMAGE 2:

Oslo bar, Hackney Central, London UK.

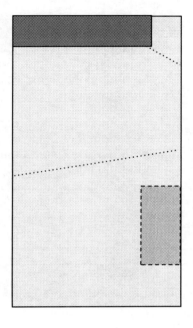

# Appendix B

Extract of khoros ode from Euripides' *Bakkhai*.

Euripides, *Bakkhai: A New Version by Anne Carson*, trans. by Anne Carson (London: Oberon Books Ltd., 2015), pp. 32–33. This version offers no line counting:

> Such Anger,
> such anger
> he shows,
> that earthborn snakebegotten Pentheus,
> son of Echion, a monster without a face.
> This is no human entity,
> he comes from giants and blood.
> he pits himself against gods.
> and soon he will have me in his prison—
> I who belong to Bromios!
> Already my comrade
> is locked in the dark.
> Do you see this, Dionysos?
> Do you see
> how
> passionately
> your prophets struggle?
> Lord,
> come down from Olympos,
> shake your thyrsos
> and crush
> the *hybris*
> of this wrongminded man!

# Appendix C

## Comment 1

Vanessa Beecroft's titling of her work is itself divorced from individuality. All of her work is designated a numbered entry in an ongoing progression; all are members of what will, after the fact, in critical discourse be termed her 'corpus' or her 'oeuvre'—each a member contributing to the greater whole. This numbering system continued until the late 2000s, when she began to work with different material (political and race-based agendas, adoption of Sudanese children, action-based durational work), and in particular when she began her current artistic collaboration with Kanye West.

## Comment 2

Mumsnet is a website and online forum for parents, especially new parents, that allows open exchange of experiences, ideas and advice. It is generally frequented by mothers, and I assume fathers, but in my research I have never encountered an entry by a man. There are bloggers (approximately 5000) who write for the site. In popular and political culture it has had recognisable impact and is seen to be a formidable form of online influence.

## Comment 3

There was a sign right next to the car that indicated that guests should not spray or shoot water into the eyes, mouth, genitals or anus of the dancers. This, at first, made me laugh at the context in which I found myself. As I watched people begin to dance on the car, though, it made me feel uncomfortable with the tone of the situation. While no one was stripping, the actions mimicking such performance created a great sense of discriminant and regrettable power dynamics in gender.

## Comment 4

The audience applauded and seemed to approve the production, but I wonder how strongly they would have approved had Ben Whishaw and Bertie Carvel

230　*Appendix C*

not been playing Dionysos/messenger and Pentheus/Agave respectively given their fame. When I much later, completely coincidentally, spoke with another person who attended the production he praised Ben Whishaw's performance but did not mention the khoros. For a text that is (1) titled after its khoros and (2) constructed with an ever-present singing/dancing/hypnotic khoros, it is notable if attendees do not comment on them.

## Comment 5

Similar examples include the videos for Beyoncé's Single Ladies, Sia's Cheap Thrills, Daft Punk's Around the World or The Chemical Brothers Let Forever Be. In the first two videos, there are distinct leaders of the groups in Beyoncé and Maddie Ziegler (although they do nothing particularly different or better than their coevals), but the group is the focus throughout; in the third video there are different characters in the form of various Halloween costumes come to life, but they all operate simultaneously as subgroups of fours and then as one large collective; in the fourth video, there is one character, but she is continuously being fractured into several multiples of herself. In all those cases, the collective is the focus point and not an intermittent feature.

## Comment 6

Incidentally, but not entirely disconnected from the topic of this text, in March 2014 Radio Free Asia reported that the ruling Workers' Party in North Korea had issued a directive that all male students should adopt Kim Jong Un's hairstyle. Further reports had stated that all male citizens were 'encouraged' to do the same. The validity of this anecdote is very hard to confirm or reject for the obvious reasons of North Korea's intense secrecy, block on sharing of information and isolationism. Nevertheless, the mere idea of this reflects a powerful and frightening move towards similarising entire demographics, and, if we return to chapter two, the enforcement of an external agency on those being similarised.

## Comment 7

Pyrrhikhe were khoros dances in 6th and 5th century BCE Greece that soldiers would perform both to demonstrate warrior prowess, success and to honour the Goddess of war, Athena, but also as a training method for soldiers to achieve finer execution of fighting actions and group cohesion.

## Comment 8

To Benjamin, the aura of the original both is unique to that work but its reproduction, in copies and simulacra, diminishes the aura. The reproduced work lacks the aura of the original. Authenticity, moreover, is a twofold dimension of reality for the work of art—it rests in its materiality and its spatio-

*Appendix C*  231

temporal biography—how time and location have affected and transformed the work. 'The authenticity of a thing is the essence of all that is transmissible from its beginning, ranging from its substantive duration to its testimony to the history which it has experienced'.[1] The work's history is carried with it and is present in its encounter. Live works of art or performance are complicated in this context as they are themselves spatio-temporal events, contingent on their existence in the present moment.

Performance works like these cases unfold live each time they occur and do not exist outside of their unique encounter. Obviously, archival materials exist beyond the encounter. The examples demonstrate how the uniqueness of the work sits with the *encounter* with it. Moreover, while performances might be a remounting of existing instances of live art or performance (such as *Bakkhai* or *Oresteia*), they are not themselves reproductions but recreations. Each performance was its own unique work of art, each experience unique and authentic. Furthermore, the liveness of these events introduced probabilities not had by static, recorded, or non-live arts. For instance, there is literally no way to recreate or reproduce the experience of the club events; there are simply too many probabilities within its liveness, indeed they were events premised on spontaneous interactions. Beecroft's installations could be restaged, but they would be different due to the changed nature of the models (even if all the same women, they would be different due to them changing in the elapsed time) and of the different audiences present. The same stands for the khoroi. One of the enduring features of the aura of these live performance instances is their sense of chance and possibility connected to both the liveness of the participants (performers) and audiences. By affecting and being affected by each other these human perspectival elements changed the aura encountered and its experience. My choice in the chapter five to explore recorded media cases situated this aura differently. In those music videos the shift in authenticity is entirely to the encounter itself. They are still live encounters for the audience, but their fixity in recording shifted their experience towards the kind of experience had in static arts. As a composite editing of takes, they locked the performers' experience in the singularity of the final copy. However, each of those moments was live and the viewer experiences that liveness through an encounter with the recorded reproduction. The viewer enters the work through the lens of the camera, which allows physical entrance to the dancing groups. The viewer also controls the experience through command and power to manipulate the time code—audiences may pause, repeat, fast-forward, rewind—but the videos are still time-bound forms. They exist in and through the experience of the continuous playing of a timeline.

## Note

1 Walter Benjamin, 'The Work of Art in the Age of Mechanical Reproduction', in *Illuminations*, trans. by Harry Zohn, ed. by Hannah Arendt (New York: Schocken Books, 1969), p. 4.

# Index

Accademia di Brera 79
aesthetic collectives: definition of 3; as
  narrators 131–132; perspectives 4; as
  static or background elements 133–134
aesthetic fields 33–36
aesthetic object 9
affect 160
affect transmission 56–59
affective convergence 145
affective dimensions 160–165
*Agamemnon* 99, 129, 136, 204
Agamemnon (king of Mycenae) 131, 204
agency 1, 9, 22, 81–83, 88–89, 108,
  110–112, 177, 179, 184–187, 201, 212;
  collective 112, 115, 125, 134–135;
  individual 111, 181; manipulating 72–79;
  perceived 88–89
agentic shift 113
agentic social beings 115
agentic states 109–116
*Alejandro* (music video) 12, 165–173, 183
Almeida Theatre 11
ambience 198
*American Dad* (television show) 158
Anderson, Ben 7, 13, 160, 162, 205
anonymity 103–104
Argives 136–137
Argos 136
Arrowsmith, William 132
art-object 9–11
*The Artworks are Containers* (White) 184
Aryanism 67, 121, 123
*As You Like It* 133
Askill, Daniel 160
atmosphere 15–16, 175–207, 213–215;
  climate 199–207; conditioning 195–198;
  encounter 176–184; foam structures
  192–195; human weather 199–207;
  immersion 184–192

atmospheric conditioning 16
atmospheric effect 6–7
attendants 25–26
audiences 25; distinction from aesthetic
  collectives 179; stagnation of crowd
  187–188
aura 175–176
Aura (goddess of the breeze) 175
Auslander, Philip 12, 154
authority 1, 62, 64, 72–78, 89, 108–115

back-up dancing groups 2, 5; affective
  experiences 159–160; entitativity 156; as
  main character 159; mood-making 159
*Bad Romance* (music video) 12,
  165–173, 199
*Bakkhai* 11, 93, 95, 97, 100–101, 103–106,
  112, 129, 131–132, 146–147, 183, 185,
  189, 191–192, 204–205; atmosphere 202;
  audience 186–187; human weather 203
Barsade, Sigal 13, 145, 148, 162, 164,
  170, 191
Beckett, Samuel 139
Beecroft, Vanessa 5, 10, 48, 62, 81,
  112–113, 155, 196; authority 72–79; de-
  individualisation of participants 106;
  directions/instruction s 79–89; earlier
  work 65; installation performances
  63–64; as Kanye West's artistic
  doppelganger 86–87; manipulation of
  participant's agency 72–79; *VB16 Piano
  Americano-Beige* 66–67, 73, 75; *VB35* 67,
  73, 76, 81; *VB40* 81; *VB45* 67–71, 73,
  76, 85–86, 121, 123, 141–142, 196,
  198–199; *VB46* 67–69, 71, 73, 76, 82,
  85–86, 111, 137–138, 177, 181–182;
  *VB48* 67–71; *VB54* 70–71, 78; *VB61
  Still Death! Darfur Still Deaf?* 70
being 11, 14

*Index* 233

being-with 8, 11, 14–15, 216
Benjamin, Walter 175
*Bewandtnis* 204
*Billboard* magazine 168
*Bindu Shards* (Turrell) 185
Bion, Wilfred 124
Böhme, Gernot 7, 15, 176, 206
Bouko, Catherine 14, 184, 191
Brennan, Theresa 7, 13, 16, 57–58, 149
Brown, Bill 4, 214

*Cabaret* (film) 167, 171
Campbell, Donald T. 8, 21, 36, 38, 41, 93, 96, 211
Canetti, Elias 44, 51–52, 187–188
Carwash 27, 113, 138
Cassandra 204
Cassils, Healther 71, 73, 75–77, 82–83, 89, 111, 136, 139–140
categorisation 63
Cavendish, Dominic 98
*CBS News* 168
CCTV footage 102–103
character 12, 76–77, 95; as characterisation 141; overview 124–125; as roles and dramatis personae 128–134
characterisation 140–147
Cheshin, Arik 165
*Choephoroi* 96, 99, 104, 129
choreography 2, 16, 43, 72, 84, 97–101, 107, 157–159, 162, 167–169, 171–172
*Chorus* 11, 95, 100, 102–103, 111, 114–115, 129, 131, 139, 193
choruses 2, 167
Clapp, Susanah 133
climate 15, 155, 199–207, 210, 215
clubbing crowd/dancing crowd 5, 197; as aesthetic collectives 26; aesthetic fields 35; collective domains 35–36; collective fantasies/enacted micro-narratives in 143; collective presence of 135; collective space of 28; cOordinated actions 42; emotional culture 145–146; immersion 178; intimate distances 51–56; and musical 30; physical contact 29–30; presence and containment 31, 33; proximity 35–36, 42, 47; spaces in 32–33; spatial regulation in 29–30, 43; synchronized movement 30; territoriality 45–46
cognition 140
collective characters 96
collective domains 33–36

common fate 8–9, 92–94, 212; agentic states 109–116; choreography 97–101; dialogue 101–105; rhythm 97–101; rôle/character 105–109; *see also* entitativity
communication 14–15, 31, 42, 46–47, 140, 177, 180, 198–199, 203, 211; cohesiveness 172; and interaction 138–139, 151; non-verbal 67, 81–82, 198; olfactory and tactile 57; physical 50; verbal 50–51
communitas 44, 56–59
co-narration 103–104
conditioned spaces 15
conditioning 195–198
conformity 88
consciousness 47
contagion 58, 147–151, 165–173; overview 124–125
container metaphors 120
convergence 150–151
*Crowds and Power* (Canetti) 187–188
Cunningham, Merce

Damasio, Antonio 47
dance clubs 5–6, 21; aesthetic fields 33–36; affect transmission 56–59; attendants 25–26; collective domains 33–36; collective fantasies/enacted micro-narratives in 143; communitas 56–59; dancing crowds as aesthetic collectives 26; discharge 42–50; encounters in 27; experiences 25; experiences in 27; immersion in 27–28; insides/outsides 28–32; prägnanz 36–43, 55; proximity 36–43, 47; touch in 51–56
dancing ensembles 2
Debbie (club) 35–36, 38–41, 46–47, 55, 142–143, 197, 200
Deitch, Jeffrey 66, 142
Deleuze, Gilles 13, 205
dialogue 101–105; co-narration 103–104; interruption 102–103; overlapping speech 193; verbalising in unison 102–103
Dionysos 131–132, 146–147, 186
discharge 43–50
distance regulation 29–30, 43
Dixon, Steve 186
DJs 6, 25–27, 43, 143–144
dominatrix model 123
Downing. Carolyn 133

effect 175, 182, 215; aesthetic 35, 71;

234    *Index*

atmospheric 6, 183, 195; collectivising 3; of dancing crowd 44; immersion 184, 186, 188; of khoros 101–102, 104, 131; mood-making 155
emotional (affective) culture 145
emotional contagion 164–165
emotional culture 145
emotions 160, 163–164
encounter 176–184
*Encountering Affect: Capacities, Apparatuses, Condition* (Anderson) 205
entitativity 6, 8, 12, 21, 64, 210; back-up dancing groups 156; common fate 93, 212; definition of 16; expansion of 63; group 115; perceived essence 115; and prägnanz 211; and proximity 211; and similarity 211–212
entrainment 57
environmental conditioning 196
essence/essentialisation 11, 134–140
essentialism 94
*Eumenides* 99–100, 105–106, 131, 134–135
Euripides 102, 129, 132, 146
*Evita* (film) 167
experiential similarity 123

Fassbinder, Irm Hermann 66
*The Feeling of What Happens* (Damasio) 47
feelings 3, 9–10, 22, 27, 43–44, 64, 71, 78, 127–129, 135, 137, 140, 145–150, 154–155, 159–161, 163, 167, 171, 176–177, 185, 197, 201, 203, 205, 213, 215–216
fields 175–176
*Fifth Harmony* (song) 142
flashmobs 2
*Foam* 13
foam structures 192–195
force of existing 205
Freud, Sigmund 124
Fuchs, Elinor 95, 108, 128, 172, 206
functional conceptualisation 21, 120, 123–125
Furler, Sia (musician) 5, 12, 160–165

Gagosian Gallery 69
GAPS + NINA 41
Gate Theatre 11, 95
gestalt phenomena 135
gestalt theory 8
gestures 72, 94
Gibson, Donald 164
Gibson, Laurieann 167

*Glee* (television show) 158
The Globe 200
Gough, Orlando 133
*The Greatest* (music video) 12, 160–165, 172, 199
Gregg, Melissa 13
Griffero, Tonino 4, 214–215
group mentality 6
Guattari, Felix 205

haka dance 162
Hall, Edward T. 31–33, 43, 45–46, 49, 121, 185
Hamilton, David L. 93
*Happy Feet 2* (film) 158
haptic contact 51–56
Haus of Gaga 165
*Hecuba* 129–130
Heffington, Ryan 160
*The Hidden Dimensions* (Hall) 31
homogeneity 63
human weather 199–207

identity project 136–138
Idhe, Don 33
immersion 176, 178, 184–192
immersive performance/audience masses 2
immersivity 9–10, 14–15
individuality 6
installations: audiences 179; immersion in 183–184
intelligent dance music (IDM) 143
interaction 186
international law 4
interpersonal spaces 52
interruption 102–103
intersubjectivity 4, 13
intimate space 31, 51–56
*Iphigenia at Auli* 102
*Iphigenia Quartet* 11, 95
Iphigenia 131

Jackson, Janet 5, 12, 157–160
Jackson, Richard 167
Johnson, Mark 17, 21, 119–123, 150, 192
joint destiny 9, 93
*Justify My Love* (music video) 167

Kashima, Yoshihisa 12, 93–94, 115, 135
Kellein, Thomas 79
Khayat. Mador 165
khoregia 5
khoroi 2, 11, 95, 105–108, 116, 124, 129,

180; atmosphere 205; audiences 179, 183; character roles 131, 142; environmental conditioning 196; immersion in 178, 183–184; pluri-use of 132–133

khoros 5, 7, 11, 92–116; agentic states 109–116; anonymity 103–104; atmosphere 202; authority 109–111; character 128; choreography 97–101; described 92–93; dialogue 101–105; essence/essentialisation of 135; rôle/character 105–109

Kid Ink 143

Klein, Steven 171

Klytemnestra 96, 131, 135–136

Knight, Andrew 145, 148, 162, 191

Kurstin, Greg 160

Lady Gaga 5, 12, 165–173, 183

Lakoff, George 17, 21, 119–123, 150, 192

Lamar, Kendrick 160

Lawrence, Francis 165

Le Bon, Gustave 58, 124, 150

Leary, Clover 71, 73–77, 82, 89

LGBTQ+ 162

Lickel, Brian 93

*The Life of Pablo* (album) 62, 87

*Like a Prayer* (music video) 167

like substances 12

*Listening and Voice; Phenomenologies of Sound* (Idhe) 33

Liu, J.H. 138

live art ensembles 5

*Liveness: Performance in a Mediatized Culture* (Auslander) 154

Madonna 167

Maori haka dance 162

Massumi, Brian 205–206

McDougall, William 58, 124, 150

McIver Lopes, Dominic M. 186

*Medea* 11, 95, 98, 100, 104, 108, 128–129, 140, 183, 185–186, 189, 191

metaphors 211

*Metaphors We Live By* (Lakoff and Johnson) 17, 119

Metropolis (strip bar) 26, 34, 39–40, 44–46, 197, 200

Milgram, Stanley 88, 109, 112–113

mimicry 150

Monkey Puzzle 160

mood 12, 140–147, 149, 162–164

mood setting 165–173

mood-making 155–160

Morrisons (club) 38, 41, 48–49, 197

motor activity 21, 120

movement 94

MTV 154

multichamber organizations 192

Museum of Contemporary Art (Sydney) 81

music videos 5, 12, 154–173; affective dimensions 160–165; *Alejandro* (Lady Gaga) 165–173; audiences 179, 182–183; back-up dancing groups in 156; *Bad Romance* (Lady Gaga) 165–173; contagion 165–173; *The Greatest* (Sia) 160–165; immersion in 183–184; mood setting 165–173; mood-making in 155–160; *Rhythm Nation* (Jackson) 157–160

Nancy, Jean Luc 216

narration 131–132

narrators 131

National Theatre 80, 133

Nazis 67, 121, 123

negative space 31

*New York Times* 168

Nietzsche, Friedrich W. 92

Noland, Carrie 72, 77, 84, 86

normative mechanisms 147

obedience 109

objectification 4

objects 4

O'Bryan, David 43

*Oresteia* 11, 95–96, 99, 101, 104, 139, 180, 185–186, 200–201, 203

Orestes 135

Orlando Pulse nightclub shooting 161

*Orphan Black* (television show) 4

Oslo (club) 28–31, 38–39, 41–43, 47–49, 143, 197–198

overlapping speech 102–103

Paglia, Camille 168

participants 25, 184

path 151

Pentheus 132, 146

perceived agency 94

perceived essence 115

perceptual conceptualisation 21, 120

personal space 29, 31, 40, 48–50, 52, 158, 196, 199–200, 211

personification 124, 135

pheromones 57

plural intersubjectivity 13

## 236    Index

popular culture 4
prägnanz 8, 36–43, 55, 211;
  *see also* entitativity
pregnance *see* prägnanz
presence 175
protoself 47–48
proximity 8, 36–43, 47, 211;
  *see also* entitativity
public space 31, 33, 35, 47
Punchdrunk 9
purposive conceptualisation 21, 120,
  123–125

*Quad* 139
quasi-things 4, 214–215

recognition 11
Red One 165
Resistance Gallery 35
Reynolds, Dee 16
rhythm 97–101
*Rhythm Nation* (music video) 12, 157–160
*Rhythm Nation 1814* (film) 157–158
rôle/character 76–77, 105–109
*Rolling Stone* magazine 168
Ryan, Maurie-Laure 186

Sala del Maggiore Consiglio of the Palazzo
  Ducale 69
Saltz, David 186
Savage (gay club) 34
scenography 196
Schechter, Hofesh 1
Schygulla, Hanna 66
scripts 48
Seghal, Tino 80
Seigworth, Gregory 13
Sena, Dominic 157–160
Shakespeare's Globe 11
similarity/similarisation 8, 94, 211–212; and
  agency 72–79; of appearance 64; and
  authority 72–79; and categorisation 63;
  and expansion of potential entitativity 63
singular being 135
singular essence 135
Sink the Pink 34
*Sixteen Dances for Soloist and Company of
  Three* (Cunningham) 84
Sloterdijk, Peter 7, 13–15, 192, 203,
  206–207
smell 57
Smith, Robertaa 66

*So You Think You Can Dance* (television
  show) 158
social distancing 31, 49
social space 31, 38
*Solo Suite in Time and Place*
  (Cunningham) 84
spatial regulation 29–30, 43, 45–46
*Spherology* 13
Spinoza, Baruch 205
stagnation of crowd 187–188
Stanislavski, Constantin 96
*Star Trek* (television show) 4
Steinmetz, Julia 73, 77, 83, 111–112, 136
*Storming the Wall* (dance performance) 1–2,
  215–216
suggestibility 150
*Suite by Chance* (Cunningham) 84
*The Sunday Times* 168

Tanghe, Jacqueline 148
Tate Modern turbine hall 80
Teevan, Colin 132
territoriality 45–46, 120
theory of spaces 31
*These Associations* 80
Thing Theory 4, 214
Tomkins, Silvan 13, 48, 160, 188, 205
Totterdell, P. 148
Tower of London 1
Toxic Titties 74
*The Transmissioin of Affect* (Brennan) 57, 149
transmission of affect 56–59
Troy 129–130
Tunick, Spencer 80–81
tuning 101, 109, 177
Turner, Victor 44
Turrell, James 184

*VB02* 81
*VB16 Piano Americano-Beige* 66–67, 73, 75
*VB35* 67, 73, 76, 81
*VB40* 81
*VB45* 67–71, 73, 76, 85–86, 121, 123,
  141–142, 196, 198–199
*VB46* 67–69, 71, 73, 76, 82, 85–86, 111,
  137–138, 177, 181–182
*VB48* 67–71
*VB54* 70–71, 78
*VB61 Still Death! Darfur Still Deaf?* 70
verbalising in unison 102–103
VH1 154
Vienna Kunsthalle Wien 67

*Index* 237

voyeurism 172

Wagner, Wofgang 136–138, 140
*The Walking Dead* (television show) 4
West, Kanye 5, 10, 62–64, 86–87
*Westworld* (television show) 4
Whishaw, Ben 186
White, Gareth 14, 184–185, 193
White, Gilbert 189–191

Wilshire, Bruce 95
Worth It 142

*X-men* 4

Yeats. William Butler 140
*Yeezy Season 3* 62, 87

Ziegler, Maddie 161

Printed in the United States
by Baker & Taylor Publisher Services